# THE FIRST RUSSIAN REVOLUTION

# THE
# FIRST RUSSIAN REVOLUTION

## THE DECEMBRIST REVOLT
## OF 1825

SUSANNA RABOW-EDLING

REAKTION BOOKS

*Published by*
Reaktion Books Ltd
Unit 32, Waterside
44–48 Wharf Road
London N1 7UX, UK
www.reaktionbooks.co.uk

First published 2025
Copyright © Susanna Rabow-Edling 2025

EU GPSR Authorised Representative
LOGOS EUROPE, 9 rue Nicolas Poussin, 17000, LA ROCHELLE, France
email: contact@logoseurope.eu

Printed and bound in Great Britain by Bell & Bain, Glasgow

A catalogue record for this book is available from the British Library

ISBN 978 1 83639 021 3

# CONTENTS

# Introduction

Near is the hour, near is the struggle, the struggle between liberty
and despotism![1]

Where are you, where are you, terror of tsars,
Proud muse of freedom?
Come, tear the laurels from me,
Smash the pampered lyre . . .
I want to sing to the world of freedom,
And strike evil on the thrones.[2]

Some people say that what Russia needs now is a revolution: a fundamental change in political power, political organization and socioeconomic
situation. Russia is no stranger to revolutions; it has experienced a number
of political revolts throughout history. The best-known of these is the
October Revolution of 1917, when the Bolsheviks led their forces in an
insurrection against the provisional government established after the abdication of Tsar Nicholas II. Much has been written about this pivotal event,
which laid the foundation for the formation of the Soviet Union. What
is perhaps less well known is the fact that the Bolshevik Revolution was
preceded by three liberal revolutions: the Decembrist revolt of 1825, the
Revolution of 1905 and the February Revolution of 1917.[3]

This book is about the first and, to a Western audience, least known of
these revolutions: the Decembrist revolt, named after the month in which
it occurred. On 14 December 1825 Russian army officers led 3,000 soldiers
to Senate Square in the centre of St Petersburg to force the senate to approve
their manifesto, which called for a constituent assembly, civil rights, a constitution and the abolition of serfdom. Two weeks later there was a second
uprising among the officers of Russia's Second Army in Ukraine, then part

of the Russian empire. Both revolts failed. Around eighty people were killed, including bystanders, more than 120 of the conspirators were sent to exile in Siberia, and five of the leaders were executed. This was the first Russian attempt to overthrow an autocratic regime by a liberal opposition movement with a structured political programme.

The Decembrist revolt became a source of inspiration for all subsequent Russian opponents of the regime. It has played a significant role in Russian history and culture, but much less so in Western historiography. Western scholars have commonly seen the Decembrist revolt as an example of the failure of liberal reform movements in Russia. Some have even argued that the unsuccessful revolt demonstrates that it is impossible for liberalism and democracy to take root in a country dominated by conservative thinking and practices. It was an 'offshoot of youthful enthusiasm inspired from abroad', which was 'bound to end on Russian soil in a political fiasco', one scholar writes.[4] This view is surprisingly similar to that promoted by Russian conservatives. According to conservative interpretations, the Decembrists were doomed to fail because they were propagating Western ideas that had not emerged organically from Russian soil, which made them alien to Russia.

However, the fact that the revolt failed does not make it any less interesting, especially considering its significance as a source of inspiration and mythmaking. Furthermore, it certainly does not mean that all future revolts are doomed to fail. There is a tendency among both scholars and policymakers to perceive Russia as a hopeless case, a country destined to be forever autocratic with a strong state, a passive population and a conservative mindset. The Decembrist societies constitute an important example in Russian history of the formation of a liberal opposition movement against an autocratic regime. In fact, this movement came close to succeeding in bringing down the monarchy. Even the tsar thought so. The revolt is also interesting in terms of political participation. It illustrates a case in Russian history when people voluntarily engaged in a dangerous political struggle in which they risked far more than they stood to gain at a personal level.

This is not to say that the Decembrists or their political programmes are irreproachable. Pavel Pestel's authoritarian ideas about the transition to a liberal state are certainly problematic, as are Nikita Muraviev's restrictions on the right to vote. Both held an ethnocentric and, in some cases, derogatory view of minorities. The fact that the same criticism can also be levelled at contemporary Western liberals does not make it any less valid.

JUST HOURS after the revolt was put down, the myth of the Decembrists began to take shape. In decrees and manifestos, Tsar Nicholas I portrayed them as bloodthirsty murderers who sought to destroy Russia. This message spread throughout the country. At the same time, censorship was tightened to give the regime a monopoly over the dissemination of information and the production of knowledge. After the mock trial of the revolt's participants in July 1826, when the five leaders were sentenced to death, Nicholas took measures to prevent these men from being made martyrs, first by discrediting them, then by trying to erase their memory from public consciousness. His strategy did not work, however. On the contrary, the next generation of liberal and socialist dissidents, above all Alexander Herzen and Nikolai Ogarev, turned the Decembrists into martyrs crushed by Russian autocracy in their fight for freedom.

Vladimir Lenin was the first to place the Decembrists in a Russian revolutionary tradition. In an article in 1912 he presented them as the originators of the Russian revolutionary movement.[5] The Bolsheviks made this myth official and used it to legitimize the Soviet regime after the October Revolution of 1917. During the rule of Joseph Stalin, the international influences on the Decembrists were toned down. Instead, an official Russo-centric, statist myth was created that presented them as patriots rather than rebels. After the death of Stalin, with the emergence of a new intelligentsia, an unofficial image of the Decembrists as freedom fighters against tyranny was recreated.[6] Conservative parts of the intelligentsia, however, criticized what they saw as an overly pro-Western outlook in Decembrist thought.

It has been suggested that it was primarily the Decembrists' moral stance, rather than their political ideas, that came to inspire the Russian intelligentsia and became significant to Russian culture.[7] However, their ethical position cannot be separated from their political values, which emanated from republican and Romantic ideals. The Decembrists' sense of honour, belief in self-sacrifice for the common good, and understanding of all acts as political and moral are associated with ideas of republican virtue, political stoicism and the Romantic cult of friendship.

The post-Soviet Russian opposition have been criticized on the grounds that, unlike the Decembrists, they have no ethical stance, no moral interest. They are accused of being selfish and unconcerned with the common good, unwilling to sacrifice themselves for a better society.[8] Nevertheless, members of the opposition to Vladimir Putin's consolidation of power have invoked the Decembrists on several occasions, most notably during the anti-government protests in 2006–8 and 2011–13.

After the fall of the Soviet Union, there was no clear official position on the Decembrists, but ever since Putin came to power, there has been a tendency to treat them with a certain scepticism. Yet it seems to have been difficult for the regime to distance itself completely from the Decembrists, who constitute an important part of the cherished Soviet patriotic heritage. Nevertheless, by the end of the 2010s, the shift to a conservative interpretation appears to have been completed. The monarchist blockbuster film *Union of Salvation* (2019), sponsored by the Russian state, manifests the new interpretation of the Decembrists in Russian history. It presents the Decembrist leaders as fanatical, power-hungry egoists, or foolish romantics, who aspire to introduce ideas alien to Russia through revolutionary means and who threaten to undermine the unity between the tsar and the people. In contrast, the new emperor, Nicholas I, is portrayed as a hero who saves Russia from the prospect of civil war and the destruction of the state. The young emperor realizes that change must evolve organically and gradually from within.[9]

At the time of writing, we are approaching the 200th anniversary of the Decembrist revolt. Because of the ongoing war in Ukraine, it is hard to predict how this event will be observed in Russia, but it is unlikely that the regime would want to honour the memory of the first liberal revolution against autocracy.

THIS BOOK EXPLORES THE UNFOLDING of the dramatic events of the revolt on 14 December 1825 and the uprising in Ukraine two weeks later. What was it all about? Why were these revolutionaries, the so-called Decembrists, willing to risk their careers and even their lives, and for what? What did they wish to achieve, what kind of society did they imagine and why did they fail? What were the consequences of the uprising for the participants and their families?

Seeking to explain the motivation behind the Decembrist revolt, the first chapter places the uprising in its national and transnational context. The actions of the Decembrists can be attributed to a combination of factors, crucial among which is the impact of Western ideas, cultures and practices. Learning about European cultures and political systems through their participation in the Napoleonic Wars, many Russian officers and future Decembrist leaders came to believe that Russia lagged behind other European countries. Moreover, the Decembrists grew up in a changing world. They were born at the time of the French Revolution.

Following the Napoleonic Wars, liberal revolts against autocratic government occurred in several European states. The Decembrists were captivated by the prevailing idea that revolutions aiming for freedom and equal rights would spread across the world until all monarchs had been toppled.

A third factor that contributed to the Decembrist revolt was the discrepancy between expectation and outcome. Members of Russia's young, educated elite were sorely disappointed in Tsar Alexander I, who began his rule with promises to end serfdom and establish constitutional government, and ended up as 'the gendarme of Europe', supplying Russian troops to quell liberal revolt in Europe. The promise of liberal change never came to fruition. Instead, Russian politics took a conservative turn.

To understand the motivations for the Decembrist revolt, it is also important to be aware of who the Decembrists were. The second chapter examines their background, education and careers and concludes that most of them were young army officers from the nobility, many with a good Western education. They were the first Russian generation to grow up in the new spirit of Enlightenment thought. In its final part, the chapter considers the origin and development of the secret Decembrist societies as part of an emerging civil society in Russia.

Part II is devoted to the revolt itself. It examines the confusion that arose over the succession to the throne after the unexpected death of Alexander I, and how this provided the Decembrists with an opportunity to revolt. This section explores the preparations made by the active members of the Northern Society and tells the story of 14 December 1825, when Russian officers marched their loyal troops to Senate Square to change the course of Russian history. It also tells the story of the lesser-known events in the southern part of the empire, present-day Ukraine, where members of the Southern Society, young officers of the Second Army, instigated a second revolt after learning about the events in St Petersburg.

The Decembrists were led by a strong belief in liberal and republican ideas. Part III explores these ideas and the political visions of a future Russian society they entailed. It also examines the origins of these ideas in contemporary Western political thought. The Decembrists believed that Russia was backward and needed to modernize, using the West as a model. Imitating Western ideas was not a problem to them, since they regarded Russia as part of Europe and saw themselves as Europeans. This view is hardly surprising, considering that Russia at the time was not only recognized as one of the great powers in Europe; after defeating Napoleon, it was regarded as the liberator of Europe. In addition, it was an important partner in the Concert of Europe.

The Decembrists expressed patriotic ideas as well, but their patriotism was not aimed at the West. It was a republican patriotism, a call to the Russian elite to engage with the problems of their own country, the suffering of their own people. It was also a protest against the superficial, Westernized Russian aristocracy, who were more interested in the latest Parisian fashions than in the plight of the Russian peasantry. Part III also analyses the interrelationship of liberalism, nationalism and imperialism, and how this was exhibited in the Decembrists' problematic view of Russia's many minorities.

The last two sections consider the consequences of the Decembrist revolt. How did the regime handle the revolt and the revolutionaries? How did the young noblemen cope with being arrested and placed in solitary confinement in the Peter and Paul Fortress? What were their reactions to the constant interrogations and the psychological pressure to confess and name other participants? How did their families react to their plight? Part IV gives an account of the arrests, imprisonment, sentencing and its execution, while Part V focuses on the fate of those sentenced to hard labour and exile.

The final chapter is not only about the men sentenced to penal servitude and deportation. It also tells the story of the women who followed their husbands or fiancés to Siberia and shared their exile. These women played a significant role for the exiled Decembrists. The Decembrist wives are usually portrayed as the ideal image of the loyal wife, an image that fits conservative historiography. However, some of them took a keen interest in political ideas. More importantly, these women were capable, resourceful individuals who worked tirelessly to mitigate the hardships of Siberian exile.

This is a book about ideas put into political action, but it is also about passion. The Decembrists were passionate in both political and private affairs. Moreover, they lived in an era when people were expected to express their feelings and to reflect on them. People's minds, emotions and actions were felt to be intermingled in a different way from today. This book is therefore not only about ideas and public actions, but about private life and emotions central to it, such as love, passion and feelings of friendship and community. We can never hope to understand the Decembrist revolt without also understanding the feelings that drove its participants to risk their lives in pursuit of a better future for their country.

# PART I
# SETTING AND
# ACTORS

V. A. Golicke, *Emperor Alexander I against the Backdrop of the Kremlin*,
1835, oil on canvas.

# 1

# State and Society

We will perhaps never fully comprehend why a group of young Russian officers chose to stand up against autocracy and privilege in December and January 1825–6. However, by exploring the world in which they lived, we may come to a deeper understanding. A key factor here is the role played by the West – Western Europe in particular – in the world view of young Russians. The Decembrist leaders were familiar with Western thought and influenced by Western culture, so they were well aware of the spread of republican and liberal principles in Western societies. Developments in their own country led many of them to believe that Russia too was about to change through liberal reforms. When their hopes were dashed, these young officers were sorely disappointed and ready to take matters into their own hands.

The Decembrist societies sprang forth from the Age of Revolutions (c. 1774–1849). In the wake of the American and French revolutions, liberal principles – legally codified individual liberties, constitutional limits on executive power, increased representation of the people in government, and an end to mercantilism – spread across Europe and the world. These principles were related to the idea of patriotism, expressed in a commitment to the common good and the welfare of the people or nation. In autocratic countries, secret patriotic societies committed to such ideals were formed. These associations often had their roots in freemasonry and its notions of social justice. Many were modelled on the practices of Masonic lodges and were dedicated to enlightenment, public welfare and moral regeneration. The Prussian *Tugendbund*, the Italian *Carbonari* and the Greek *Filiki Eteria* are the best-known, but a number of secret societies with similar agendas could be found across Europe, dedicated to the national liberation of their fatherland or the constitutional reorganization of society, and sometimes a combination of the two. On several occasions, these secret societies staged liberal revolts against autocratic rule in both Europe and the Americas. Such tendencies were reinforced by the patriotism awakened by the Napoleonic Wars.

In Russia, it seemed a new dawn rose when a young tsar with the aspiration to bring liberal reform to the nation came to power in 1801. Alexander I was a child of his era. He was brought up in the spirit of the Enlightenment and considered himself a free-thinker. His grandmother Catherine II, who supervised his education, had chosen as his tutor Frédérick César de La Harpe, a Swiss republican who wielded great influence over the young prince. Before Alexander ascended the throne, he was often critical of monarchic rule and spoke in favour of the rights of man and of nations. Even after his coronation, he continued to express aversion to tyranny and slavery. He was committed to bringing about changes in the political, social and economic life of Russia. Thus the new emperor conveyed his desire to abolish serfdom, reform political institutions and promote enlightenment through improved education.[1]

With the intention to plan for ambitious reforms, the tsar appointed a consultative body called the Unofficial Committee, consisting of a close circle of like-minded friends. Like Alexander, these friends were inspired by the economist Adam Smith and ideas about free trade. They opposed mercantilism in the name of commercial freedom. Their ideas informed the Russian customs tariff of 1801, although the tariff retained some restrictions to protect Russian industries.

Alexander's accession to the throne was greeted with unanimous and sincere enthusiasm by members of the Russian educated elite.[2] After a period of severe political repression and arbitrariness under Paul I, it was felt that there was finally hope for progressive change. The provisions of the Charter to the Nobility of 1785, which had consolidated the prerogatives of the nobility, were restored. Among other things, it reinforced property rights and the right of assembly and guaranteed trial by peers, freedom from the poll tax and compulsory army duty, the right to travel abroad and exemption from corporal punishment. The Secret Expedition, Paul I's secret police, was abolished and about 12,000 prisoners, who had been sentenced without a trial, released. Fugitives abroad were granted amnesty for crimes other than murder and the ban on travel was lifted. Alexander I reinstated discharged officials and officers and declared that future cases of dismissal could result only from lawful prosecution. Finally, he appointed a commission to draw up a new law code. One of its members was the well-known radical Aleksandr Radishchev. His appointment was of clear symbolic value and revealed the liberal leanings of the new emperor. Alexander I at first intended to announce additional plans for reform at his coronation, but his 'young friends' in the 'Unofficial Committee' dissuaded him from moving too fast.

## Liberal reforms

In 1801 both the Russian economy and the government were organized along premodern lines. In an overwhelmingly agrarian state, the soil was tilled by serfs tied to landed estates. The country was governed by an autocratic ruler with a minimum of constitutional restrictions on his exercise of power. It was an empire that fell far short of the principles propagated by the Age of Revolutions and of the ideals embraced by the youthful tsar. Alexander I's reign was dominated by the impulse to reform the system of government and to abolish serfdom. But in the quarter of a century that followed his coronation, the hope awakened in Russia's enlightened elite gradually turned to bitter disappointment.

In the period before the end of the Napoleonic Wars, Alexander initiated but ultimately failed to deliver the liberation of Russia's millions of peasant serfs (just over a third of the population). Serfdom was not the same thing as slavery, which was banned in Russia in 1723. The system of serfdom meant that peasant serfs were given a plot of land for their own use by landlords (the nobility, the state or the Church). In return, they had to provide service to the landowner, usually through agricultural labour. Although by law serfs were not the property of landlords and had legal rights, in practice landlords had absolute control over their serfs' lives and could buy and sell them at will. The conditions for serfs on state land were somewhat better. In Siberia, where land belonged to the state, peasants were practically free.[3]

During the first years of his rule, the new emperor commissioned several constitutional projects, as well as studies of the feasibility of emancipating the serfs. A number of suggestions for the reform of serfdom were presented, originating in both the court bureaucracy and the Unofficial Committee. There can be no doubt as to Alexander's negative view of noble privilege and of serfdom, an institution he regarded as inhuman and degrading. Measures to restrict the rights of landlords over their serfs were discussed in the Unofficial Committee from the outset of his reign, but the tsar moved cautiously. He did not want to make enemies of the nobility, who were afraid of losing a valuable asset. It was not just that they depended on free labour; many nobles had mortgaged their serfs to state credit institutions.

Shortly after his accession, Alexander presented a memorandum to the Permanent Council, the highest advisory body of the state, which proposed a prohibition on the sale of serfs without land to cultivate. But the conservatives in the Council argued that the measure was premature. The Council also opposed the proposal that the obligations of the peasants to their landlords should be specified more clearly by law. However, the Free Agriculturalists Law was passed in February 1803.[4] According to this law, landowners were permitted to free their serfs collectively. Landlords were allowed to petition the tsar for permission to free whole villages of serfs and thereby create a new social class of free peasants or agriculturalists. Each peasant was to be given a strip of land, the size of which was to be determined by the landlord. The peasants could compensate for this by paying cash, in instalments or in kind. But few landowners took this opportunity to free their serfs. The abominable practice of selling serfs openly at markets, something both Russians and foreigners reacted to, was not banned by law until 1808.

Projects for governmental reform fared little better in this period and they, too, would fail to bear fruit. When Alexander came to power, he expressed his desire to restore the former prestige of the senate as an institution of supervision and control, and perhaps even transform it into a legislative institution. In June 1801 he issued an order to the senate, demanding a report about its rights and duties. However, when the senate failed to agree on this matter and presented a report containing conflicting recommendations, Alexander chose to issue an edict that accomplished little.

In 1803 State Secretary Mikhail Speranskii was commissioned to work out a plan for political reform, but the formation of the Third Coalition against Napoleon now occupied Alexander's attention and the project was shelved.[5] In 1808 Speranskii was once again commissioned to draw up a plan for political reconstruction, and the document he presented to Alexander in 1809 was entitled 'An Introduction to the Code of State Laws'. It was an elaborate project, containing both a treatise on the general condition of Russia and proposals for constitutional reforms. Speranskii recommended the granting of civil rights to 'the better classes'. His plans for institutional reorganization were based on the theory of separation of powers between the executive (the State Council), the judiciary (the senate) and the legislature (the state Duma). However, since the emperor held supreme power, there was no real separation of power. The Duma would not have any actual legislative authority, but it would have the right to reject a law (proposed by the ministers) if it were thought to be harmful, as well as the power to make formal complaints if it believed fundamental laws had been broken. This meant that the power of the tsar would be restricted to some degree.

Speranskii had drawn up a proposal based on the commission he had received from Alexander. But the emperor did not approve it. He may have felt that the time was not ripe for reform, or that Speranskii's plan was too far-reaching. He may also have been frightened by the realization that he was eroding his own power. Alexander believed himself to be indispensable to the regeneration of the country. Another reason for his action may have been that he was preoccupied with managing international relations. Whatever the cause, the only part of the plan to which he agreed was the establishment of a new Council of State, replacing the Permanent Council, and additional ministries.

Another key reform project that came to nothing was the codification of Russian laws. A commission was set up in 1801 and a Russian law code finally completed in 1812. It was accepted by the State Council, which had replaced the Permanent Council in 1810, but was never enforced.[6] Even though Alexander clearly had the ambition to establish some form of limited monarchy and rule of law, the bottom line is that not much came of the planned political reforms.

Alexander's progressive ideas also found expression in an ambitious liberal vision of Europe. In 1804 he presented a proposal to the British prime minister William Pitt for the reorganization of Europe into a league of constitutional states founded on 'the sacred rights of humanity', under the protection of Russia and Britain. He also suggested that codes of law and the rights of man should be introduced for the whole of Europe.[7] This outlook is reflected in his decision to recognize the liberal Spanish Constitution of 1812, as well as in his attitude to constitutions in the years immediately following the Napoleonic Wars. Alexander showed that his constitutionalism was not merely empty words, but something he truly believed in.[8] All this had a great impact on the young, educated elite who had started to dream of a constitution for Russia.

The Age of Revolution was also an age of war. The Napoleonic Wars, which in Alexander's case began with Russia's participation in the War of the Third Coalition (1805–6) and ended in Paris in 1814, enhanced both the status of the Russian state and the tsar's reputation as a liberal ruler and defender of a free Europe, especially after Napoleon's invasion of Russia in 1812. In war propaganda, Napoleon was portrayed as a bloodthirsty tyrant with an insatiable hunger for expansion, who was depriving the peoples of Europe of their liberty. Napoleon's tyranny, aggression and immorality were contrasted with Alexander's defence of the liberty of Europe and its peoples. In a pamphlet, the classical scholar and imperial administrator Sergei Uvarov wrote, 'To liberate nations, to topple odious tyrants. To restore lawful rule, to act as a tsar, having fulfilled the knight's duty on the battlefield . . . these are the deeds of Alexander.' The Russian Orthodox Church presented Napoleon as the enemy of Russia and of the liberating mission with which Russia had been entrusted. At the time of the invasion, the Church proclaimed that Providence was calling on Russia to stop the atrocities of 'godless Napoleon' and free Europe from his grip. The prominent poet Gavriil Derzhavin depicted the war as a struggle between good and evil.[9]

Since Russia was on the side of good, it was expected to win. Thus the French occupation of Moscow came as a horrendous shock. The Decembrist Nikolai Lorer recalled in his memoirs the moment when the news reached St Petersburg. His entire household was 'in great sorrow and confusion . . . There was a terrible [feeling of] emptiness in the city.'[10] Sorrow and confusion prevailed everywhere. Hence, when Napoleon's Grande Armée was crushed and Alexander I led Russian troops into Paris on 31 March 1814, Russia's educated elite regarded the tsar as a liberator who had freed Europe from Napoleon's tyranny and saved the Russian people.

After the war, Alexander continued to promote moderate constitutional reform in Europe. He was convinced that civil and political rights would lead to stability and peace. For that reason, he supported the proclamation of constitutions in the German states and in Switzerland. He sent his foreign minister, Ioannis Kapodistrias (John Capodistrias), to Switzerland in November 1813 to help establish Swiss unity and independence, and supported Kapodistrias's efforts to introduce a new federal constitution there. The young Russian tsar also insisted on a constitution for the restored monarchy in France. The *Charte Constitutionelle*, adopted in June 1814, was thus not only approved, but encouraged by Alexander. It guaranteed equality before the law and religious toleration. The king was given executive power, but a bicameral assembly was formed based on a limited franchise, with the right to reject a bill proposed by the king. Thus Louis XVIII would return not as an absolute monarch but as a constitutional monarch. Alexander believed that by guaranteeing these rights and thus incorporating parts of the French revolutionary principles, stability would be ensured.

These events were followed closely by the educated Russian elite.[11] There were two important constitutional events in Russia itself, or rather in the Russian empire, that also had an impact on the country's educated elite. Following the Swedish defeat in the Finnish War (1808–9), Finland was incorporated into the Russian empire as an autonomous grand duchy. To receive the support of the Finns, the tsar promised to respect Finnish laws and the existing political structure. This was seen as a sign of Alexander's positive attitude to the rule of law. Even more important was his granting of a constitution to the Kingdom of Poland on 27 November 1815. According to the Treaty of Vienna of that year, Alexander had accepted the crown of the new independent Congress Kingdom of Poland. The kingdom had its own government and judiciary, a separate civil service and army. The new constitution provided Poland with an elected legislature (the Sejm) and civil rights.[12]

On 15 March 1818 Alexander opened the first session of the Polish Sejm in Warsaw. This was a highly symbolic moment. Lorer, who was in Warsaw at the time, recalled how the emperor appeared in the hall in traditional Polish dress, bowed to the people's representatives and in a firm voice said, 'Représentants du Royaume de Pologne! [Representatives of the Kingdom of Poland]'. 'It took my breath away and tears welled up in my eyes. This conversion was of course new for all of us, subjects of the autocratic sovereign.'[13] In his speech, the tsar expressed his hope one day to be able to extend the liberal institutions of the Polish Charter 'to all the lands entrusted by Providence to my care'.[14] Contemporaries heard in this speech the promise of a Russian constitution. Vladimir Shteingel, another Decembrist, recalled the significance of this speech that flattered the hopes of Russian liberals.[15] It was quickly translated into Russian and published in *Vestnik Europy*, the *St Petersburg Gazette* and *Dukh zhurnalov*. Shortly thereafter, at the Congress of Aix-la-Chapelle, in an interview with the high-ranking military officer Marquis Nicolas Joseph Maison, Alexander renewed his declaration: 'The peoples must be delivered from arbitrary regime; I have re-established this principle in Poland, I will establish it in my other States.'

When news of the emperor's speech reached Russia, all members of the educated elite were affected. Russian officers drank to their country's future constitution at St Petersburg restaurants.[16] The liberal law professor and philosopher Aleksandr Kunitsyn of St Petersburg University published a highly noted article in *Syn otechestva* (Son of the Fatherland) in 1818, defending constitutionalism against its conservative critics.[17] Western literature on constitutions was widely read both in the original and in translation. Russian journals, such as *Dukh zhurnalov* (The Spirit of Journals), published laws and constitutions from foreign countries. But not everyone was pleased by the emperor's speech and the public discussion of constitutions that followed. In a letter to a friend, the historian Nikolai Karamzin warned that 'the Warsaw speech had a formidable effect on young hearts: they dream of a constitution.' Later, Count Rostopchin, former governor general of Moscow, made a similar assessment, saying that the speech of the emperor in Warsaw had excited young people, who now demanded a constitution from him.[18]

When Nikolai Novosiltsev, one of the tsar's closest associates, was secretly commissioned sometime in 1818 or 1819 to write a charter for Russia, it seemed that Alexander was ready to follow through on his intention to give Russia a constitution. He approved the first draft in October 1819. It was made public in November, when the French newspaper *Le Constitutionel* reported that the tsar intended to grant his country a constitution, which would lay the foundations for a representative government. Constitutionalism was now the talk of the town. In early summer of 1820 it was reported that Alexander was still positive about the project, clearly wanting it to continue. Yet he took no action to implement it.

The end of the Napoleonic Wars also brought the resumption of projects for the emancipation of the serfs. Parts of the educated elite and the peasantry felt that the serfs had earned their freedom through the patriotism they displayed in the war of 1812. During the French invasion, serfs had played a major role in Napoleon's defeat by preventing supplies from reaching the French army and by attacking the French rearguard. An intense discussion of peasant reform in such journals as *Vestnik Evropy* (The Messenger of Europe) and *Syn otechestva* followed the war. Meanwhile, Alexander commissioned several projects for the emancipation of the serfs in the years 1817–19. But, as with constitutional reform, the emperor held back. The strong resistance expressed by many leaders of the provincial nobility appears to have made him hesitant. Still, there was some movement. Peasants were liberated in the Baltic provinces in 1816–19, in Estonia in 1816, in Courland in 1817 and in Livonia in 1819 – yet in all cases without being provided with land of their own. These measures led some Russians to believe that emancipation would soon be underway in Russia too. After all, the serfs had been liberated in the Duchy of Warsaw and in Prussia in 1807. Some liberal landowners tried to assist Alexander through private initiatives, but their attempts were rebuffed. Leading officials addressed the tsar, urging the abolition of serfdom. In 1815 Mikhail Orlov wrote a memorandum to the tsar, signed by many leading officials, among them Count Vorontsov, Count Bludov and General Vasilchikov. It was followed the next year by another memorandum by Count Pavel Kiselev. These initiatives came to nothing.

The many millions of Russian serfs could thus not look forward to brighter times. On the contrary, their lives were destined to change for the worse. In 1810 military colonies were being established in Russia, and by 1825 colonies were formed in St Petersburg, Novgorod, Mogilev, Ekaterinoslav and Kherson provinces. Military colonies were made up of soldiers and peasants. The soldiers and their families would assist the peasants in peacetime, while the peasants would provide for the soldier and his family when he was called up to war. The colonists were to receive financial support and welfare: better housing, roads, healthcare and education.

There were several reasons for the introduction of military colonies. The cost of maintaining a standing army commensurate to Russia's new standing as a European great power was prohibitive, and state finances were in a critical state after the exertions of the Napoleonic Wars. By settling soldiers on the land, the army could become self-supporting. The colonies also promised to overcome the resistance to compulsory service among the peasantry. Another important reason for introducing military colonies was to create modern (Westernized) villages. The idea was that the colonies would contribute to forming well-organized villages with better infrastructure and well-educated inhabitants at no cost to the government. In practice, they brought even greater hardship to the peasantry.

The military colonies fundamentally transformed the lives of the Russian peasants. Villages were converted into military camps whose inhabitants were subject to a military regime around the clock. Peasants were forced to wear military uniforms, to shave their beards and cut their hair short. A brutal system of discipline meted out corporal punishment for the slightest offence. Sons were forced to become soldiers, daughters to marry within the colony. Nor were the promised economic benefits realized. The colonists had to perform obligatory construction work in return for low salaries. Constant interference in the peasants' lives by ignorant officials resulted in crop failures. Even though women were officially required to give birth annually, the conditions in the colonies were so bad that the death rate exceeded the birth rate.

The military colonies provoked bitter resentment among the peasants. Numerous petitions were sent to the tsar and riots broke out in several colonies. In 1819 some 28,000 peasants rose up in rebellion in the south.

General Arakcheev, the organizer of the military settlements, led two army divisions to suppress the uprising. Hundreds of rebels were put on trial and dozens were flogged to death. Among liberal members of the educated elite, the military colonies came to be seen as a symbol of despotism and oppression.[19]

## The conservative turn

In 1820 Alexander I ultimately abandoned his liberal ambitions and embraced the conservative politics of the Holy Alliance. This was a gradual process that had started in 1819. In March that year August Friedrich von Kotzebue, a German playwright who worked for the Russian intelligence service, was murdered in Mannheim by a student. Shocked by the assassination, Alexander started to suspect that revolutionary ideas were once again spreading from France. Still, this did not mean that he immediately abandoned his view that constitutions created stability. This outlook changed in stages.

At the beginning of the 1820s revolts broke out in Spain and Naples, aiming to introduce representative government. In March King Ferdinand VII of Spain was forced to restore the liberal constitution of 1812. When Alexander learned about the revolt in Madrid, he advised Ferdinand to accept the liberal constitution the rebels demanded. In Naples a few months later, a revolt broke out that threatened the position of Austria on the Italian peninsula. Alexander initially supported his foreign minister Kapodistrias's suggestion that Naples should have a national constitution. However, the Austrian foreign minister, Klemens von Metternich, who needed Alexander's support in suppressing the revolution, tried to undermine Kapodistrias and convince Alexander that Europe faced a revolutionary threat through the spread of secret societies. Metternich argued that constitutional demands were in themselves subversive and a threat to the social and political order in the whole of Europe. At the Congress of Troppau in October 1820, Metternich finally won Alexander's support for military intervention if a state were threatened by a change of government owing to revolution, which put other states at risk.[20]

In the autumn of 1820 Alexander was also becoming disillusioned with the constitutional government in Poland. The tsar's relationship with the parliament was amicable at first, but when delegates in the second Polish Sejm, which met in September 1820, questioned his actions and regarded them as unconstitutional, he acted in the true sense of the autocrat he was, telling them through an emissary that he could remove the constitution as easily as he had introduced it.[21]

During the liberal revolts in Europe, Alexander had maintained that Russia was immune to the revolutionary threat; that religion, reason and wise government guaranteed stability. However, while the emperor was busy with foreign affairs attending the Congress, there was a mutiny in the prestigious Semionovskii Guards regiment in St Petersburg. The soldiers of the First Company revolted against the cruel treatment of soldiers under the brutal new commander F. E. Schwartz. The whole company was arrested and brought to the Peter and Paul Fortress. When the rest of the regiment supported them, they were also sent to the fortress.[22] Alexander was convinced that the mutiny was the work of Russian liberals, who disliked his participation at the Congress. But he also believed that it was connected to the revolutionary movement in Europe.[23] It was now apparent to him that the French Constitution had not prevented the survival of revolutionary ideas. The Semionovskii revolt caused him finally to lose faith in constitutions as pillars of stability.

By 1821 Alexander had become a staunch adherent of Metternich's political doctrine. When revolts broke out in Piedmont in February 1821, he described this as a threat to the Christian religion and blamed it on the influence of French Enlightenment ideas. At about the same time the Greek secret society Filiki Eteria (Society of Friends) started a revolt against the Ottoman empire in Moldavia and Wallachia as part of a plan for Greek independence. The leader of the society, Alexandros Ypsilantis, had been a major general in the Russian army. Ypsilantis turned for support to the Russian emperor, as the protector of the Orthodox faith, but Alexander, who had now started to fear revolutions, did not approve. He regarded the Greek revolt as part of a larger European revolutionary conspiracy, attempting to prevent the Holy Alliance from crushing the revolution in Naples.[24] Without Russia's support, the Greek uprising was defeated. However, in June another began in the Peloponnese (Morea) and spread to Crete, Macedonia and central Greece.[25]

There was widespread sympathy in Russia for Greek independence. Officers of the Guard, agitated by the news of the Greek uprising, asked to join army regiments that were expected to fight. When Alexander refrained from helping 'fellow orthodox believers', people were upset. A few years later Shteingel expressed these feelings in a letter to the new tsar, Nicholas I: 'The Greeks were left to their fate; the bond of one faith which had been indestructible for eight centuries ... was suddenly destroyed.'[26] At the Congress of Verona in late 1822, the situation in Spain was discussed by the Quintuple Alliance (Austria, Prussia, Russia, France and Great Britain). Alexander not only supported the French invasion to crush the liberal movement and reinstate monarchical power, but promised to send Russian troops to assist them.

Liberal-minded Russians were distressed and hugely disappointed by Alexander's new foreign policy and his hostile attitude to the freedom of peoples. How could 'the liberal tsar' contribute to the oppression of the Spanish revolutionaries, who desired to uphold the very constitution he had supported a few years earlier? The way Russian troops were used to suppress liberal movements, not just in Spain but everywhere, was shameful. The disappointment many educated Russians felt about the tsar was conveyed in a letter sent by the Decembrist Piotr Kakhovskii from his cell after the defeat of the Decembrist revolt: 'Was it not he who fanned the light of freedom in our hearts, and was it not he who then so cruelly extinguished it not only in our own country, but in the whole of Europe? He helped Ferdinand suppress the legitimate rights of the people of Spain and did not foresee the evil that this caused to all thrones.'[27]

Alexander's changed perception of European stability also made him wary of risking social disorder and antagonizing the nobility by emancipating the serfs. Many landowners were reluctant to free the serfs, fearing that it would lead to economic loss and peasant revolt. Between 1815 and 1825 flight, disturbances and complaints among peasants increased significantly. In addition to dissatisfaction with the military colonies, a possible reason for this is that news about serf reform was spreading to the peasants. It is also possible that landowners were exploiting them more in intensive farming and factory production after the war.[28] Whatever the reason, Alexander feared that emancipation would create social unrest that would add fuel to the revolutionary movement he now believed was threatening the political and social order of Europe.

Another area affected by the more reactionary view of the regime was education. At the beginning of his reign, Alexander had introduced a reform of the educational structure. Schools were open to all classes and genders and were free of charge for the poor. In 1809 two decrees intended to improve the level of education were instigated by Speranskii. However, in 1819 under the new minister of education, Aleksandr Golitsyn, former chief prosecutor of the Holy Synod, a change in policy was evident. Kazan University was the victim of a purge, during which it was completely reorganized and several professors expelled. A couple of years later, in 1821–2, a number of professors were dismissed from the University of St Petersburg. They were accused of sympathizing with atheism and constitutionalism. At the University of Dorpat (now Tartu) and Vilna, professors were expelled for teaching rationalistic philosophy. In July 1822 the government banned the University of Dorpat from enrolling students who had attended foreign universities, since these individuals were believed to bring with them practices of insubordination. In February 1823 Russian students were forbidden from attending certain German universities because these were considered places of antireligious and immoral ideas. This reactionary educational policy disillusioned many young men.

Members of the reform-inclined educated elite were also upset by the tightening of censorship. At the beginning of Alexander's reign censorship had eased somewhat and the prohibition of foreign books was lifted, although certain subjects, such as serfdom, were still outlawed in the press. However, in the year before the French invasion of Russia, censorship became stricter and more arbitrary. Numerous regulations silenced the press and subjected authors to the whims of narrow-minded censors. After the war things did not improve; quite the opposite. The government ruled that journalists must now adjust their statements to the intentions of the regime and assist in promoting peaceful relations. The journal *Dukh zhurnalov* closed down in December 1820. The import of foreign books was prevented. Aleksandr Kunitsyn's popular book about natural law published in 1818–20 was banned from teaching and removed from the libraries in 1821.[29] Nevertheless, political commentaries and republican poems, such as Kondratii Ryleev's 'Volynskii' and 'Nalivaiko's Confession', sometimes slipped through.

After the revolt, several Decembrists expressed their dismay at Alexander's change in political direction. To Vladimir Shteingel, the problem was that the emperor's conservative turn occurred 'just as the minds of dreamers of freedom in Russia had been ignited'.[30] Nikolai Basargin concurred. He argued that the events leading up to the Decembrist revolt followed a similar pattern in Russia to those in other European states. The people began to express their discontentment when they saw no clear signs that their expectations were being met. This provoked a reaction from the sovereign. The people, now convinced that they could expect nothing from their government, began to act on their own. They decided to advance public affairs by the formation and spread of secret societies.[31]

## A nascent civil society

As early as the end of the eighteenth century, a tentative civil society was emerging in Russia. The process was accelerated by the war of 1812, when Napoleon invaded. In the Decembrist Ivan Iakushkin's words, 'the war of 1812 roused the people of Russia to life and constituted an important period in its political existence.'[32] The war not only inspired patriotism, but changed people's mentalities and the way educated Russians saw themselves and their country. It made them visualize Russia in the context of larger historical events and a wider geopolitical context, and it contributed to shaping a sense of public responsibility and civic consciousness.[33]

The Decembrists developed this sentiment into a programme of civic nationalism. This programme marked a shift among large parts of the nobility from the role of subjects to that of citizens, from concern with aristocratic privilege and rank to civic consciousness and a concept of the common good. It was a rejection of the idea of the autocrat as the principal agent of social change and progress. The tsar was no longer seen as the embodiment of the state.[34] This transformation was captured by Sergei Volkonskii when he recalled his association with 'free-thinking people' in the circle of his schoolfriend Mikhail Orlov in Kyiv: 'From that time on, a new life began for me. I set out with a proud sense of conviction and duty, not as a loyal subject, but as a citizen, and with a firm intention to fulfil my duty at all costs solely out of love for the Fatherland.'[35] Hence, while the middle classes were instrumental to this process in the West, the nobility played a crucial part in the development of civic and national consciousness in Russia, just as it did in countries in Eastern Europe.

The Russian nobility in the early nineteenth century was fragmented and insecure. It lacked representative estate institutions and a firm local base, and it was economically weak; status and careers were insecure. Noblemen were expected to serve the state.[36] Yet things were starting to change. The Charter to the Nobility of 1785 accorded the gentry of each province the right to meet every three years to discuss local affairs, and to elect a district and a provincial marshal of the nobility to manage welfare functions and a land captain to serve as a local police official. They also had the right to petition the tsar. An active social life began to develop in the provinces.[37] Meanwhile, enlightened nobles joined different types of association in the cities to discuss cultural, social, economic and political subjects.

In the early nineteenth century a large number of voluntary associations were formed in Russia, especially after the Napoleonic Wars. Organizations of various types, including dining clubs, theatre clubs, literary societies, philosophical societies and Masonic lodges, emerged or were resuscitated. Many future leading Decembrists were attracted by Freemasonry, which had a revival in Europe at the beginning of the nineteenth century. The Masonic movement was founded on the precept that all men are created equal, and many Masons promoted ideas of social justice. This liberal tendency appealed to many Decembrists, and some were active participants in lodges for a long time. Pavel Pestel, Ryleev, Sergei and Matvei Muraviev-Apostol, Vilgelm Kiukhelbeker, Mikhail Lunin, Ivan Pushchin, and Aleksandr and Nikita Muraviev were all members. But gradually they became disenchanted with the Masonic movement. Freemasonry promoted gradual reforms through the enlightenment of the individual; there was no action and never would be. Still, the lodges served as a model for the organization of the Decembrist societies and brought many of the members together.[38]

Future Decembrists were involved in various associations that provided opportunities for self-expression and knowledgeable company. Most were educational and reform-orientated, such as the Moscow Agricultural Society, which was aimed at improving knowledge of agriculture and disseminating better agricultural practices in Russia. Some were more informal and had a creative and free-thinking purpose, such as the literary society Arzamas or the unconventional literary club the Green Lamp. Commonly, future Decembrists preferred the more serious Free Society for Lovers of Russian Literature or, to a lesser extent, the Free Society for Lovers of Literature, the Sciences and the Arts. An association with close ties to the Decembrists was the Order of Russian Knights, formed by Orlov, with the purpose of assisting the tsar in carrying out constitutional reforms and the emancipation of the serfs. Other pre-Decembrist societies were the officers' clubs (*artels*) of the Semionovskii and Izmailovskii regiments, formed for the reading of foreign newspapers and conversation about Russian life, and the Sacred Artel, formed in 1814 by young Guards officers interested in republicanism.[39]

These associations and the opportunity they offered of meeting like-minded people fulfilled an important function for the young generation, both psychologically and sociologically. Looking back on this period, many Decembrists – most of whom were army officers – agreed that the associations satisfied a need for companionship and purpose after the war.[40] Here, they were able to talk openly about pressing issues with people they could trust and with whom they shared a common purpose: to serve their country and the common good. Moreover, the experience of communion with friends fostered a feeling of belonging to a community of citizens. Ivan Pushchin recalled how discussions about the evil of the existing order and the possibility of change created uncommonly close bonds between the members of the Sacred Artel. These conversations made a profound impression on him. He felt chosen, part of something greater, a movement that 'would sooner or later have its beneficial action'.[41] Nikolai Turgenev remembered the meetings of the Union of Welfare as the happiest moments of his life: 'In these all too brief moments, I was in the company of people who for me were always noble and filled with the purest aspirations and selfless devotion to their friends.'[42]

In the voluntary associations, young Russian officers found an outlet for their newfound civic consciousness and a new way to serve their country in peacetime. There were many who felt that the true purpose of men was love for their fatherland, desire for its well-being and the sacrifice of self for its benefit. They were greatly inspired by the idea of spreading civic virtue and enlightenment and achieving the freedom of the peasants.[43] Basargin remembered the evening reading circle formed by Pestel for officers at the headquarters of the Second Army in Tulchyn. Here, young officers met not only for personal enjoyment but for self-improvement, and with the ambition to promote the common good. They discussed contemporary events and topics, as well as literature and philosophy. According to Basargin, the evenings when they got together and gave one another an account of what they were doing, reading and thinking constituted the best kind of entertainment.[44]

Volkonskii also attached great significance to the fact of associations having a higher purpose. He fondly recalled his first stay in Kyiv, when he entered a circle of people who believed that their existence and deeds were not limited to the empty life of St Petersburg drawing rooms and military garrison life. This group, Volkonskii wrote, believed that their lives and deeds should be dedicated to the benefit of the fatherland and its civil transformation, taking Russia to the level of civil life found in Europe and introducing to it the rights of man and peoples. Evgenii Obolenskii emphasized that the secret society of the future Decembrists, the Union of Welfare, 'satisfied all the noble aspirations of those who sought in life not pleasure alone, but the true moral benefit of their own and all their neighbours'.[45] Similarly, Iakushkin recalled that the society's members occupied themselves with questions about everything that could contribute to Russia's prosperity.[46]

Some Decembrists tried to be useful to their country by leaving the army, which they felt was of no use in peacetime, for less prestigious public positions. In his memoirs, Basargin narrates how he left the Guards Artillery and transferred to public service in Moscow, where he was appointed court judge. Both friends and relatives were shocked by his decision because in those days public service, especially that at a lower level, was considered beneath the dignity of a rich and noble gentleman. But Basargin wanted to show that you can serve your country honourably anywhere. Another example is Pushchin, who resigned his commission as an officer in the prestigious Horse Guards Artillery for the civil service, working first in the St Petersburg Criminal Chamber, then as a judge in the Moscow Court of Justice. He hoped to be of use in this field and to encourage others to take on similar responsibilities, to disregard 'shiny epaulettes' for 'the benefits that they could bring to the lower courts', introducing 'that noble way of thinking, those pure motives that adorn a person both in private life and in the public arena'.[47]

Ryleev, another case in point, left the army to work as an assessor at the St Petersburg Criminal Court. According to his own account, he had served the fatherland while it needed the service of its citizens and did not wish to continue when he saw that he would serve only the whims of an autocratic despot. He felt that as a judge he would better serve humanity. In this position, he would shed his blood for the freedom of his fatherland and the happiness of his compatriots, 'for the acquisition of legal rights for oppressed humanity'.[48] He subsequently accepted a position as manager at the Russian-American Company.

The Decembrists were very much part of an emerging civil society in Russia, not only in the way they involved themselves in voluntary associations, discussed social and political issues and wrote political programmes, but in the way they sought to shape public spirit, engage public opinion and enact public protests. The position they took in front of the senate at the time of the revolt was not only a means to achieve certain political changes. It was a public demonstration against the traditional political order.[49]

Another example of a public demonstration occurred a few months before that, when the Decembrists made use of the funeral of Ryleev's cousin Konstantin Chernov, on 27 September 1825, to arouse public opinion. Funerals were public occasions well suited to this, and in the second half of the nineteenth century members of the radical intelligentsia often used them for this purpose, but the Decembrists were already aware of their symbolic public role. Chernov, whose family was of modest social status, was killed in a duel with the high-born aristocrat and aide-de-camp Vladimir Novosiltsev. Novosiltsev had become engaged to Chernov's sister Maria but did not keep his promise to marry her. More than a year after the betrothal, when Novosiltsev still showed no willingness to marry Maria, her brother had challenged him to a duel. The Decembrists turned the occasion of his subsequent funeral into a public demonstration against the privileged aristocratic elite and their arrogant behaviour towards people of lower social status. Iakushkin designated it 'their first public protest'. More than two hundred carriages and numerous people on foot took part in the procession. Shteingel described the occasion as expressing 'a new, hitherto unprecedented public spirit [*dukh obshchestvennosti*]'. Aleksandr Bestuzhev regarded it as a democratic achievement. After the funeral, he argued, people could no longer claim that there was no public opinion in Russia.[50]

Civic poetry was also employed to influence public opinion. Another means of shaping public sentiment used more extensively by the Decembrists was parodic songs. Ryleev and Bestuzhev wrote numerous subversive poems condemning Russian reality, based on well-known Russian songs. They were intended to be spread among the people, and although it is hard to tell whether they actually were, it is fair to say that some were quite widely known.[51]

In a letter to Nicholas I, written in the Peter and Paul Fortress in January 1826, Shteingel contended that Russian society was already so enlightened that shopkeepers were reading newspapers that reported on the debates in the Chamber of Deputies in Paris.[52] Not all Decembrists were equally positive, but most maintained that in the last years of Alexander's reign their secret societies began to influence public opinion, and that the idea of constitutional rule gained supporters.[53] To root out free thought in Russia, Shteingel concluded his letter to the new tsar, you would have 'to destroy an entire generation'.[54] Nicholas did not destroy an entire generation, but he stifled many of its members and forced them to move underground.

# 2

# The Decembrists

The Decembrist associations had their origin in a secret society called the Union of Salvation, formed in 1816, later also known as the Society of True and Faithful Sons of the Fatherland. The Union of Salvation was influenced by secret societies in Europe but was modelled more directly on the Tugendbund (Society for Virtue). This was a secret quasi-Masonic society founded in the spring of 1808 in Königsberg, Prussia (now Kaliningrad, Russia), with the purpose of bringing about the moral and political regeneration of the fatherland, including its constitutional reorganization, and the overthrow of French rule after the Prussian defeat by Napoleon. Its members were mostly army officers.

The founders of the Union of Salvation included several close friends who later played a key role in the Decembrist societies: Nikita Muraviev, Sergei Trubetskoi, Ivan Iakushkin, Mikhail Lunin, Aleksandr N. Muraviev, Matvei and Sergei Muraviev-Apostol, all of them officers in the Imperial Guard and members of the high nobility. Soon Mikhail Fonvizin, Ivan Pushchin, Mikhail Muraviev (Aleksandr's brother), Ivan Burtsov and Pavel Pestel joined. Other active members were Fedor Glinka, Pavel Grabbe, Prince Ilya Dolgorukov, Prince Fedor Shakhovskoi and Ivan Shipov. In his memoirs, Iakushkin recounted that it was Aleksandr and Nikita Muraviev who suggested the formation of a secret society. Likewise, Lunin writes that he was present at the meeting in Sergei Muraviev-Apostol's St Petersburg home when, on the night of 9 February 1816, his cousin Nikita suggested that a secret society be formed. This first Decembrist organization was small, with only about thirty members, but it was active both in the capital and in Moscow. The Moscow members met at Fonvizin's, where Iakushkin also lived, or in the quarters of Aleksandr Muraviev.[1]

There are slightly different opinions among contemporaries about the society's goal. According to some testimonies, it was formed to promote moral revival and to support the tsar in his efforts at reform. Others claimed that this was only a facade; that its true aim was the abolition of serfdom and the introduction of constitutional monarchy. Iakushkin stated that the society's goal was representative rule and the refusal to take the oath of allegiance to a new tsar unless he agreed to rule as a limited monarch. But he added that not all members were aware of this. Pestel, who later became the leader of the Southern Society, stated that the purpose was to form a revolutionary organization. It appears that the main goals of the Union of Salvation were to abolish serfdom and to introduce constitutional monarchy. At this point, it was still believed that the tsar was in the process of introducing liberal reforms in order to 'arrange the good of Russia'.[2] According to Trubetskoi, the Society consisted of young officers who had promised to assist the emperor in all his designs for the good of the people. These officers wished to show their love for the fatherland not only by fulfilling the duties assigned to them by their military service, but by dedicating all their means and abilities to promoting the common good in all its forms. This was seen as their patriotic duty, and the Tugendbund had shown that collective action could achieve a lot of good.

Soon political divisions arose between the conservative and radical members of the Union of Salvation. A committee was elected to draft a constitution and propose a reorganization of the society. This committee, consisting of Pestel, Dolgorukov, Trubetskoi and Shakhovskoi, completed a draft constitution in February 1817, but it was criticized for being too radical. The committee had abandoned the idea of peaceful transformation through existing institutions. Instead, it was proposed that a revolt would be staged at the time of the tsar's natural death. This was not acceptable to the conservatives, who wanted to influence public opinion gradually to secure widespread support for the society's aims.[3]

In the autumn of 1817, when Pestel was stationed in Mitava, leading members decided to reform the society. New statutes were drawn up, influenced by the constitution of the Tugendbund.[4] These statutes, called the 'Green Book', were presented to the members in January 1818. At the same time a new society was formed, called the Union of Welfare. Fundamental concepts in the new constitution were justice, virtue, civic obligation and the common good. The stated goal of the new society was to spread virtue and enlightenment to fellow citizens, as well as 'assisting the government in raising Russia to the level of greatness and prosperity that its Maker intended'.[5] In the enquiry after the Decembrist revolt, Lunin, who was a member of the council of the new Union of Welfare, asserted that the objects of the Society had been twofold: allegedly 'to spread abroad enlightenment and humanitarianism', but in reality to introduce the Union's constitution and 'a free and legal government'. Similarly, Evgenii Obolenskii wrote that the ultimate goal of the Union of Welfare was the political transformation of the fatherland so that 'general education would be accessible to the people'. Meanwhile, they should strive for a solution to 'the most important issues'.[6]

To reach their goal, Obolenskii maintained, members had to work on their moral improvement and spiritual education. Each member should strive to direct society, through his personal actions in his own social circle,

> to the solution of the most important issues, both political, general
> and contemporary, by the influence that each member could have,
> and by his personal education and by the moral character that was
> assumed in him . . . In the . . . distance, one could see the final goal
> – the political transformation of the Fatherland.[7]

The 'secret' goal of the Union of Welfare – that is to say, representative government and the abolition of serfdom – was included in the second part of the Green Book. This part was not formally accepted by the Decembrists and has not survived.[8] In his memoirs, A. M. Muraviev recalled additional goals contained in the Green Book, such as the equality of citizens before the law, transparency in public affairs and of legal proceedings, the abolition of the wine monopoly, the destruction of military colonies and reducing service for soldiers.[9] However, it is unclear whether these ideas were part of the original statutes or were expressed by the Society at a later stage.

The Union of Welfare was a patriotic association in the sense that it was focused on the good of the fatherland and tried to direct people to the needs of that fatherland. The Society's members criticized the superficial culture of the Russian nobility, who seemed more interested in French fashions than in the development of their own country or the conditions of the Russian people. These aristocrats had not understood the importance of civic virtue, the dedication to common welfare necessary for a state to flourish. The Union of Welfare even discouraged parents from educating their children in foreign lands, because of the danger that children would become infatuated with foreign things and thus not be devoted to the improvement of their native land. Today, we often associate patriotism with conservative nationalism, but at the beginning of the nineteenth century it was associated with liberalism and republicanism. A patriot worked towards national independence, civic rights and the common good. The Union of Welfare declared that 'to strive for the common good is the concern of every citizen ... The nation's common weal demands the good of the individual, and ... every man, whatever his estate, has a right to it.'[10]

The Society's members also took a keen interest in the improvement of the lives of the peasantry, of education and of the nation's economy. Each member pledged to free their serfs when they passed into their inheritance. They were supposed to work to improve the fields of philanthropy, education, justice and national economy, based on the idea that there is an unbreakable tie between a people's virtue and its welfare. Education was particularly important. To be of use to their fatherland, the members of the Union needed detailed information about the state of their country as well as knowledge of the sciences that could improve civil life. The acquisition of this information and knowledge was therefore an indispensable duty.[11] The Decembrists' attention to national welfare also made them interested in the nation's economy, the foundation of its wealth. They studied books on political economy and attended lectures at the university. 'Through trade and industry', they said, the nation's economy 'binds together not only all estates, but all the vast territories of the state'.[12]

The Union of Welfare became a larger and more long-lasting organization than its predecessor. It had more than two hundred members. In addition, many Russians who were not formally members shared its views and were in close association with its members. Meetings were held in the apartments of Nikita Muraviev, Nikolai Turgenev, Dolgorukov and Shipov. Members were divided into four groups according to their occupation, and each group was divided into councils. All the councils were under the leadership of the Supreme Duma, or Main Council, in St Petersburg, composed of 24 members.[13] Foreigners, who had left their homeland to serve a foreign state, were not considered trustworthy citizens and were not admitted, with the exception of those who had rendered important services to Russia. Women were not considered full citizens and were thus not admitted either.[14]

The Society's attitude to women may seem jarring to modern sensibilities, but it was typical of the era. Although not admitted as members, women were to be encouraged to do philanthropic work in the spirit of the Union, and the members were charged with turning women from enjoying 'idle pleasures' to the dissemination of patriotism and true enlightenment. The most esteemed calling for the female sex, according to the Green Book, was the education of children.[15] The ideal of republican womanhood expressed in American and French revolutionary rhetoric is similar. The role of women was to spread republican values to the next generation, rather than to exercise civic rights themselves. Republicanism encouraged the education of women, but at the same time upheld the idea of a domestic sphere for women separate from the public sphere of men.[16]

In late 1818 and early 1819 the Union of Welfare developed a southern branch in what is now Ukraine.[17] In the autumn of 1818 Pestel was transferred to Tulchyn (Tulchin) as aide-de-camp to the newly appointed commander-in-chief of the Second Army, General Piotr Vitgenshtein. There, Pestel started organizing a second branch of the Society. He was assisted by Ivan Burtsov, who arrived in the spring of 1819 as General P. D. Kiselev's adjutant. Among the members recruited at this stage were Nikolai Komarov, Aleksei Iushnevskii, Semion Krasnokutskii, Pavel Avramov, Dr Ferdinand Volf (Wolf) and Vasilii Ivashev. Pestel, who belonged to the radical wing of the Southern branch, met opposition from such moderates as Burtsov and Komarov, but he managed to make some progress nevertheless. Meanwhile, in the north, the Union faced difficulties. Few new members were recruited and the important Moscow branch lacked leadership. The situation in other cities, such as Smolensk, Nizhnii-Novgorod and Tambov, was not much better. Pestel concluded that for a revolution to succeed, a national organization was needed. The two main branches had to be coordinated. For this purpose, he travelled to St Petersburg in 1819 with a view to establishing a closer relationship between the two main groups.

The second important development at this time was the radicalization of the Society. Again, Pestel was the main mover. According to his testimony to the investigating committee after the revolt, both branches of the Union of Welfare agreed to transform Russia. Their difference of opinion primarily concerned the means by which change was to be effected and the form of government that would replace the current regime. At the beginning of 1820, a meeting of the leaders of the Union of Welfare was called in St Petersburg. Pestel, who was in town on official business, took the opportunity to argue for his newfound republicanism. It had taken him some years of study to conclude that this was the best system of government for Russia. Now he was given an opportunity to present his arguments to the board of the Union of Welfare. The meeting took place in the apartment of Colonel Glinka at 18 Teatralnaia Square. According to Pestel's testimony to the investigating committee,

Prince Dolgorukov proposed that the Board request me to set forth all the advantages and disadvantages of monarchical and republican government so that each member could then express his arguments ... Finally, after long discussions, the debate was concluded and it was announced that a vote would be taken ... In the end, everyone unanimously accepted a republican government. During the speeches only Glinka spoke in favour of monarchical government.[18]

There is good reason to question the veracity of Pestel's account of the meeting. If he is to be believed, he succeeded in convincing the assembled members of the superiority of the governmental system of the United States of America and the desirability of establishing a republican form of government in Russia. In his testimony, Pestel observed that all the newspapers and political essays at the time praised the increasing welfare in the United States highly and ascribed it to the country's republican rule. This seemed to him clear evidence of the superiority of republican over monarchical government. However, there are conflicting testimonies as to whether there actually was agreement in the meeting about the possibility of introducing such a system in Russia.[19] The political discussions of the Decembrists typically revolved around ideals rather than practical policy or reform.

Lunin's testimony provides a different account of the meeting. According to his recollections, the meeting instead ended with an agreement that the best system for Russia was a constitutional government with limited executive power under a monarch or a president performing a similar function to the monarch. It is known that some influential members, among them Nikita Muraviev, later reverted to the plan for a constitutional monarchy. In general, it appears that members changed their view frequently, and it is impossible to say which form of administration the Union would finally have chosen had their revolt been successful.[20]

To most members, limited government and political representation were the main issues, and whether executive power was invested in a king or president was of secondary concern. It was quite possible to be in favour of republican values and to support a form of civic republicanism without seeking to abolish the monarchy.[21] Although it is a kingdom, the limitations on the monarch and the power of Parliament had led many political writers to describe Britain as a republic at least since the middle of the eighteenth century, for example.

Another controversial subject raised in the meeting was the question of regicide. Already in the Union of Salvation, several members had suggested that the tsar had to be killed. Now it was Nikita Muraviev who argued that regicide was needed to establish a republic. The proposal was heatedly discussed, but in the end the majority of those present believed regicide would throw Russia into anarchy. Yet these debates show that at the time of the January meeting, both republicanism and regicide were on the agenda in the northern branch of the Society. When Pestel returned to Tulchyn, the majority of the members of the southern branch accepted the new republican platform.[22] The southern organization became the radical wing of the movement. Its ranks increased during 1820, with new members including Sergei Volkonskii, Vasilii Davydov, Nikolai Basargin, Mikhail Fonvizin, Nikolai Kriukov and Aleksandr Bariatinskii, turning it into the largest branch of the Union of Welfare.

Pestel testified to the investigating committee that the strategy of the Society was to increase its membership to the point where the views of the Union of Welfare came to prevail in public opinion. In this way, public opinion would support the goals of the revolution and facilitate the successful transformation of Russia. It is apparent that Pestel, in common with other leading members, was well versed in the current Western literature on the significance of public opinion. To that effect, the members of the Union should be dispersed throughout the country to organize support.[23] However, the increased vigilance of the government following the revolutions of 1820 and the Semionovskii revolt made it difficult both to increase membership and to shape public opinion. Secret societies have to keep constant guard against infiltration, and the Union of Welfare was no exception. At the end of the 1820s it became apparent that the government knew both of the Union's existence and the names of some of its members. There were also concerns that the broad enrolment of members had brought untrustworthy persons into the Union. These suspicions proved justified when it was discovered that Mikhail Gribovskii, a former member of the Main Council and now chief of the secret police force formed in the wake of the Semionovskii revolt, had betrayed the Society to the tsar. However, Alexander did not act on the information, presumably because Gribovskii insisted that the Union no longer existed.[24]

The failure to increase membership and achieve any form of progress led to dissatisfaction among the members of the Union of Welfare, many of whom believed that the situation required more powerful measures and better-defined political goals. A conference was convened in Moscow in January 1821 to decide the future of the Society. All the founding members of the Main Council were invited, and every branch was to send representatives. Iakushkin travelled to Tulchyn to discuss the conference with the southern branch. During these discussions, Burtsov told Iakushkin that if Pestel went to Moscow, everything would be spoiled 'with his acerbic opinions and his stubbornness'.[25] Pestel appears to have antagonized some people through both his ambitious character and his radical ideas. Yet his close friends described him as unselfish, honest and of remarkable intelligence and education, although he often got carried away and was sometimes a bit arrogant.[26] In the end, the matter was easily solved. It turned out that Burtsov and another moderate member, Komarov, had leave of absence at the time of the conference as well as credible reasons to go to Moscow, so it was decided that these two men were to represent the southern branch.

Led by Turgenev and Fonvizin, the Moscow conference consisted of three weeks of heated discussion, out of which came several important decisions. Most importantly, the participants decided on a ruse. They would pretend to dissolve the Union of Welfare to mislead the government and help rid the Union of unreliable and passive members. The conference also agreed to revise the constitution and reorganize the Society. Four main dumas or councils would be established, in St Petersburg, Moscow, Smolensk and Tulchyn, under the leadership of Turgenev, Fonvizin, Iakushkin and Burtsov. New regulations for the new society were approved. According to these so-called Moscow Rules, the aims of the society were to be 'the preparation of the state to accept a representative system of government' and 'the limiting of autocracy in Russia'. According to some testimonies, an additional goal of the conference was to isolate Pestel and reduce his influence in the southern branch.

To the extent that the Moscow conference had hoped to reduce the influence of Pestel, its actions misfired badly. Returning to Tulchyn, Burtsov gathered the members and declared the Union dissolved. His intention was to create a new branch in the south. Instead, the members turned against him and rejected the decision. From that moment, Burtsov was isolated and lost all influence. Instead, Pestel and Iushnevskii reconstituted the former organization under the name of the Southern Society. Its members were drawn from the regiments of the Second Army, based at Tulchyn. Pestel, Iushnevskii and Nikita Muraviev were elected to its directorate, with Pestel as chairman. In 1825 Sergei Muraviev-Apostol was also elected to the directorate. The aims of this Society were to overthrow the emperor by revolutionary means and to establish a republican form of government, abolish serfdom and redistribute land.

The Southern Society had several branches, among them one in Tulchyn, led by Pestel and Iushnevskii; one in Kamianka (Kamenka), 200 kilometres (125 mi.) southeast of Kyiv, led by Volkonskii and Davydov; and one in Vasylkiv, 20 kilometres (12 mi.) from Kyiv, headed by Sergei Muraviev-Apostol and Mikhail Bestuzhev-Riumin, both disgraced officers from the Semionovskii regiment. A St Petersburg branch was established, led by Fedor Vadkovskii. It was supposed to act as an intermediary between the two societies' directorates. Until 1822 there was also a branch in Kishinev, Moldova. The distance between the branches, as well as the fact that from 1822 onwards Pestel did not live in Tulchyn, but in Illintsi (Lintsy), where his regiment was quartered, complicated matters. The leaders of the Southern Society came up with the idea of meeting at the January trade fair in Kyiv, to which they could all travel without suspicion. At the first Kyiv conference in 1822, Pestel presented the main content of *Russian Justice*: his plans for transforming Russia into a republic and his project for land reforms. Such a radical document required time for reflection. Consequently, the leaders of the Southern Society decided to defer a decision on whether to adopt *Russian Justice* as its constitution until the next year's conference, when they did indeed adopt this as its (albeit unfinished) programme.

The Northern Society that formed after the dissolution of the Union of Welfare consisted mainly of junior officers of the Guards regiments in St Petersburg. Key figures in the establishment of the new Society were Nikita Muraviev, Lunin, Turgenev, Trubetskoi and Obolenskii. However, its creation was hampered when the Guard Corps, including the most active members, were sent to the Vilna region for fifteen months in the spring of 1821. The Northern Society was formally constituted on their return in the autumn of 1822, yet few new members were recruited, and people were afraid of expressing their views openly. This changed with the recruitment of Kondratii Ryleev in 1823. He replaced Trubetskoi in the Main Council when the latter received an appointment in Kyiv. Ryleev was intense, energetic and enthusiastic, and gathered around him a group of dedicated supporters. According to Lunin, membership increased dramatically at this point. In contrast to the programme of the Southern Society, the aim of the new Northern Society was to establish a constitutional monarchy, although a few of the leading members, including Ryleev, developed republican views.

At this point the Southern Society was completely independent from its northern counterpart. Still, Pestel kept insisting that both organizations must be seen as part of a common national organization. As early as 1822 attempts were made to unite the societies and emissaries were exchanged.

But it was difficult to come to an agreement. Pestel had not expected Nikita Muraviev to change his mind in favour of supporting constitutional monarchy. Nevertheless, in early spring 1824 Pestel went to St Petersburg to explain the main ideas of *Russian Justice* to the members of the Northern Society. His mission was to unite the two societies behind this document, but he failed to make the leaders of the north appreciate his programme. The northerners were especially critical of his proposal for land reform, which involved the distribution of land to the peasants. Trubetskoi and Muraviev opposed Pestel's proposals strongly and had done so for some time. However, he had great influence on Ryleev both regarding the goals of the Society and the means to achieve them.[27]

Obolenskii, who like Ryleev was impressed by Pestel, recalled how at the first meeting with members of the Main Council in St Petersburg (that is, Trubetskoi, Nikita Muraviev and Obolenskii),

> Pavel Ivanovich [Pestel], with the usual fascinating gift of speech, explained to us that the ambiguity of the goal and the means to achieve it gave the Society such an indefinite character that the actions of each member separately were lost in vain efforts, whereas being directed towards a definite and clearly recognized goal, could serve to the earliest achievement thereof.[28]

Pestel's proposal thus appears to have been attractive to at least some of the northern members. But 'for all the dignity of his mind and the persuasiveness of his words, each of us felt that, having once accepted the proposal of Pavel Ivanovich, each must abandon his own conviction and ... follow the path indicated by him.' Moreover, they could not give Pestel a decisive answer without putting his reform programme to the members of the Society, many of whom were absent. The Main Council therefore postponed a conclusive response.

Having failed to persuade the northerners to accept *Russian Justice* as the whole Society's programme, Pestel decided to revise it and present a new version at the next joint meeting, which was scheduled for 1826. However, he was successful in making the Main Council agree to coordinate the actions of the Southern and Northern societies. At the St Petersburg meeting, a decision was made to take advantage of the next succession or some other important political event 'to fulfil the ultimate goal of the Union, that is, for a *coup d'état* by those means that will be ready for that time'.[29]

## The actors

While the Decembrists cannot be seen as a unified group, many of the leading members of the secret societies came from similar backgrounds and had much in common, such as class, education, age, occupation and experiences.[30] All these factors may help to explain who these people were and why they were willing to risk their careers and even their lives to introduce representative government in Russia. The Decembrists belonged to the privileged layers of Russian society; some were very rich aristocrats, whereas others were noblemen of modest means. The majority belonged to the educated elite. Many leading Decembrists, among them Trubetskoi, Obolenskii and Volkonskii, had received a home education by private tutors from abroad. Volkonskii was educated at home until he was twelve, when he attended Abbé Charles Dominique Nicolle's expensive Jesuit boarding school of the Fontanka. Other future Decembrists, such as Bariatinskii, Mikhail Orlov, Piotr Svistunov and Iosif Poggio (Podzhio), were also among the Fontanka pupils. Trubetskoi received a home education until he went to university at sixteen. Others, among them Matvei and Sergei Muraviev-Apostol, went to school in Paris. However, most of the Decembrists were educated at St Petersburg schools.[31] Fonvizin, Aleksandr Brigen and Aleksandr Kriukov went to the Lutheran St Petrischule, the oldest school in St Petersburg, attached to St Peter's Lutheran church. Basargin, Pushchin, Vilgelm Kiukhelbeker (Wilhelm Küchelbecker) and Vladimir Volkhovskii attended the highly prestigious Alexander Lyceum at Tsarskoe Selo, founded in 1811. This was a boarding school for the sons of the nobility, where pupils were trained for leading positions in government. The syllabus focused on modern languages and literature, and in senior courses, the school taught natural rights, comparative political systems and social contract theory.

One of the Lyceum's most famous pupils was the poet Aleksandr Pushkin, a classmate and close friend of the future Decembrist Ivan Pushchin. Pushkin socialized in the same circles as the Decembrists and sympathized with their ideas, composing such radical poems as 'Liberty' (Vol'nost; 1817), 'The Village' (Derevnia; 1819) and 'The Dagger' (Kinzhal; 1821). However, he was never invited to become a member of the secret society. Pushkin was known for his lack of discretion and his dissipated lifestyle, and according to some accounts, the Society did not trust him. Others have claimed that his officer friends did not want to expose him to the great risks involved.[32]

There were also military schools that catered for the sons of the nobility, including future Decembrists. The quality of education in these schools may not have been particularly high, but they prompted pupils to discuss contemporary topics and form a sense of their own worth. The schools forged strong personal ties, fostered a sense of fellowship and contributed to the formation of a kind of military intelligentsia.[33] The Corps des Pages (founded in 1802) is the best-known of these institutions, but the First St Petersburg Cadet Corps, the Corps of Infantry Cadets, the Mining Cadet Corps, the Naval Cadet Corps and the School of Guards Sub-Ensigns were also attended by future Decembrists, including Glinka, Ryleev, Andrei Rozen, Vladimir Shteingel, Aleksandr Beliaev and Dmitrii Zavalishin. A popular school for slightly older students was the Moscow Academy of Column leaders, and a number of Decembrists are found among its alumni.[34] Pestel attended the Corps des Pages, as did Svistunov, Ivashev and Aleksandr Gangeblov. This school was known for teaching polished manners and flawless French, rather than encouraging intellectual pursuits. However, there were exceptions among its roll. Pestel developed his interest in the political sciences at the Corps. This was largely thanks to an influential teacher, Karl German (Carl Hermann), who encouraged his pupils to read works by Montesquieu, Gabriel Bonnot de Mably, Jean-Jacques Rousseau, Jeremy Bentham, John Locke and Adam Smith. Among Pestel's papers are notes from a lecture by German on political economy.[35]

While several of the future Decembrists went to lectures at foreign universities, many of them also attended Moscow University. Professor Kunitsyn's lectures on political economy became particularly popular. Obolenskii, who attended his lectures in 1819, recalled that they were based on the ideas of Heinrich Storch and Jean-Baptiste Say.[36] The aforementioned Professor German also gave widely popular lectures on political economy at Moscow University. As we have seen, political economy was considered an important subject of study by members of the Society because it focused on national welfare. The Decembrists wished to serve the common good, so knowledge of how to procure national welfare was essential.

In addition to political economy, leading Decembrists studied classical literature and history, contemporary European literature, law, philosophy and political economy. They spoke French fluently; some knew German, and some English. Aleksandr Bestuzhev, who knew both French and English, became familiar with liberal ideas by reading speeches made in the House of Commons in London and in the Chambre des députés in

Paris.[37] Many had taken advantage of the opportunity to travel abroad to improve their knowledge and gain experience. In the early nineteenth century, study abroad became commonplace among the Russian nobility, and Germany, where they attended lectures by well-known thinkers, was a particularly popular destination. An increasing number of young Russian men studied at universities in Leipzig, Heidelberg, Berlin and Göttingen.[38] Pestel went to Germany with his brother in 1805, when he was only twelve years old. He took a break from his studies at the Corps des Pages for four years to stay at his grandmother's house in Dresden, in order to study with a local teacher.[39]

Many Decembrists were well read. They read Greek and Roman writers, as well as modern Western thinkers, including Smith, Bentham, Say, Rousseau, Nicolas de Condorcet, Cesare Beccaria, Louis de Bignon, Benjamin Constant, Jean-Louis de Lolme, Benjamin Franklin, Germaine de Staël, Antoine Destutt de Tracy, Gaetano Filangieri, Niccolò Machiavelli, Voltaire and Montesquieu. Romantic writers, such as Sir Walter Scott and Lord Byron, were also popular, as well as domestic writers, among them Pushkin, Aleksandr Radishchev, Denis Fonvizin, Aleksandr Griboedov, Denis Davydov and Ivan Krylov. Pestel was one of the most well read. His friend Nikolai Lorer recalled that he had lots of books, mainly political, economic and of an educational nature, as well as constitutions of all kinds in many foreign languages.[40] Nikita Muraviev, one of the leaders of the Northern Society, had received an excellent education, learning several languages including English. He had access to the substantial library of his father, the poet Mikhail N. Muraviev, who died when Nikita was only eleven years old.

According to Shteingel, the root of the Decembrists' liberal thinking was found precisely in this kind of upbringing and education, which the government itself had encouraged. It 'fed them, like milk, with liberal ideas'. As a consequence, a whole generation grew up as free-thinkers. This meant that there was a large number of people who did not belong to the Society but who shared their ideas and feelings.[41] These people met to discuss politics in private apartments, clubs and salons, and they crowded into halls for public lectures.

The Decembrists had yet another feature in common. They were young. The vast majority were under thirty, some of them barely twenty. Many felt restrained by the older generation, who were obsessed with formality, hierarchy and service, held all the major positions and were satisfied with things as they were. The majority of older Russian nobles were conservative and cared only about personal ambition.[42] Young people wanted liberty and a constitution. In the words of Mikhail Fonvizin, 'the young generation, which entered state service in the first ten years of the reign of Alexander and was brought up under the influence of freedom-loving principles that he himself had proclaimed, fully realized to what extent Russia lagged behind Europe and true civilization.' They expected the tsar to make changes, to modernize Russia.[43]

It might be expected that their youth would make the Decembrists more prone to radical ideas, since there is a tendency for people to grow more conservative with age. Perhaps less expected is the fact that they acted against the interests of their own class. Existing social and political conditions favoured them. The privileges the Decembrists wished to remove were their own, and they would clearly be disadvantaged by the reforms they promoted. The role of criticizing and opposing aristocratic birth privilege

Pyotr Sokolov,
*Nikita Muraviev*, 1824,
oil on canvas.

has in most countries been filled by the middle classes. But in Russia it fell to young noblemen to attack aristocratic privilege in the name of republican and liberal political ideas and a capitalist economic development. The Decembrists hence took on a role that should logically have belonged to the middle classes. As Count Rostopchin – recently returned to Russia from France, where he had lived for eight years – pointed out so eloquently, 'In France, cooks wanted to become princes, but here princes wanted to become cooks.'[44]

What is more, the Decembrists did not only belong to the privileged elite; the vast majority were or had been army officers, many serving in the prestigious Imperial Guards regiments, which were an excellent platform for establishing informal contacts with members of the imperial family. The high aristocracy monopolized three of the Guards cavalry regiments and two of the Guards infantry regiments. The cavalry Guards regiments had the most serving future Decembrists. There is a common belief that military officers believe in discipline, hierarchy and authority and thus are supporters of the established social order. This group should, then, have been among the most conservative. But in reality, nineteenth-century military officers were often inclined towards modernization. This was a group of highly educated individuals, well informed of the situation in other countries and motivated by a patriotic will to serve the common good of their country. The liberal revolutions of 1820–21 in Spain, Naples, Portugal and Greece were all instigated by military officers. In early nineteenth-century Russia, the army was one of the main institutions in which a concentration of the Europeanized elite could be found, and it became a hotbed of political ideas.[45]

In addition to having class, age, education and profession in common, several Decembrists shared experiences from the Napoleonic Wars. The foreign campaigns in Germany and France had made Russian officers aware of the workings of liberal societies and systems, and introduced them to new political ideas. These experiences made a strong impression on them. 'Spending a whole year in Germany, and then several months in Paris, could not but change, at least a little, the views of thinking young Russians,' Iakushkin recalled in 1854.[46] Future Decembrists became familiar with societies and regimes more liberal than their own. They attended lectures and debates, studied political literature and discussed political and social issues with German and French officers. According to Fonvizin, they absorbed these officers' free manner of thinking and desire for constitutional institutions.[47] Volkonskii recalled the great impression the meeting with French officers at Tilsit made on him; how free they seemed and how well they treated their soldiers. He was also fascinated by the stories told by officers who had participated in the American War of Independence about the new country, where all citizens had equal rights.[48] Russian officers in Germany and France learned about secret societies and patriotic constitutional movements, such as the Tugendbund and the Carbonari. Some of them were initiated into radical Masonic lodges while in Paris, and they were especially imbued with republican ideas.

## Experiences of war

The officers who returned to Russia after the war brought home their experience of liberal societies and constitutional movements, as well as their newfound awareness of republican and liberal ideas. Returning to Russia after the glorious victory over Napoleon, when Alexander I led his troops into Paris, these officers felt an urgent need for reform. They saw the backwardness of Russian life more clearly against the backdrop of European practices. Commenting on this experience, Iakushkin wrote that his stay abroad during the military campaigns first 'drew my attention to Russia's social structure and compelled me to see its defects'.[49] The young officers could now compare all that they had seen abroad with what confronted them at home: 'slavery of the majority of Russians, cruel treatment of subordinates by their superiors, all kinds of government abuses and general tyranny'.[50] 'The army, from generals to privates, upon its return, did nothing but discuss how good it is in foreign lands,' Bestuzhev recalled. 'A comparison with their own country naturally brought up the question: Why is it not so here? . . . Did we liberate Europe in order to fasten its chains upon ourselves?'[51]

The Decembrists later recalled the anger they felt when the peasants, who had been fighting against Napoleon, returned to Russia and were once again forced into serfdom. After fighting alongside regular soldiers, the officers felt strongly for these unfortunate people. 'Can I see the enslavement of the people, of my fellow citizens, the paltry dress of the sons of the Fatherland . . . and not suffer with them?' Vladimir Raevskii asked. The common good demands change, he continued.[52] Testimonies of the great shame felt by the returning officers abound. Alexander I, 'the liberator of Europe', was in Russia a despot who ruled over a backward country, where peasants were oppressed by landowners, soldiers were abused by their commanding officers and corruption was widespread. In a letter to Nicholas I written from the Peter and Paul Fortress shortly after the Decembrist revolt, Piotr Kakhovskii complained about 'the condition of the people in our country. The security of people and property completely deprived of protection, a total absence of law and justice in the courts, oppressive taxes levied not on profit, but destroying capital, damage to trade, repression of enlightenment and freedom'.[53]

In the digest of the Decembrists' testimony concerning the internal conditions of Russia, compiled after the revolt, a number of similar grievances are recorded.[54] Throughout these statements are complaints about arbitrary rule and the absence of clear and concise laws that prevent abuse and corruption. Above all, the Decembrists were unhappy about the plight of the Russian people. The collection of taxes was imposed arbitrarily and led to abuse and misery. Moreover, the incessant road-construction duty ruined villagers. Comparing serfdom with American slavery, Bestuzhev stated that, 'Negroes working on plantations are more fortunate than many serfs. The sale of peasants independently of their families, the violation of peasant girls, the corruption of peasant wives – all this is done quite openly and considered of no significance.'[55] In Shteingel's words, this was 'derogatory for the Russian nation'.[56]

Conditions in the military were another common complaint among Decembrists. Alexander had outlawed cruel punishment in the army, but little improvement was made in practice. Running the gauntlet, for example, was still in use. Brutality was the main reason for the Semionovskii revolt in 1820. Sergei Muraviev-Apostol, a captain in the Semionovskii regiment, told his brother Matvei that officers were even themselves harassed if they were not brutal to their subordinates.[57] Yakiv Andriyevych (Iakov Andreevich), one of the most active members of the Society of United Slavs, which had merged with the Southern Society, told the investigating committee that he was upset to witness 'the unbridled and inhuman behaviour of our commanding officers towards the wretched soldiers'. The government was the reason for their degradation. 'Now tell me,' he said, 'was it possible, seeing every day the indignation and murmuring of these wretched pillars of our native land, not to feel for their situation?' Andriyevych told the Committee that he wished to sacrifice his life to redeem these unhappy people, his fellow men.[58]

The introduction of military colonies made conditions even worse. One of the main purposes of these settlements was to ease the hard lot of the Russian soldier, but the Decembrists believed that shortening the term of service for soldiers from twenty-five years to eight or twelve would satisfy this goal. This measure would also disseminate the military spirit throughout Russia and allow peasants to return to their families, marry and 'follow the peasants' calling'. Instead, regiments were settled on the land and soldiers forced to combine agriculture with military duties. State peasants were transferred to these colonies with or without their consent and compelled to undergo military drills and exercises, as well as cultivate the land.[59] The peasants who lived in the military colonies were doomed to military service for life.

Iakushkin described indignantly how badly the peasants in Novgorod province were treated when they protested against the transformation of their villages into military settlements. General Arakcheev sent in the cavalry and artillery against them. They were fired at, cut down, many were made to run the gauntlet . . . Then it was announced to the peasants that their houses and possessions no longer belonged to them, that they were all to become soldiers and their children were to become cantonists, that is to say, educated in special canton schools attached to military regiments.[60] Pestel wrote, 'the very thought of the military settlements fills every decent soul with pain and horror.' In his view, their removal was the prime duty of a future government. There were also other reasons for removing them, according to some Decembrists. Trubetskoi argued that they formed a special caste in the state, which could become an instrument of the oppression of the people. They would constitute a force that nothing in the state could resist. Another danger was that the military colonies would be controlled by a few people, who could make them an instrument of their ambition. Finally, military colonies were less orderly than military regiments. Trubetskoi warned that a small cause for displeasure could give rise to a riot, which could easily spread through the whole settlement.[61]

According to the Decembrist testimonies, they did not consider only peasants and soldiers to be ill treated. As Bestuzhev put it, everywhere honest people suffered while informers and swindlers rejoiced. All around one could see discontented faces. The village clergy was in a wretched state, without any salary. They also needed education. The merchants, hampered by guild restrictions and difficulties of transportation, as well as the inconsistency of tariffs, had suffered great losses since 1812.[62]

The Decembrists were extremely critical of the tariff policy, which was governed by motives of foreign policy and oscillated between protectionism and free trade. 'The instability of the tariff resulted in the impoverishment of many manufacturers and discouraged others,' Bestuzhev maintained. 'It destroyed confidence in the government among Russian as well as foreign merchants. Consequently, there was a great decline in our foreign credit and general complaints against the lack of cash.'[63] Shteingel wrote extensively about this in the letter he sent Nicolas I from the Peter and Paul Fortress. He told the emperor that the tariff of 1810 had been beneficial to Russian manufacturing, but it was suddenly replaced in 1816 by a twelve-year tariff that favoured Austria, Poland and Prussia. Then, in 1819, when the merchants had started to adapt to this tariff, things changed again. The government introduced a new general permission to import foreign goods, which soon flooded Russia. Many merchants and manufacturers went bankrupt, and it was especially difficult for petty traders. The error was corrected by the tariff of 1823, but the damage was irreversible: 'Thus our commerce is in a paralytic state, while other countries are doing well and are flourishing.' Bestuzhev concurred, arguing that while petty traders and townspeople in other countries were respected, in Russia they were 'insignificant, poor, burdened with obligations, deprived of means of livelihood'.[64]

We have seen that the reform-minded Russian officers who returned home after the Napoleonic Wars became dissatisfied with the many inadequacies in their country, but the homecoming also affected them in other ways. Life for young officers in post-war Russia was difficult, and they found it hard to readjust to civilian society. Decembrist testimonies and memoirs express bitterness and frustration. Common to most of them are feelings of emptiness and inactivity and, above all, a lost sense of purpose. 'For two years we had had great events before our eyes that had decided the fate of nations, and had taken some part in them,' Iakushkin recounted; 'now it was intolerable to behold the empty life of St Petersburg and listen to the chatter of old men who praised all that was old and censured any movement forward. We were a hundred years ahead of them.'[65] There was also a growing frustration at not being heard, at not having their opinions taken seriously. Russian officers who had participated in the Napoleonic Wars felt proud about what they had achieved, what the Russian army had achieved. To them, the war was associated with patriotic honour and glory, with fighting for the fatherland and for the liberation of the people. Peace left these officers with an emptiness of purpose. Many of them felt oppressed by peacetime army life: the endless marching drills and strict rules, the military pedantry.

After the Napoleonic Wars, life in Russia was militarized by incessant military parades. When the army returned home, they continued drill training, practising marching including posture and length of steps. Obsessed with discipline and order, the emperor was meticulous about the precision of the movements of the regiments as they marched and insisted that their arms and equipment be in excellent condition at all times. This parade mania prompted Ryleev to call Alexander 'the Russian German', referring to the contemporary negative image of Germans as over-meticulous and keen to follow rules.

The Guards regiments became the tsar's substitute for the army. Their numbers rose rapidly, and they became increasingly important. Not only were the most talented soldiers transferred to the Guards, but the most hand-some. Beauty and symmetry signified order and order signified modernity, the fact that Russia was a progressive empire. The parades were attended by the foreign diplomatic corps and clearly intended to impress them. External appearance was important to Alexander, so the parades were great spectacles intended to display the supremacy of the tsar.[66] Conversely, the young officers hated this military pedantry, and service became unbearable to them. For whole days, regiments marched all over St Petersburg. Drumming was heard from early morning until late at night.[67] The life of young reform-minded officers in St Petersburg had become suffocating.

While the experience of the war created great discontent with the state of their homeland among the young returning officers, it also brought a pos-itive spirit of change. The foreign campaigns revealed to them how strong, widespread and dominant liberal and republican ideas were, especially among young Europeans similar to themselves, and they were influenced by the prevailing 'spirit of change'. This experience made them feel that liberty and a constitution were also feasible goals for Russia. In Fonvizin's words, 'the spirit of freedom also blew over Russia.'[68] That this was the right way forward was confirmed by the way revolutionary ideas were spreading across Europe and the rest of the world in the wake of the American and French revolutions.

In his reply to the investigating committee's question regarding the origin of his revolutionary ideas, Pestel wrote,

> Every age has its distinctive features. Ours is marked by revolution-ary thinking. From one end of Europe to the other, everywhere the same thing is seen, from Portugal to Russia, without the exception of a single country, even England and Turkey, these two opposites. The whole of America presents the same spectacle. The spirit of transformation causes minds everywhere to simmer, so to speak.[69]

This was a time of high expectations in Russia. After the war many officers, who had not done so before, started to read political works and journals, as well as foreign newspapers. They discussed politics and constitutional forms of government. Learning about 'these bold political systems and theories', Fonvizin observed, 'it was quite natural that they wanted to see them applied to their Fatherland.'[70]

These young Russian officers saw themselves as Europeans, and Russia as part of Europe. They spoke French much better than they spoke Russian.[71] They followed European cultural trends and read Western literature, philosophy and history, as well as books on Western politics, economy and law. They kept abreast of social and political development in the West through Western journals and newspapers. Events in Europe were also regularly reported on in Russian periodicals. The Decembrists never doubted that Western ideas were applicable to Russia, nor that changes occurring in the rest of Europe would also come to Russia. This did not mean that they did not love their country. On the contrary, they were committed patriots. They wanted what was best for Russia and for the Russian people, which to their mind was freedom, representative government and the rule of law.

After the revolt, Nikita Muraviev testified that the Decembrists had been inspired by the introduction of constitutional rule in several European monarchies, not least the establishment in November 1815 of a constitutional government in the Kingdom of Poland, which after all was under the domain of the Russian tsar. They were further encouraged by the emperor's speech before the Sejm of the Kingdom of Poland in March 1818, when he spoke highly of free institutions and announced his intention of introducing them in the entire Russian empire.[72] 'When granting the Poles a constitution,' Lunin recalled, 'Emperor Alexander promised before the whole of Europe to spread the blessings of a representative form of government to all the peoples entrusted to his care.'[73]

The young freedom-loving Russians were impatient. They wanted reform without delay. 'I am . . . crushed by the thought that I will not, in my lifetime, see Russia free and governed by a wise constitution,' Turgenev noted in his diary in 1817. Twenty months later, worried about his country, he returned to this theme: 'Is it possible that this glorious, intelligent, good nation will never rise to its true dignity?'[74] To the Decembrists, it was self-evident that Russia was ripe for reform. They did not accept that it should be any different from the rest of Europe, and were upset that Alexander seemed to regard Poland as more civilized and more European than Russia: 'Who can think that our people is not endowed with all the abilities possessed by other nations? A state enlightened for several centuries by the Christian religion, having relations with foreign peoples as with its brothers, cannot be in a state of ignorance.'[75] Lunin later recalled these times of high expectations, when everyone was hoping that the tsar would grant Russia a constitution. Ultimately, they realized that Alexander was too attached to autocracy and did not really care about the welfare of his subjects. After 1820, those ideas of improvement that he himself had propagated were considered subversive.[76]

# PART II
# REVOLT AGAINST
# AUTOCRACY

# 3

# Revolution in St Petersburg

In September 1825 Alexander I and his wife, Elisabeth, travelled to the town of Taganrog on the Sea of Azov to spend the winter in a more temperate climate. The empress suffered from a lung condition, and the humid air of St Petersburg was detrimental to her health. In late October Alexander made a trip to the Crimea. On the way back to Taganrog, he was taken ill. At first it appeared to be a common cold, but soon his condition deteriorated and he developed a high fever. His physicians concluded that he had contracted a disease, most likely typhus, that was prevalent in the Crimea at the time and was characterized by intermittent fever. The tsar refused any medical treatment and, on 19 November, he passed away in Taganrog.[1]

## The interregnum

The death of Alexander came as a great shock. He was only 47 years old and in good health. News of his death did not reach St Petersburg until 27 November. A service was being held in the Winter Palace on that day for the emperor's health but, when the news arrived, it quickly turned into a requiem. A number of Decembrists were present, among them Sergei Trubetskoi, who recalled how the death of the tsar inspired fear. People were used to Alexander, and for all his shortcomings he was considered a better ruler than his brothers. 'Perhaps any change in the ruling face in a despotic government inspires fear,' Trubetskoi mused. 'You get used to the despot's shortcomings, when they are not great vices, and the change of an autocratic ruler leads to involuntary fear.'[2]

Alexander I had no children, but he did have three brothers: Constantine, Nicholas and Michael. Grand Duke Constantine, the eldest, was commander-in-chief of the Polish army and the expected successor to the throne. Thus, learning of Alexander's death on 27 November, Grand Duke Nicholas immediately swore allegiance to his brother Constantine. However, in pledging allegiance without the publication of an accession manifesto drafted by the heir, Nicholas appeared to break the law of succession to the throne. To prevent a dynastic crisis and give legitimacy to Nicholas's oath, the senate – the highest judicial and supervising body subordinate to the emperor, which had supreme legal authority in the absence of an heir – published a manifesto. This document contained an announcement of Alexander's death together with an order to pledge allegiance to Constantine. Enclosed was the text of the oath Nicholas had delivered.[3] Following the publication of the manifesto, the Guards regiments swore allegiance to Constantine.

At the time, most people were not aware that Constantine had renounced his right to the throne in a secret document known only to a few. The reason for his decision was that he had entered into a morganatic marriage with the daughter of a Polish chamberlain. In 1797 Paul I had promulgated a law requiring that dynasts be born of authorized marriages, and in 1820 a new law further stipulated that only children of Romanovs born of marriages with people of equal status – members of a royal family – could inherit succession rights. Constantine had married his long-time mistress Countess Joanna Grudna-Grudzinska in Warsaw on 24 May 1820 after his marriage to Juliane of Saxe-Coburg-Saalfeld, who left him in 1801, never to return to Russia, was officially annulled on 20 March 1820. This meant that he could not produce a legitimate heir, causing him to renounce his claim to the throne.

Constantine's renunciation of the throne, which transferred the right to succession to his younger brother Nicholas, had been placed in a manifesto drawn up by Metropolitan Philaret and signed by Alexander I in August 1823. The original document was deposited in the Cathedral of the Assumption, and sealed copies were sent to the State Council, the Synod and the senate in St Petersburg, with the inscription: 'in case of my decease, to be opened before any other steps are taken'. Evidence suggests that Nicholas was aware of the existence of this document, but the problem no one seems to have foreseen was that an unpublished document did not have the force of law.[4] Furthermore, the Russian sovereign could not dispose of the inheritance of the throne through a personal will. A law dating from 1722 gave the sovereign the right to select the heir to the throne, but that right was eliminated in the law of 1797. If Nicholas ascended the throne without Constantine's public abdication, it could be considered usurpation. This was particularly sensitive because Nicholas was not popular, especially among the military, owing to his poor treatment of officers and cruelty to soldiers.[5] Nevertheless, his first impulse was to assume the throne, but he was discouraged by high officials who insisted on observing the legal succession. M. A. Miloradovich, Governor General of St Petersburg, was instrumental in persuading Nicholas to swear the oath to Constantine, arguing that the troops would not back him if he took independent action.[6]

Meanwhile, in Warsaw, Constantine declared his loyalty to Nicholas but did not officially renounce his claim to the throne. Nicholas, who feared civil war and thus did not dare to declare himself emperor, tried to persuade Constantine to come to St Petersburg and abdicate in public. For two weeks letters were sent back and forth between St Petersburg and Warsaw by courier, until finally it became clear to Nicholas that Constantine would not return to the capital. *The Times* in London reported at the time that in Russia there were 'two self-denying emperors and no active ruler'.[7]

This unclear situation, this interregnum, presented the reform-inclined men of the Northern Society in St Petersburg with an unexpected opportunity to overthrow the autocracy. Autocracies are at their most vulnerable during the transition of power, especially if there is uncertainty about the succession. To complicate matters further, unlike most absolute monarchies, in post-Petrine Russia there was a need to legitimize the new ruler. Peter the Great, who did not want his son to rule, removed primogeniture in 1722 and decreed that the legal qualifications for a successor were, first, appointment by the reigning monarch and, second, that the heir designate should be worthy of royal office. This new law, which was extremely unpopular, destabilized the process of succession in Russia. Accession documents had to be produced that were addressed to the public and defended the legal right of the new ruler. These documents pointed to four qualities that provided legitimacy: appointment, dynastic inheritance, worthiness and election.[8] This has important implications for our understanding of the Decembrist revolt. A volatile transfer of power was relatively common in Russia, so the Decembrists' decision to act at the time of a succession crisis made sense. Moreover, at this moment there was also some room for participation in the political process because legitimacy was not automatically bestowed on the successor. Monarchs had been elected on several occasions in recent Russian history, for example in 1598, 1613, 1645 and 1682.

However, the members of the Northern Society did not immediately realize the existing possibilities. The evening after the Guard regiment's ceremony of oath-taking to Constantine on 27 November, Society members gathered at the quarters of the poet Kondratii Ryleev on 72 Moika River Embankment, near the Blue Bridge in St Petersburg. This apartment was often used for social gatherings, both political and literary.[9] Ever since being recruited, Ryleev had assembled around him the more radical members, most of whom were staunch republicans. This group, consisting of such people as Ivan Pushchin, Evgenii Obolenskii, Aleksandr Odoevskii, Aleksandr Iakubovich, Piotr Kakhovskii, Vilgelm Kiukhelbeker, Vladimir Shteingel, Konstantin Torson, Aleksandr Sutgof, Anton Arbuzov and the Bestuzhev brothers, gained influence during 1824 and became the driving force behind the revolt of 14 December.[10]

The Society had long agreed that the death of the tsar would be the signal for action, but they had not expected it to happen so soon. They were taken completely by surprise. According to Obolenskii's account, the members assembled at Ryleev's agreed that it would be impossible to undertake anything decisive before the new emperor assumed the throne. Before concluding the meeting, they decided that with the accession of the new emperor it was necessary to suspend the Society's actions temporarily. 'Sadly, we went home,' Obolenskii recalled, 'feeling that for a long time, and maybe forever, the realization of the best dream of our life was distant!' Nevertheless, when only Nikolai and Aleksandr Bestuzhev remained with Ryleev, they decided to prepare the soldiers for an uprising after all. They began to write proclamations to be disseminated in the barracks, but then decided it was better to address the soldiers in person, so the three men wandered the streets of St Petersburg looking for soldiers. Nikolai recalled 'the avidity with which the soldiers listened to us'.[11] After two nights of walking around the city, Ryleev developed a sore throat.

Shortly after the meeting at Ryleev's, rumours that the new emperor planned to abdicate spread through St Petersburg. At the same time, the will of the deceased tsar and the probable accession to the throne of Grand Duke Nicholas became known to the public. As Obolenskii put it, 'Then everything began to move and again the hope of success flashed in all hearts.'[12] It was 'a great opportunity,' Pushchin declared, 'and if we don't take it we will rightly be regarded as utter scoundrels.'[13]

Ryleev's apartment once again became a centre for news, meetings and debate. Many in the Society were acquainted with members of the senate and the Holy Synod and managed to get access to important information, which they brought to the evening meetings. Fedor Glinka, who worked for Count Miloradovich, Governor General of St Petersburg, had particularly important insight into the course of events. 'An opportunity presented itself to use the moment of taking the new oath to the Grand Duke Nicholas,' Nikolai Bestuzhev recalled. The swearing of a new oath so soon after the old one would create confusion among the soldiers. The members of the Society decided to agitate among the troops against a new oath: 'We worked harder, prepared the Guards, fostered and stimulated the spirit of hostility towards Nicholas that existed among the soldiers.'[14] Ryleev, still recovering from his cold, intensified his efforts to recruit new members. Aleksandr Bulatov and Andrei Rozen were among the newcomers.

Prince Trubetskoi later gave the following reasons for the Society's decision to act: that it had not happened before that a legitimate heir relinquished the throne voluntarily; that Grand Duke Nicholas was unpopular; that the highest elite was dissatisfied with the strange situation; and that the members of the Society were sure that several of the state's prominent dignitaries would collaborate with and even join them once they realized that a sufficiently strong military force backed them up.[15] However, despite all the efforts of active Society members, they could not be sure how many troops they could count on. Members pledged to lead various regiments, but because they were not regimental commanders, nobody could vouch for the commitment of a whole regiment. Company commanders could be responsible only for their own companies.

Many who participated in the frenzied preparations for the uprising observed that there was a general feeling of doubt about its success. Nevertheless, the majority of the members believed in the need to act for the freedom of Russia. An example was called for to arouse 'the sleeping Russians'. Ryleev often said that 'a shock was necessary[;] the tactics of revolutions consist in one word: dare, and if this is unfortunate, we will teach others by our failure.'[16] Obolenskii recalled that hardly any of them were convinced of the possibility of success: 'Everyone hoped for favourable events, for unexpected help, for what is called a lucky star; but ... everyone felt that he was obliged to the Society to fulfil his given word – he was obliged to fulfil his purpose.'[17] Aleksandr Muraviev concurred, noting that the members of the Society had sacrificed their lives to their fatherland long ago. They intended to 'make a grand statement against the autocracy and indicate to the nation [нации] that ... we had only one thought, one desire – the freedom of the country!'[18] The Decembrists acted not for the sake of their own personal benefit, then, but for the common good: for the nation, the people and their country. Although their notion of the common good, like that of contemporary Western liberals, was not all-inclusive, it is clear that their goal was not to gain power for themselves. As Ryleev later told Nikolai Bestuzhev when he learned that they had been betrayed by Iakov Rostovtsev: 'I am sure we will perish, but the example will remain. Let us make a sacrifice for the future freedom of our fatherland.'[19] This idea of heroic sacrifice (which can also be found among other European revolutionaries) was prevalent among the Decembrists at the time.

When Odoevskii stepped out on to Senate Square on the day of the uprising, he allegedly cried out: 'We are going to die, brothers, oh, how gloriously we are going to die!'[20] Scholars have found in his words a key to how the Decembrists perceived themselves and the rebellion. The uprising had not yet begun, and it was still possible that it would succeed. But the figure of the dying hero gave the event the character of high tragedy, elevating the participants in their own eyes and in the eyes of their descendants to the level of characters in a theatrical plot. They were not their real selves, but actors playing a role. The revolt made it possible for them to situate in real life the Romantic persona they had created for themselves.[21]

However, this does not mean that the Decembrists' revolt was all make-believe, or that the Decembrists did not act on the basis of real ideals and real objectives. They believed they were making a political statement by bringing their Romantic characters to life through action. They wished to do something of importance for their country, to make a difference. After all, they were prepared to die for freedom. This realization made them feel proud, because they could place themselves next to other civic heroes in history, such as Brutus, who assassinated Julius Caesar, and Rafael del Riego, the leader of the Spanish revolution of 1820. There is no reason to doubt the sincerity of the Decembrists just because they realized the significance of symbolic action. Symbolic action constituted a central part of rebellious action. It was a way of giving the revolt meaning and communicating this publicly.

Although the Decembrists were unsure whether they would succeed, they tried to plan the revolt as best they could in the short time at their disposal. To begin with, the uprising needed a leader. Prince Trubetskoi was the obvious candidate. He was from one of the most prominent families in the country and had an excellent military record. On Ryleev's initiative, Trubetskoi was appointed 'dictator' on 12 December. Colonel Aleksandr Bulatov was to be his second in command, with Iakubovich as an assistant, and Prince Obolenskii was to be chief of staff. The use of the term 'dictator' has sometimes been interpreted as a sign of the totalitarian view of the Decembrists. However, they used this term not in the modern sense of an autocratic ruler who has commonly obtained power by force, but in its ancient Roman republican sense, meaning a chief magistrate appointed by the senate to rule the republic in a state of emergency. The use of this term was therefore a way of legitimizing the revolt by placing it in a republican context.

According to Rozen's account, the plan of the leaders of the Northern Society was to march as many troops as they could trust to Senate Square on the day of the oath-taking to Nicholas, under the pretext of defending Constantine's rights. Should the number of troops be sufficient, it was decided to seize the Winter Palace, the main governmental buildings, the banks and the post office. The occupation of the Peter and Paul Fortress would take place after the imperial family had been arrested. If the number of troops should be insufficient and the attempt fail, they were to retreat to the military settlements in Novgorod, 190 kilometres (120 mi.) south of the capital, or to Kronstadt, the naval base on Kotlin Island in the Gulf of Finland.[22]

Ryleev was convinced that it was necessary to deliver the first blow, since this would create confusion and provide the Decembrists with a new chance to act. He therefore argued that Mikhail Bestuzhev of the Moscow regiment, Anton Arbuzov of the Guards Naval Crew or Aleksandr Sutgof of the Grenadier regiment – whoever reached the square first – should seize the palace and arrest members of the royal family. They were to be held until a Grand Council (constituent assembly) had been convened, whose duty it was to decide the future of Russia. The Decembrists would then surround the senate to prevent the senators from swearing the oath to Nicholas; they would instead compel them to read aloud to the people a manifesto that had been drawn up by the Decembrists and signed by Prince Trubetskoi.

Trubetskoi had assigned Ryleev the task of writing that manifesto in the name of the senate. He was to explain that the tsar had renounced the throne and the former government had been abolished. Consequently, the senate had found it necessary to appoint a provisional government that would lead the country until a constituent assembly was convened. This would be a Grand Council of popular representatives from all the social estates, whose task it would be to decide the fate of the nation and adopt a constitution.[23] The senate played this crucial part in the Decembrists' plan for revolt because of its distinctive role as the political and legal authority and symbol of power during the interregnum.[24] In the end, rather than Ryleev, Baron Shteingel came to write the manifesto.

Ryleev and Obolenskii were hoping that six regiments would refuse the oath to Nicholas, a number they thought sufficient to realize the plans of the

Society. These were the Izmailovskii Life Guards regiment, the Finliandskii Life Guards regiment, the Moscow Life Guards regiment, the Jaeger Life Guards regiment, the Grenadier Life Guards regiment and the Guards Naval Crew. However, they felt they could rely only on the Grenadier regiment, the Moscow regiment and the Guards Naval Crew. After the revolt, Ryleev confessed to the investigating committee that Trubetskoi had expressed doubts about the number of troops they would be able to muster, and had considered it unlikely that all companies would follow the example of a few who refused to swear the oath. According to some reports, Bulatov was also doubtful. Ryleev, however, believed they had sufficient support, considering the soldiers' 'resentment towards their demanding commanders'. When he asked Trubetskoi what force he thought sufficient to carry out their plans, Trubetskoi allegedly answered: 'One regiment is enough.' On hearing this, Ryleev said to him: 'Then we have nothing to worry about; we can, in all probability, be certain of two or three.'[25] Unbeknown to Ryleev, it seems, Trubetskoi was making plans to coordinate the revolution in the capital with a revolt in the south. The idea was that Sergei Muraviev-Apostol would march on St Petersburg. This never happened.[26]

While the members of the Northern Society were making plans for revolt, momentous events took place in the Winter Palace. On 12 December 1825 Nicholas received two disturbing reports. The first was a detailed one from Adjutant General and Chief of Staff Ivan Ivanovich Dibich (Hans Karl von Diebitsch) about the discovery of a secret society in Ukraine and the imminent arrests of several members of the Southern Society. The other was from the former Northern Society member Second Lieutenant Iakov Rostovtsev, who informed the tsar of the plans for an uprising in St Petersburg, but without naming any names. When Nicholas found out that a revolt was imminent, he decided to seize power with immediate effect, in what has been called 'a virtual *coup d'état*'.[27] Nicholas dared not wait any longer for Constantine's official abdication. He presented his accession manifesto to the State Council on the evening of 13 December and made sure it was approved immediately.

Meanwhile, through their friends in the senate, the Decembrists learned that the oath of allegiance to the new tsar would be taken the following day. The news reached them during their evening meeting on 13 December, and the atmosphere in Ryleev's apartment grew excited. Everyone present realized that this was the opportunity the society had been waiting for, and that there would be only one chance. Rostovtsev's betrayal made this clear. For reasons unknown, Rostovtsev had presented a copy of his report to Obolenskii, who informed Ryleev. When Ryleev learned about the betrayal, he contacted Nikolai Bestuzhev immediately to discuss their options. They both agreed that the best course was to act, rather than wait for arrests to be made.[28]

The final details of the plan for the uprising were developed. According to some sources, Ryleev asked Kakhovskii if he was still willing to assassinate the tsar, telling him that this was the moment to deliver on his old promise. There are contradictory accounts of Kakhovskii's reaction. Some say he accepted the proposal but changed his mind later and refused, owing to moral doubts. Others claim there is no evidence that he refused to carry out the assassination. Because much of this information was brought to light in interrogations under pressure, it is impossible to establish the veracity of these accounts with any certainty.[29] Iakubovich said he would go to the Artillery and the Izmailovskii and bring both regiments to Senate Square. But he was a notorious braggart and several of the society's members doubted his word, so Ryleev promised them he would go in Iakubovich's stead.

Mikhail Bestuzhev left an account of the noisy, turbulent meeting in Ryleev's rooms. Those present were in a feverish, somewhat exalted state:

> How handsome Ryleev was that evening! He was not good-looking, he spoke simply, but not smoothly; nonetheless when he found himself on his favourite topic – love for his fatherland – his physiognomy revived, his eyes, black as pitch, lit up with unearthly light, speech flowed smoothly, like fiery lava.[30]

It was almost midnight when the members of the Northern Society hurried home to be ready for the fateful day. Later that night, Rozen discussed with his wife 'the forthcoming dangers', which he and his companions had talked about constantly over the previous days. Contrary to what might be expected, he included his wife in the secret plan: 'I was able to be completely frank with her,' he recalled. 'Her mind and heart understood everything.'[31] The claim made by some scholars, that the wives of the Decembrists were unaware of the Society, is thus not true.

By swift and shrewd action, Nicholas delivered a fatal blow to the Decembrists' plan before the uprising had even begun. In the early hours of 14 December, a messenger arrived at Rozen's house with an order to all officers to present themselves at the residence of the colonel of the Finliandskii regiment at seven o'clock in the morning. Nicholas had summoned the chiefs of the Guards regiments to the palace, where, through

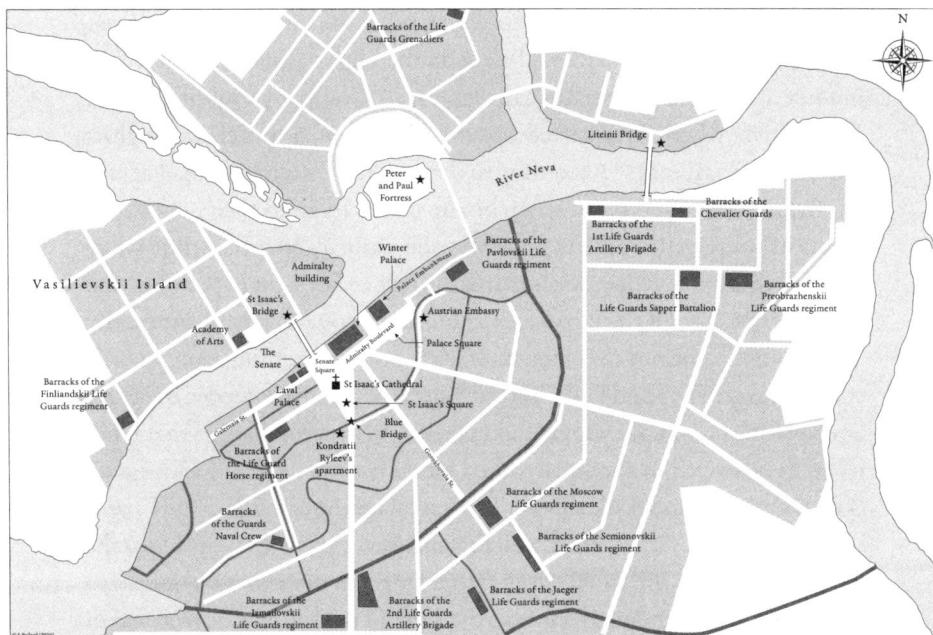

Map of St Petersburg on the day of the Decembrist revolt, 14 December 1825.

flattery and promises of reward, he convinced them to administer the oath. Afterwards, the generals hurried to their regiments and began to swear them in to the new emperor even before the break of dawn. The oath to Nicholas I thus came to be taken separately in the Guards regiments, and at different times, which made it difficult to coordinate the uprising.[32]

## The revolt

When 14 December dawned, it soon became clear to the rebels that things were not going their way. Nicholas had pre-empted their plan by rescheduling the oath-taking to an earlier time. Fewer troops marched to Senate Square than they had hoped. Trubetskoi, the designated leader, lost his nerve at the last moment and did not show up. Moreover, the logistics of organizing the revolt presented some challenges. Society members could not just make a phone call or send a text message if they needed to get in contact with someone; they had to get to whomever they wished to communicate with in person. However, communication was made easier by the fact that most Guards regiments were located in the city centre and the Decembrists lived relatively close to one another. Trubetskoi and Ryleev, for example, lived only about 1 kilometre (½ mi.) apart.

Just before 7 a.m. on 14 December, with the city still in darkness, Trubetskoi went from the Laval Palace on the English Embankment to the modest apartment in the Russian-American Company building on the Moika River where Ryleev lived with his wife, Natalia, and their daughter Nastenka (Anastasia).[33] According to the plan the Decembrists had agreed on, Ryleev was supposed to be up before 6 a.m. to go to the Guards regiments and urge the soldiers to refuse the oath to Nicholas. But when Trubetskoi arrived, Ryleev was still in bed. Trubetskoi went back home, and a short time later Ryleev passed his quarters, together with Pushchin. Trubetskoi had begun to doubt their plan, but said nothing. After a brief conversation, Ryleev and Pushchin bid him farewell and proceeded to Senate Square. On the way, they met Kiukhelbeker, who accompanied them, but when they arrived in the square, they found it empty save for Odoevskii. Ryleev, Pushchin and Kiukhelbeker then set off for the barracks of the Guards Naval Crew at the Griboedov Canal Embankment, and then went across the Fontanka River to the Izmailovskii Barracks. From there they went east, to the Cavalry-Pioneer Guards close to the Liteinii Bridge. Ryleev, who was in civilian clothes and thus could not enter the barracks, talked to officers outside the buildings, urging them to refuse the oath and march to Senate Square. Afterwards, the three friends walked the streets, waiting for troops to appear.

When no troops appeared, the men returned to Ryleev's quarters. There they found Shteingel, who was completing his work on the 'Manifesto to the Russian People'. Suddenly, Rostovtsev arrived and reported that most of the Guards had already taken the oath. Because Rostovtsev was a traitor and not to be trusted, the others decided to return to the square to present their manifesto to the senate. As Ryleev was about to leave, he met Nikolai Bestuzhev in the yard and asked him what he intended to do. Bestuzhev replied that he was going to the Naval Crew to see if they would come out for the cause. Ryleev then reported that he would go to the Finlandskii and the Grenadiers but was first going to Senate Square. If any troops marched to the square, he planned to join the ranks of the soldiers. Ryleev and Bestuzhev embraced and said their goodbyes. At that moment, Ryleev's wife came running out, seized Bestuzhev's hand and burst into tears. 'Leave me my husband,' she said. 'Do not take him away. I know he is going to perish.' Both men tried to reassure her, but she would not listen. Instead, she called out to their daughter, '"Nastenka, beg your father for your sake and for mine." The little girl ran out sobbing and hugged her father's knees while her mother fell on his chest almost unconscious.' Ryleev brought her into the apartment, 'placed her on the sofa, tore himself from her and her daughter's embrace, and ran away'.[34]

In another part of the capital, Nikolai's brothers Mikhail and Aleksandr Bestuzhev made their way to the Moscow Life Guards regiment. Mikhail wrote in his journal that he did not get much sleep that night. He had been forced to spend the night with Dmitrii Shchepin-Rostovskii, a staff captain in his regiment. Although not formally a member of the secret society, Shchepin-Rostovskii attended the meetings at Ryleev's apartment where plans for the uprising were discussed. The night before the revolt, Bestuzhev found him in a state of excitement and had to calm him down. At dawn all the officers of the regiment were ordered to their commander, General P. A. Frederiks, who read out Constantine's abdication and Nicholas's accession manifesto. When Mikhail finally returned to his quarters, he found his brother Aleksandr there, impatiently waiting for him. However, Iakubovich, who had promised to be present, remained at home. Apparently his talk the night before about bringing the Artillery and the Izmailovskii regiment to Senate Square had been no more than empty promises.

Mikhail and Aleksandr made their way hastily to the quarters of the Moscow Life Guards regiment on 90 Fontanka River Embankment, about 2 kilometres (1¼ mi.) from Ryleev's apartment. Aleksandr went to talk to the troops there. He made up a story about the new emperor Constantine, that he was held up on the road to St Petersburg while powerful people tried to compel the Guards regiments to swear allegiance to Nicholas. 'We don't want Nicholas!' the soldiers replied. 'Hurrah for Constantine!' Aleksandr's younger brother, the 25-year-old staff captain Mikhail, issued live ammunition and sent trusted men to the other companies with orders to bring live cartridges and march out with them. For two days his soldiers had been working hard to convince soldiers from other companies to refuse the oath. The company commanders had given their word that they would not prevent soldiers from following Bestuzhev.

Mikhail lined up his troops in the courtyard, where they were already preparing for the oath-taking ceremony. Staff Captain Shchepin-Rostovskii lined up his troops behind, followed by a group of soldiers from different companies. On the way out, as Mikhail and Shchepin's troops were about to seize their banners, a struggle broke out with the soldiers who had lined up to swear the oath. Once the melee was under control and the companies had resumed their march, several officers who had noticed the scuffle tried to stop them. In the commotion, Shchepin-Rostovskii wounded both the brigade commander Major General Shenshin and the regimental commander Major General Frederiks.

Finally, the companies of the Moscow Life Guards regiment led by Mikhail and Aleksandr Bestuzhev and Shchepin-Rostovskii left the barracks and filed towards Senate Square. Marching down Gorokhovaia Street, one of the city's major thoroughfares, they passed the quarters of Aleksandr Iakubovich. Bestuzhev later recounted how Iakubovich ran into the street to join them: 'his sword drawn and his white-plumed hat waving magnificently on its tip, [he] approached us with triumphant cries: "Hurrah! Constantine!"'

It was nearly nine o'clock when the Life Guard companies reached the snow-covered, completely empty square. No other regiment had arrived. 'What did I tell you?' Iakubovich exclaimed. 'I was obviously not the only one who thought you had undertaken an impossible task.' 'You couldn't have said that if you had kept your word and brought either the Artillery or the Izmailovskii here before us,' Aleksandr Bestuzhev replied angrily. Now they had to place their hope in Ryleev, who had promised that he would lead the Artillery, Izmailovskii, the Semionovskii and the Jaeger regiment to the square.[35]

Unfortunately for the Decembrists, Ryleev failed to lead any of these regiments to Senate Square. After his meeting with Nikolai Bestuzhev in the yard, he went to the square for the second time that morning. He had put on a soldier's bag and a sling, and when he found that the Moscow Life Guards regiment had arrived, he joined the ranks of the soldiers. However, he soon had to leave to expedite the arrival of the Grenadier regiment.[36] According to several witnesses, Ryleev was rushing between the barracks trying to drum up more support. Meanwhile, waiting for other troops to join them on Senate Square, the Moscow regiment formed into a carré (the shape of a square). Mikhail Bestuzhev's company, including privates from other companies, made up two sides, one facing the senate building and the other facing the monument of Peter I. Shchepin-Rostovskii's troops, which also contained men from other companies, formed the two sides facing St Isaac's Cathedral and the Admiralty.

By now it had become clear to the rebels in the square that the plan so hastily drawn up by Society members in the days after the death of Alexander had suffered yet another setback. After Rostovtsev's denunciation of the rebellion, Nicholas called the senate to an early meeting. Thus, when the Moscow regiment arrived, the Senators had already sworn allegiance to Nicholas and left. This ruined the plan to compel the senate to sanction the revolt and declare the government overthrown. Nevertheless, the actions of the Decembrists remained meaningful, because the stand on Senate Square was not only an attempt to force the Senators to proclaim the Decembrists' manifesto, but a public demonstration against the autocratic state.[37] For more than two hours the Decembrist contingents remained in place, without any government troops appearing to quell the rebellion.

Andrei Rozen spent the early morning at the residence of the colonel of the Finliandskii Guards regiment on Vasilievskii Island, where the officers of the regiment swore the oath to the new tsar. The colonel announced Nicholas I as the new emperor and read out Alexander's will, Constantine's renouncement of the throne and Nicholas's manifesto to the officers. He subsequently ordered them to return to their battalions to oversee the taking of the new oath by the troops. The first battalion swore the oath at the barracks, with the exception of Rozen's section of sharpshooters, who were on guard duty. The entire second battalion was also on guard. When Rozen returned home, he found a note from Ryleev telling him that he was expected in the quarters of the Moscow regiment. Rozen hurried away at once. As he approached St Isaac's Bridge in his sleigh, he saw a crowd at the other end and a division of the Moscow regiment on the square, on the other side of the Monument of Peter I. It was now between ten and eleven in the morning. Rozen pushed through the crowd and was greeted with loud cheers. He saw Mikhail Bestuzhev with his company and a dozen men from other companies. Prince Shchepin-Rostovsky was next to him. Pushchin was also there, 'dauntless and steadfast' in civilian clothes. 'Where can I find the dictator Trubetskoi?' Rozen asked. 'He has vanished,' replied Pushchin. 'If you are able, bring us more men.' Rozen hurriedly returned to the barracks of his regiment, where he found that his section had been released from guard duty. He ordered all four companies to get ready. But he was too late. Nicholas had already ordered troops into position. When Rozen's sharpshooters were ready to depart, their brigadier received orders to lead the battalion to St Isaac's Square.

During the morning Nicholas was informed by the chief of staff of the Guards Corps that several companies of the Life Guards of the Moscow regiment had refused to swear the oath and had marched under their banners in the direction of St Isaac's Square. Nicholas immediately ordered the Semionovskii regiment to pacify them and the Horse Guards to stand at the ready. The emperor himself went to the palace's main guardhouse and ordered the Finliandskii regiment on guard to load their guns and take up a position at the main gate of the imperial palace. Meanwhile, Nicholas received intelligence that the rebellious companies had entered Senate Square and that a crowd had gathered. A command was sent to the first battalion of the Preobrazhenskii Life Guards regiment to march to Palace Square without delay.

Subsequently, Governor General Count Miloradovich came to see the emperor, bringing with him the news that the crowd were shouting, 'Hurrah, Constantine!' At that moment, Nicholas realized the seriousness of what was happening. The Life Guards Sapper Battalion and three companies of the Pavlovskii Life Guards regiment were ordered to occupy the Winter Palace, while the third battalion of the Preobrazhenskii regiment and the Life Guard Horse regiment were ordered to join the emperor immediately on Palace Square. A number of attempts were also made to appease the rebellious troops. Miloradovich addressed them in the belief that his reputation as a war hero would make them listen, but to no avail. Instead, he was mortally wounded by a shot fired by Piotr Kakhovskii.[38] By this time the Horse Guards regiment had arrived, followed by three companies from the Pavlovskii regiment. The emperor moved closer to the rebels in the hope that his presence would make them surrender, but this manoeuvre seems to have had the contrary effect.[39]

As these events unfolded on the square, Rozen stood on St Isaac's Bridge, a pontoon bridge leading to Senate Square, with his four companies of the Finliandskii Guards. In the morning, when ordering his troops to get ready, his plan had been to join the rebels. Then the order to join the government troops had come. Moreover, when he reached the square, he realized that the revolt was without a leader. Trubetskoi, the appointed leader, had lost his head, probably because he believed the revolt would fail and innocent people would suffer. Instead of going to the square, he went into hiding at the Austrian embassy, where his brother-in-law Ludwig Lebzeltern served as the Austrian empire's minister to St Petersburg. The reason for his cowardly behaviour remains a mystery. Trubetskoi most likely did not care so much for his own life. After all, he was an experienced officer who had seen action and had fought bravely in many battles. Writing his memoirs several years later, Rozen still had no idea why Trubetskoi was not at his post. All his friends agreed that he was an able, energetic man, someone to be trusted in an emergency.

Having convinced himself that the revolt had no leader, Rozen did not want to sacrifice his soldiers in a hopeless fight, but joining the other side was out of the question. For this reason, the moment the brigadier gave the order to advance across the bridge, Rozen decided to disobey and to halt his men at their station. In this way, he prevented his soldiers from turning against his friends, and also successfully blocked the regiments behind them from crossing the bridge to attack the rebels. The brigadier tried to make the sharpshooters move, but Rozen held his position on the bridge. Every moment he expected his friends to break through to the bridge, where he was ready to assist them with his eight hundred men.[40]

Back in Senate Square, the emperor decided to make an attempt to scare the rebels and commanded the cavalry to attack. From his position on the bridge, Rozen saw a squadron of the Horse Guards advance and place themselves at short range from the rebels. The soldiers of the Moscow regiment prepared to shoot. Mikhail Bestuzhev gave the order to 'reverse arms', but a few bullets had already been shot and a few horsemen fell, whereupon they retreated. According to Bestuzhev's own depiction of the incident, the cavalry made several attacks. Rushing down on the rebels in their first attack, the Horse Guards were greeted with a shower of stones and firewood from the onlookers and had to return to their original position in disarray.[41]

According to another account it was Ryleev who incited the onlookers to deflect the attack by throwing firewood at the advancing cavalry.[42] But the Moscow regiment had to withstand the second and third attacks without the assistance of the crowd. After the third attack, the Horse Guards galloped to the senate building and started to line up. The soldiers on the square immediately took aim, preparing to fire a volley that would probably have killed them all. At the last minute Mikhail Bestuzhev ran out in front and commanded, 'Halt!' The soldiers lowered their guns, but several bullets whistled past him and a number of Horse Guards fell. Next the Mounted Pioneers rode past the Horse Guards, but Bestuzhev's men fired volleys at them, forcing them to retreat. In his report to the emperor, the war minister later blamed the failure of the attacks on the cramped space and the favourable position of 'the rebellious gang'.[43]

The shots fired on the square were heard in the nearby barracks of the Guards Naval Crew, which was responsible for the maintenance and manning of the imperial yachts and rowing vessels as well as for court and garrison guard duty. The soldiers had gathered to swear the oath to the new tsar when Nikolai Bestuzhev appeared at the entrance to the barracks telling the soldiers to refuse the oath. When they heard the shots fired to repel the attack of the Horse Guards, Nikolai shouted, 'Lads, we are under attack, follow me.' Led by Nikolai Bestuzhev and Anton Arbuzov, the men followed. According to conflicting accounts, both Lieutenant Mikhail Kiukhelbeker (younger brother of Vilgelm) and Nikolai's younger brother Piotr Bestuzhev are credited with rousing the troops. In any event, at lunchtime a full battalion of marines could be seen coming down Galernaia Street to assist the rebels. Leaving in haste, they had neglected to bring cannon from the arsenal, but they counted on being reinforced by the Guards Artillery, who were expected to join the rebellion.[44]

On the square, the Naval Crew positioned themselves to the right of the Moscow regiment and sent their sharpshooters forwards under Kiukhelbeker's command. Ryleev greeted Nikolai Bestuzhev and took him aside: 'Our prediction is coming true,' he said. 'Our last minutes are close, but these are the minutes of our freedom: we breathed it, and I willingly give my life for it.'[45] Shortly thereafter, eight companies of the Grenadier Guards regiment led by three young officers, Aleksandr Sutgof, Nikolai Panov and Andrei Kozhevnikov, all in their early twenties, arrived to join the rebels.

According to Pushchin's account, Lieutenant Piotr Konovnitsyn, a young member of the society, rode with Odoevskii to the barracks of the Grenadier Guards regiment to find out why they had not appeared on the square. There, they learned that the Grenadiers had already sworn the oath to Nicholas and that the men had been dismissed. Surprised and disappointed, they went to Sutgof (a member of the Society) to reproach him for not having led his company to the designated assembly place of Senate Square.

Vasily Timm, *Life Guards Horse Regiment during the Uprising of 14 December 1825 on St Isaac's Square*, 1853, oil on canvas.

Sutgof, who pleaded ignorance of these instructions, immediately ordered his company to seize their guns. Live cartridges were issued and the whole company set out towards Senate Square. Battalion Adjutant Panov, who happened to be nearby, rushed off to the other companies urging the soldiers to keep up with Sutgof's company. Miraculously, he managed to persuade all seven companies to grab guns and cartridges and follow him out of the barracks. The admonitions of Colonel Ludwig von Stürler, commander of the Grenadier regiment, were to no avail.

The barracks of the Grenadier Guards were in the Petrogradskii district on the other side of the Neva River from Senate Square. The companies took the shortest route across the ice, which meant marching through the Peter and Paul Fortress. This means they could easily have seized the fortress, and things would have turned out very differently if they had. Instead, the Grenadiers pushed on. When they had crossed the river, they entered the courtyard of the Winter Palace without facing any resistance. Guards were stationed at the main gate. According to the plan, the Decembrists were supposed to enter the palace to arrest the tsar and his family. This never happened. In the courtyard, instead of brothers in arms, they found Colonel Aleksandr Gerua, commander of the Life Guards Sapper Battalion, protecting the palace. In vain, the colonel tried to bring the Grenadiers to the side of the emperor. Panov called out, 'This is not our side,' and led the detachment out on to the Palace Embankment. The Grenadiers followed the Embankment to the Palace Square, where a cannon was standing. Here, they missed another opportunity. Had they taken possession of the cannon, it is likely that the outcome of the revolt would have been different. On the way to Senate Square, on Admiralty Boulevard, Panov's Grenadiers came face to face with the emperor himself, leading the first battalion of the Preobrazhenskii regiment. Nicholas stopped the Grenadiers and asked where they were going and if they were on his side. 'If so, turn right; if not, turn left,' he said. 'To the left,' a voice replied. The troops dispersed and allowed the Grenadiers to pass. Subsequently, Nicholas claimed that he ordered his troops to disperse to avoid bloodshed.[46]

Reading Nicholas 1's reminiscences of the events of 14 December, it becomes apparent just how close the Decembrists were to succeeding at this moment. Nicholas describes the danger he found himself in when

> a troop of Royal Grenadiers led by officer Panov was advancing with the intention of seizing the palace and, should there be any resistance, wiping out our entire family. They reached the main gates

of the palace in a certain degree of order, so that the commandant thought they were the detachment I had sent to occupy the palace. However, Panov suddenly noticed the sapper battalion of the Life-Guards regiment which had just arrived ... and, calling out 'Those are not ours!', began to wheel the detachment round and ran out with them back on to the square. If the sapper battalion had arrived but a few minutes later, the palace and the whole of our family would have been in the hands of the insurgents, while I, preoccupied with what was happening on Senate Square and totally unaware of this extreme danger ... would have been totally unable to offer any resistance.[47]

Through these dramatic events, Commander Stürler had accompanied the Grenadiers, all along trying to persuade the soldiers to turn back. As they entered the square and lined up next to the Moscow regiment, Kakhovskii shot at Stürler, who was mortally wounded. As the Grenadiers were lining up, young cadets of the Naval and First Cadet Corps approached the Decembrist troops offering their help. 'We are sent as deputies from our corps to request permission to come to the square and fight in your ranks,' said one of them breathlessly. Mikhail Bestuzhev recalled that their offer made him smile but that he resisted the temptation to give them permission to fight, since he did not want to put the boys in danger.[48]

There were now about 3,000 rebels gathered on the cold and windy Senate Square. In addition, there were thousands of spectators surrounding them, many of whom were sympathetic and appeared willing to support the revolt. In hindsight, Rozen was confident that had there only been a single efficient leader, the availability of so many men would easily have led the revolt to a more favourable end. This was especially so considering that some regiments assembled around the tsar appeared inclined to join the rebels. In Rozen's view, had offensive action been taken, many of the battalions would have joined them. Instead, 'as if bound by a spell, the soldiers who had earlier shown themselves so ardent now stood inactive when, with relatively little difficulty, they could have seized the cannon which were now being used against them.'[49]

Aleksandr Beliaev's recollections corroborate Rozen's view. He remembered how they all saw the guns being aimed at them in the early evening, but they did not dare to act. According to Beliaev, Captain Aleksandr Kornilovich of the Southern Society, who was visiting St Petersburg and participated in the revolt, said, '"now we need to go and take the guns," but since none of the leaders were on the square, no one dared take it upon themselves to move the battalions against the guns and perhaps begin a deadly struggle, which decided the fate of this unfortunate attempt'.[50] Aleksandr Bestuzhev was of the same opinion. In his view, the greatest misfortune was the absence of Trubetskoi, which affected both the officers and their men. Without military titles and with few epaulettes, nobody dared to take command.[51]

Colonel Bulatov, who was second in command, had also vanished. When his disappearance had been established, the command was offered to Mikhail Bestuzhev, who declined. At last, Prince I. P. Obolenskii was persuaded to accept the post, but he was not a suitable leader. According to eyewitness accounts, total anarchy now prevailed. Rozen recalled how everyone shouted commands that nobody obeyed. The rebels could not make up their minds to attack, which, at this early stage, might have produced a significant result.

Of the loyal forces, the Imperial Horse Guards, commanded by Alexei Orlov, were the first government troops to appear on the scene. They positioned themselves with their backs to the Admiralty building, which was between Senate Square and the palace, and their right flank towards the river. Next, the men of the Preobrazhenskii regiment arrived, accompanied by Nicholas, closing off the exit from St Isaac's Bridge, where Rozen was waiting with his troops, and barring the English Embankment, which ran along the banks of the Neva from the northwest corner of the square. The Pavlovskii regiment lined up against the Lobanov-Rostovskii Palace, just southeast of the square, while the men of the Izmailovskii formed up along the street next to it and the Semionovskii regiment lined up along the Imperial Horse Guards Manege in St Isaac's Square to the south. Other regiments were stationed along the main streets leading to the palace, St Isaac's Square and Senate Square. Thus the rebellious troops were finally encircled. However, the arrival and disposition of the government troops were not instantaneous but gradual and slow. This meant that there were opportunities for the revolutionaries to strike had they only found a leader to take action.

On Admiralty Boulevard stood the carré of the Preobrazhenskii regiment. Here the emperor, on horseback and with his suite, took up position. His eldest son, seven-year-old Aleksandr Nikolaevich, was in the middle of this carré with his tutor. In front of the imperial carré were placed cannon covered by a section of the Horse Guards. Behind the Horse Guards stood a battalion of the Pavlovskii Guards. They blocked the entrance to Galernaia Street, which ran parallel to English Embankment from the southwest corner of the square. Sappers were deployed in the courtyard of the palace.

The troops surrounding the rebels were four times their number. Nevertheless, the members of the Society did not despair. They were convinced that the regiments facing them were friendly. Mikhail Bestuzhev insisted that the men of the Izmailovskii regiment were 'brought out against troops whom they were waiting for an opportunity to join at any moment! As commander of this regiment, the new emperor had not even received a formal response to his threefold greeting: "Hello lads!" and had left in embarrassment.' Furthermore, the Horse Guards had been exposed to such a consistent campaign of persuasion by members of the Society that, 'had our regiment moved, they probably would have joined us.' According to Bestuzhev, the men of these regiments had let the Decembrists know their intentions by means of the people surrounding them on the square.[52] Beliaev tells a similar story about soldiers who approached them, sent by the infantry regiments, asking the rebels to hold out until evening, when they promised they would all join the uprising.[53]

Rozen's account concurs with Bestuzhev's story. He agreed that Nicholas could not rely on the loyalty of these troops and that the soldiers were wavering: 'When the 2nd Battalion of the Jaeger Guards received the order to advance over the Blue Bridge towards St Isaac's Square, Iakubovich gave the order, "Left about face," and the entire battalion turned about so that only two regiments could be made to move.' The Izmailovskii regiment, too, was wavering. This regiment included numerous Society members among the officers. One of them, Captain Bogdanovitch, committed suicide later that day because he had failed to support his friends. Furthermore, the cannon were guarded by a section of the Horse Guards led by a member of the Society, Lieutenant I. A. Annenkov, but no one thought of taking advantage of this. The revolutionaries also failed to exploit the fact that the guard in the Winter Palace that day was taken by the 2nd battalion of the Finliandskii regiment under the command of Colonel A. F. Moller, for many years a member of the Society. Moller had promised to act, but the day before the revolt he told Nikolai Bestuzhev that he had changed his mind, fearing the failure of the uprising. Yet another turn of events that would have changed the outcome of the revolt was Bulatov's failed attempt to kill the tsar. He stood for two hours at Admiralty Boulevard, twenty paces from the emperor, carrying two loaded pistols, without plucking up the courage to shoot.

The more time passed, the more worried Nicholas became. He was reluctant to shed blood on his first day as emperor, but all efforts to make the rebels surrender failed. Everyone who approached them and tried to induce them to disperse was driven away. Miloradovich and Stürler were both shot by Kakhovskii. General Voinov was shot by Vilgelm Kiukhelbeker. Grand Duke Mikhail Pavlovich, who had just returned from Poland, also tried to talk to the troops. He promised them an unconditional pardon, as had Miloradovich before him, but was obliged to withdraw when Kiukhelbeker pointed his gun at him. Finally, Metropolitan Serafim approached the rebels, accompanied by the Metropolitan of Kyiv and several priests. He begged them for the love of Christ to return to their barracks. But they told him to go back to the church and pray for their souls. The presence of the emperor himself had no effect whatsoever on the rebels.

Thus neither political, military nor spiritual authority had any impact on the Decembrists in Senate Square. Furthermore, crowds of civilians sympathetic to the rebels had gathered on the square and resisted the attempts of the police to disperse them with projectiles of stones and pieces of wood. 'The mob was on the side of the insurgents,' the frightened empress wrote in her diary. Some civilians asked the rebels to give them weapons. If Obolenskii as the appointed leader had decided to go on the offensive, involving the many onlookers and handing them weapons, the revolt could have stood a chance. According to Rozen, many in the crowd were already armed with axes and hatchets.[54]

The short winter day was drawing to a close. Nicholas, fearing that the revolt might spread to the crowd, finally made the momentous decision to resort to severe measures and gave the order to bring up the artillery. In the emperor's own words, 'workers from the construction site began to throw pieces of wood at us from behind the fence. It was necessary to bring the situation to a rapid conclusion, otherwise the rebellion might communicate itself to the mob, and then the troops, surrounded by them, would be in a most difficult position.' The government later argued that the civilian crowd was bribed with money and wine, but never said by whom.[55]

Nicholas ordered four cannon to be brought against the rebels. The government troops broke ranks to let the weapons through, and the cannon were placed just 18 metres (60 ft) from the rebels. By now the crowds on the square were dwindling and the police had become bolder in dispersing them, but many stayed put. Nikolai Sukhozanet, adjutant to the chief of artillery, galloped up to the rebels to tell them one last time to surrender; otherwise, they would be shot.

'Get back,' we cried out, Mikhail Bestuzhev recounted, 'and send someone who's less dirty than you!' added Pushchin. Galloping back to the battery, Sukhozanet took the plume out of his hat, which was the agreed signal to fire, and a shot rang out. The cannon was aimed over our heads. The crowd of people did not move.[56]

According to Rozen, it was Count Toll who approached the emperor and said to him, 'Sire, give the orders that this square be swept by cannon, or resign the throne!' The first cannon shot was loaded with blank cartridges. The second and third shots hit the wall of the senate or flew over the Neva. The shots were answered with resounding 'Hurrahs' from the rebels. The guns were then loaded with grapeshot and aimed at the troops in the square. The emperor gave the command to fire. But the artillery soldier refused to obey, whereupon Captain Bakunin ran up to him, seized the slow match out of his hand and lit the charge. A moment later grapeshot was fired into the ranks of the rebels. People fell or scattered in different directions. Many innocents were also hit. The rebels fled down Galernaia Street and over the river to the Academy of Arts. The guns were immediately moved. Several more shots were fired down the narrow Galernaia Street after the running soldiers and across the Neva. Soldiers fell. When the square was empty, the Horse Guards regiment crossed St Isaac's Bridge to Vasilievskii Island to prevent rebel reinforcements.[57]

Mikhail Bestuzhev remembered how he ran to the front of his company facing the Neva as the shots were fired. Many of his soldiers fell to the ground, groaning in torment. Others ran to the river. 'Follow me, lads!' he cried to the men from the Moscow regiment and went down to the Neva. In the middle of the frozen river, he stopped the soldiers and with the help of his non-commissioned officers began to form into a column, with the intention of marching over the ice to occupy the Peter and Paul Fortress. The fortress would have been an ideal point to gather the revolutionaries and begin negotiations with Nicholas with guns trained on the palace.

Bestuzhev had already managed to line up three platoons when a cannonball hit the ice, ricocheting along the river:

I turned back to see where the fire came from, and through the smoke from the guns saw a battery positioned near the middle of St Isaac's Bridge. I kept on building the column, although cannonballs were taking rows from it, now on the right, now on the left. The soldiers did not lose heart ... The tail of the column was already being completed, when suddenly there was a cry: 'We are drowning!'

. . . The ice, under the weight of all the people and crushed by cannonballs, could not hold and was giving way.[58]

Had the ice held, Bestuzhev might well have succeeded in capturing the Peter and Paul Fortress. Instead, the soldiers rushed for the safety of the riverbank, reaching it beside the Academy of Arts building. Bestuzhev realized that if they could seize the halls of antique statues and paintings that surrounded the courtyard of the Academy, they would be able to defend themselves for a long time. However, when they ran towards it, the doorman lowered the weights of the gate and it slammed shut in front of their noses. Bestuzhev then told his men to fetch a log from the bottom of a broken wooden barge lying in the river. With its help, the men tried to knock the gate from its hinges. 'The gate was already cracking under their blows when we caught sight of a squadron of Horse Guards rushing towards us at full speed,' Bestuzhev later wrote. 'The soldiers dropped their hands . . . "Save yourself as best you can, lads!" I shouted. The soldiers scattered in different directions.' Bestuzhev himself moved slowly through the alleys to his family's house on the seventh line of Vasilievskii island, just north of the Academy.[59] There, with his mother and sisters, he finally got some rest.

Meanwhile, Rozen had led his companies to the riding school. He was ordered to withdraw while his soldiers took the oath of allegiance to Nicholas, and then to take his section to patrol the Andreevskii market and the shops on Bolshoi Avenue, not far from the Academy of Arts. By six o'clock the insurrection had been suppressed. St Petersburg was like a city after a storm. In the dark night, bonfires were burning on the squares; troops were deployed in every district; patrols were roaming the streets in whole detachments.[60] Many rebels were arrested during the evening. According to Nikolai Lorer, the emperor wanted to shoot summarily at midnight all those who had been arrested, but State Secretary Mikhail Speranskii prevented him. Speranskii hurried to the palace and begged the tsar to show mercy: 'You make each of these unfortunate heroes, martyrs . . . All of Russia, all of Europe is watching your actions.'[61]

That evening Mikhail Bestuzhev, dressed up in his brother's old naval uniform and a fur coat, took a cab across the river to see his friend Torson on St Isaac's Square. The driver informed him that they were washing out the blood, sprinkling new snow and shoving dead men under the ice.[62] Not far from St Isaac's Square, they were stopped by a gendarme and Bestuzhev continued on foot. As he approached the square, he saw that it was illuminated by bonfires at which the soldiers were warming themselves:

Through the smoke and flickering flames, the shining muzzles of
the cannon, placed at all the exits of the main streets leading to the
square, appeared and disappeared . . . Inside this cherished circle,
where during a few hours the fate of the tsar and Russia had been
settled, working folk were busy washing away and destroying all
traces of the unlawful attempt made by unreasonable people who
dreamed of alleviating, if only a little, the burden of their bitter lot.
Some scraped off the red snow; others sprinkled white snow on the
washed and scrubbed places. The rest removed the bodies of the
dead and took them to the river.[63]

Anne Disbrowe, wife of the British diplomat Sir Edward Cromwell
Disbrowe, had heard the cannon shots from her house. At half past nine
in the evening she wrote to her father, Robert Kennedy, 'It was dreadful to
hear the firing. Every round went to my heart. I do not know particulars
for certain except that at this moment, all is quiet and some say the muti-
neers have retreated across the river and dispersed.'[64] No matter how much
they scrubbed, traces of blood were still left when she went out two days
later: 'The traces of the sad event on Monday were horrid: pools of blood
on the snow and spattered up against the houses. The Senate House dread-
fully battered.'[65] However, she appears to have been of the opinion that the
rebels had themselves to blame. She was clearly dissatisfied with the turmoil
the uprising caused to the implicated families and to the Russian nation.[66]

In general, there was a lot of public interest in the events at Senate Square.
Newspapers reported on the arrests made and on the extensive investigation into the circumstances of the revolt. People were surprised to hear
that so many young members of prominent families were involved. Why
would these people take part in a revolt and run the risk of losing everything?
Aleksandr Bulgakov, Moscow Postmaster, noted: 'Rebellion is the business
of vagabonds who gain everything and lose nothing from the riots.'[67] Nevertheless, the persistent feeling that spread through Russian society was fear.
Many were eager to show their loyalty to the new tsar.

# 4

# Revolution in Ukraine

At almost the same time, about 1,387 kilometres (860 mi.) to the south, another revolt was in the making. This uprising, organized by members of the Southern Society, was even more disorganized than the one in St Petersburg, but for different reasons. The members in the south had no time to plan their revolt or to coordinate their actions. Their uprising was a response to a government attack on the Society. Furthermore, they were scattered over a large area of Ukraine, so communication was problematic. However, this southern revolt did have an advantage over that carried out in the north: it had a resourceful leader.

Notwithstanding the failure of the Secret Society in the capital, there was still a chance of success in the south. By 1823 the Vasylkiv (Vasilkov) branch was the most active part of the Southern Society, with a larger membership than the main organization at Tulchyn and a more active leadership. Sergei Muraviev-Apostol and Mikhail Bestuzhev-Riumin were the leaders of the Vasylkiv branch, both former officers of the insurgent Semionovskii regiment, many members of which had been transferred to the Russian southern armies.[1] To broaden their support, they established contact with the Polish Patriotic Society, founded in 1821 under Major Walerian Łukasiński. As with its Decembrist counterpart, the members of this society were mostly army officers. Its main objectives were to reunite all Polish lands, uphold the constitution granted in 1815 and promote national independence. Several Decembrists had personal relationships with Poles and sympathized with their liberal aspirations. However, they never fully supported a completely independent Polish state. Such members as Mikhail Lunin, Pavel Pestel and Bestuzhev-Riumin accepted the necessity of granting Poland some form of independence, but they were not happy about it. Lunin felt that a union like the one between England and Scotland would be the best solution.

Contact between the Vasylkiv branch of the Southern Society and the Polish Patriotic Society was established in the spring of 1823. The Decembrists wanted the Poles to assassinate Grand Duke Constantine, commander-in-chief of the Polish army, at the time of a future uprising. In return for assisting the Southern Society, the Poles wanted a guarantee that all territories seized by Russia would be restored to Poland. According to Muraviev-Apostol, the Southern Society offered Poland the restoration of her former independence, but conceding territory was a tricky question. Pestel hoped to solve it in a way that was not detrimental to Russia. Many members of the Northern Society were against yielding Russian territory and unhappy with the Southern Society's contact with the Poles.[2] Sergei Volkonskii recalled meeting representatives of the Polish Society together with Pestel. Volkonskii and Pestel wanted to know whether the Polish Society accepted that provinces conquered from Poland be 'annexed' to Russia. According to Volkonskii, Pestel said:

> We should not set conditions about the border, we must strive for a common cause. The union between Poland and Russia should not be to the detriment of the latter . . . What has been Russian for a long time must remain Russian; we will form a federal whole based on nationality . . . You will find brothers in us, and the line between us will not be the arbitrariness of any class.[3]

The Southern Society made several plans for a revolt. One idea was to use the occasion of an imperial inspection of the troops of the Third Infantry Corps at the village of Bila Tserkva (Belaia Tserkov) in the summer of 1824 to assassinate the tsar. The plan, which was drawn up by Bestuzhev-Riumin, Muraviev-Apostol, Pestel, Iosif and Aleksandr Poggio, Vasilii Davydov and commander of the Aleksopol Infantry regiment Ivan Povalo-Shveikovskii, was for several officers at the changing of the guard to break into the emperor's apartment and murder him in his sleep. The leaders were then to instigate an uprising in the camp and lead the troops to Moscow and Kyiv. From Kyiv Muraviev-Apostol would go to St Petersburg to incite the members of the Northern Society. In the end the emperor cancelled his visit to Bila Tserkva and the plan came to naught. The rebels then talked about executing their scheme in the summer of 1825, but ultimately decided to wait until 1826, when a meeting of delegates to reconsider a possible unification of the Northern and Southern societies was planned.

In the autumn of 1825 Pestel made plans for an uprising to take place in January 1826, which would start with his own Vyatka regiment. That regiment would take advantage of guard duty to seize the headquarters of the Second Army. Simultaneously, brigade commander Volkonskii would incite the Nineteenth Infantry Division and the Twenty-Seventh Mounted Artillery Company. The Vasylkiv section was to rouse the Third Infantry Corps and Davydov the military colonies. However, the actions of the Northern Society would be crucial to their success. The Northern Society had to take control of the capital. That was why Pestel was so disappointed after the talks in St Petersburg failed to unite the two societies. In the summer of 1825 he heard rumours of betrayal, which made him pessimistic about the Society's future, and he became increasingly discouraged as time passed. Instead, Muraviev-Apostol became the more prominent advocate of rebellious action, even more so after the death of Alexander I. Together with Bestuzhev-Riumin, he had developed several plans for a revolt in the south rather than in St Petersburg.[4]

At the end of the summer of 1825 members of the Southern Society learned of the existence of the Society of United Slavs. This group, formed in Novohrad-Volynskyi in 1823 by the officers Andrei and Piotr Borisov and the Polish nobleman Julian Lublinski, had 51 members, almost all of whom were junior officers. It shared the democratic ideas of the Southern Society, but – in contrast to the latter, which embraced ethnocentric centralized ideas – the aim of the United Slavs was to form a federation of ten democratic Slav republics. On the initiative of Muraviev-Apostol and Bestuzhev-Riumin of the Vasylkiv council, the United Slavs merged with the Southern Society at the beginning of September 1825, forming within it a new branch called the Slavic council (duma). The Slavic council became one of the most vigorous branches, conducting propaganda among the soldiers and preparing them for rebellion.[5] The extent to which the Decembrist officers stationed in Ukrainian villages were influenced by anti-Russian sentiment among the local population is hard to tell. However, they were certainly conscious of the peasants' negative attitude to the imperial army.[6]

## The Society is exposed

The Southern Society had greater potential to succeed than the Society in the north. Being far from the capital, it was monitored less by the government. Moreover, Pavel Dmitrievich Kiselev, chief of staff of the Second Army at its headquarters in Tulchyn, was unusually permissive and tolerant,

Unknown artist, *Sergei Muraviev-Apostol*, 1828, oil on cardboard.

forming close friendships with several of the Society's members.[7] The Society's major problem was infiltration. In the summer and autumn of 1825 information was reaching the government about the Southern Society. One of the informers was Ivan Vasilievich Sherwood (Shervud), a junior officer of the Third Ukrainian Ulan regiment. He managed to win the trust of Fedor Vadkovskii, one of the founders of the St Petersburg branch of the Southern Society, who recruited him to the Society.

Although Sherwood did not obtain detailed information, he did report that there was a secret society in the south that was conspiring against the regime. He was brought before Alexander I on 17 July and asked for proof of his claims. Soon afterwards the emperor received another report, from General I. O. Witte (Vitt), about a conspiracy in the Eighteenth Infantry Division, and this confirmed Sherwood's claims. Witte had hired an agent, Aleksandr K. Boshniak, who managed to infiltrate the Southern Society and was able to name some of its members, including Pestel. Witte, who was summoned to Taganrog on 19 October, told Alexander that Pestel was the leader. The emperor also received a second testimony from Sherwood, who reported from another meeting with Vadkovskii about the plans for a revolution. He was also able to identify members of the Society with the help of a secret letter that Vadkovskii had handed him to be dispatched to Pestel. In this letter, several members were mentioned. The tsar received information about these plans late on 26 October, while in Crimea. He did not return to Taganrog until 5 November. Although his chief of staff, Ivan Ivanovich Dibich, accompanied him to Crimea, the emperor did not give Dibich the order to arrest Vadkovskii until 10 November. It is most likely that Alexander hesitated because he did not want to draw attention to any opposition to the regime. The tsar's illness and death further delayed action, and Vadkovskii was not arrested until the beginning of December.

Another report reached Dibich in Taganrog after the death of Alexander I. This one was from Captain Arkadii Maiboroda, a fellow officer of Pestel's in the Vyatka regiment. Pestel himself had recruited Maiboroda to the Southern Society, where, serving directly under Pestel, he was privy to a great deal of confidential information and therefore a more dangerous informer. Pestel had accused Maiboroda of having robbed regimental funds. Revenge or fear of the consequences of being exposed were the probable reason for his betrayal. In his memoirs, Lorer claims that he warned Pestel about Maiboroda, but that Pestel refused to listen. In a detailed statement, Maiboroda provided Dibich with a list containing the names of 46 members of the Society and naming Pestel as the leader.[8]

On 5 December, by order of Dibich, Lieutenant General Aleksandr Chernyshev was sent to Tulchyn to inform Pestel's commanding officer, General Vitgenshtein, about the suspected conspiracy, and to arrest Pestel and Volkonskii. Chernyshev's intention was to visit the army regiments and arrest officers according to his list of suspects, but the commander-in-chief advised him against this, since it was likely to arouse suspicion. Instead, Vitgenshtein sent Chernyshev with his chief of staff, Pavel Dmitrievich Kiselev, to Pestel's quarters in Illintsi (Lintsy) in Vinnytsia region, where his regiment was stationed, with orders to search them. At the same time Vitgenshtein summoned all the commanders from Pestel's division to

Tulchyn 'for instructions'. When Pestel arrived, he was immediately arrested, as was Aleksei Iushnevskii. This took place on 13 December, the day before the rising in the north. The next day Lorer's servant informed him that Pestel's valet had been brought back from Tulchyn in chains. Lorer managed to see him in his temporary prison and the valet told him that Pestel had been placed in a convent under strict guard. Driving to Tulchyn, the valet had spotted from a distance a platoon with sabres drawn. When he told his master, Pestel stopped the carriage, wrote a note and ordered the valet to deliver it to Lorer by any means while he continued alone to the city. However, after a mile or so the valet was overtaken by officials, who stopped him and brought him to Tulchyn. There Chernyshev took the note.

Pestel was interrogated for two weeks before being transferred to St Petersburg. In the meantime, Chernyshev and Kiselev searched frantically for Pestel's secret papers. Even the garden was searched, yet after three days they had not found anything incriminating. Meanwhile, the interrogation of other officers led nowhere.[9] Despite the absence of proof, on 23 December Nicholas wrote to his brother Constantine in Warsaw that 'those arrested in the Second Army are the most important ringleaders . . . It is particularly important to me to have Pestel and Sergei Volkonskii.'[10] When Nicholas wrote these words, Volkonskii was still at large, albeit fearing imminent arrest. His pregnant wife, Maria, recalled how, one night in mid-December, he returned home after midnight and rushed into her room, shouting 'Get up at once!' She woke up trembling, scared by the sudden noise:

> He began to light the fireplace and burn some papers. I helped him as best I could, asking what the matter was. 'Pestel has been arrested.' 'For what?' No answer. All this secrecy disturbed me. I saw that he was sad and worried. Finally, he told me that he had promised my father to take me to his village for my confinement, and so we set off.[11]

Lorer recalled the anxiety members of the Southern Society felt when they first received the news that Alexander I was dead and then, a few days later, Chernyshev turned up in Tulchyn. They burned all their papers. On the evening of the swearing of the oath to Constantine, everyone dined at Pestel's as usual. After dinner, Lorer and Pestel were left by themselves. They were sitting in the study when suddenly a staff officer materialized on the threshold and handed Pestel a small note written in pencil: 'The Society has been found out. If a single member is taken, I will begin the affair.' It was signed S. Muraviev-Apostol.[12] The next day they found out that they had been betrayed by Maiboroda.

The whole affair was embarrassing for Kiselev, who had ignored reports of the existence of a secret society of officers in his regiments. He now felt betrayed, especially by Pestel, whom he held in high regard.[13] Lorer recalled that Kiselev and Chernyshev summoned him and pressed him about his membership of the Society. However, according to his own account, Lorer kept quiet. The following day all the soldiers of the 1st Battalion were interrogated about Pestel, but nothing incriminating came to light and the generals left for Tulchyn. Less than two days later, on 22 December, Lorer was called to Tulchyn. At the inn where he stayed, he was told that several sympathetic regimental commanders had been arrested and that Muraviev-Apostol, Povalo-Shveikovskii and Vasilii Tizengauzen, commander of the Poltava Infantry regiment and member of the society, had been placed under guard.

The next morning, 23 December, Lorer went to the house of the commander-in-chief, where Kiselev lived and Chernyshev was staying. Chernyshev again accused him of being a member of the Society and said that unless he admitted as much, he would be confronted with Maiboroda. To avoid such an embarrassing encounter, Lorer decided to confess to being a member but allegedly revealed nothing more. The following day he was ordered to prepare to go to St Petersburg, following Chernyshev in his own carriage. En route to the capital, he learned about the uprising of 14 December. On approaching St Petersburg, Chernyshev made another attempt to persuade Lorer to make a full confession and tell him where *Russian Justice*, the programme of the Southern Society, was hidden. Lorer claims that he remained silent.[14]

While the search for *Russian Justice* was going on, members of the Southern Society were discussing what to do after Pestel's arrest. Some wanted to wait and see what would happen, while others believed the best strategy was to stage an uprising as soon as possible. Ivan Horbachevskii (Gorbachevskii), who represented the Society of United Slavs at the Vasylkiv council, recalled that most members agreed to gather their companies and march directly to Kyiv, where Muraviev-Apostol, who was seen as second in command to Pestel, could join them. On 20 December Horbachevskii received a note from Bestuzhev-Riumin saying that it would be possible to begin the uprising as early as February, and that they should meet in Kyiv on 15 January. While work on these plans was proceeding, members of the Southern Society were waiting to hear from St Petersburg about the uprising there, but all was quiet. The decision was made to send Bestuzhev-Riumin northwards to act as liaison. However, as an ex-officer of the Semionovskii regiment, he did not have the right to leave of absence. Thus, on 24 December, Sergei Muraviev-Apostol and his brother Matvei left for the headquarters in Zhytomyr (Zhitomir), 150 kilometres (93 mi.) west of Vasylkiv, to ask Commander Rot for leave of absence for Bestuzhev-Riumin. At the last staging post before Zhytomyr, the brothers heard of the uprising in the capital from a courier. This information was later confirmed by Rot over dinner in Zhytomyr.

During Sergei Muraviev-Apostol's absence, gendarmes arrived in Vasylkiv from St Petersburg with an order for his arrest. The soldiers entered his apartment, where Bestuzhev-Riumin was then staying, went directly to Muraviev-Apostol's office and removed all his papers. The members of the Society hurriedly decided that Bestuzhev-Riumin should go after the soldiers and try to overtake them, in order to warn Muraviev-Apostol. The officers who stayed would prepare for the uprising. In the meantime, Sergei and Matvei had continued to Lyubar (Liubar), 85 kilometres (53 mi.) south-west of Zhytomyr, to discuss plans for an uprising with their cousin Artamon Muraviev, commander of the Akhtyrsky hussar regiment and also a member of the Society. While they were talking, Bestuzhev-Riumin suddenly entered

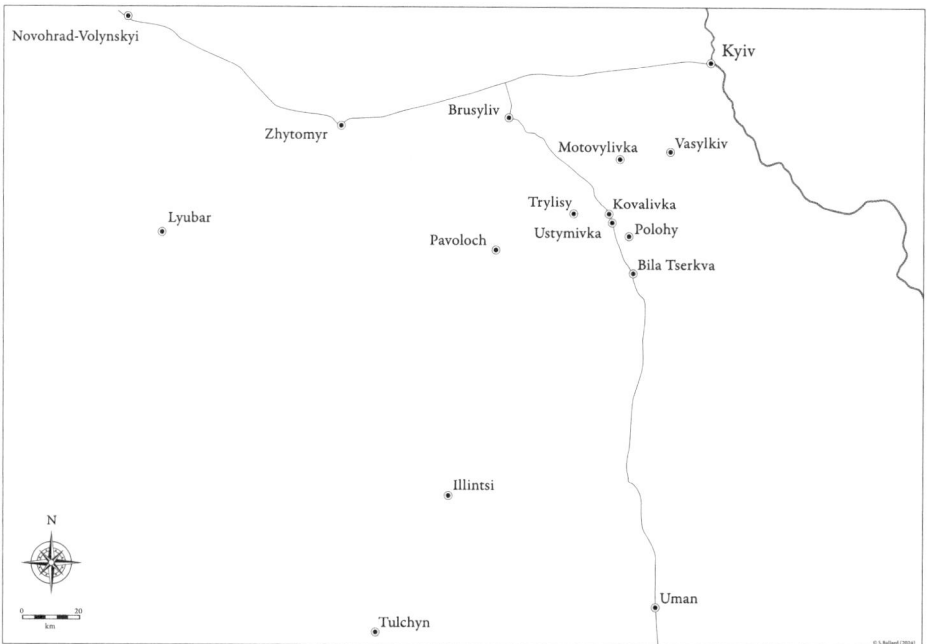

Map of the revolt in Ukraine, 29 December 1825 to 3 January 1826.

the room. 'You have been ordered to be arrested,' he said breathlessly to Sergei. 'All your papers have been seized by [Gustav] Goebel [commander of the Chernigov/Chernihiv regiment], who is on your tail with the gendarmes.' Sergei briefly considered going into hiding, but concluded that attack was the best defence. Unexpectedly, Artamon, who had acted so bravely and made so many promises, now adamantly refused either to raise his regiment or to notify the United Slavs of the danger they were all in. After a brief moment, Sergei wrote a message and asked as a last request that Artamon take it to the United Slavs in the 8th Brigade. Artamon received the message, but tore it to pieces as soon as his cousins had left. He even refused to provide them with fresh horses.[15]

## The revolt of the Chernigov/Chernihiv regiment

Losing the support of the Akhtyrsky regiment was a major setback. Most of the troops loyal to the Society were artillery- or infantrymen and needed the cavalry to protect them. But what was worse was that the leader of the Society had been arrested and the second in command was being pursued by gendarmes. Muraviev-Apostol realized that the best strategy was to return to his regiment in Vasylkiv as quickly as possible and gather troops loyal to the Society there. The headquarters of the Chernigov/Chernihiv regiment were in Vasylkiv, but its companies were scattered in villages west of the town all the way to Trylisy (Trilesy). The 5th Musketeer Company, led by one Lieutenant Kuzmin, a member of the United Slavs and one of the most active members of the Southern Society, was stationed in Trylisy. On the way back to Vasylkiv, the Muraviev-Apostol brothers stopped for the night in Trylisy, at Kuzmin's lodgings. There, the gendarmes found them later that evening. Sergei and Matvei were arrested and sentries placed around the house. Fortunately for the prisoners, Sergei had sent Kuzmin a note earlier in the evening informing him of their arrival in Trylisy and asking him to come there with three other members of the United Slavs to discuss further plans.

Early the next day Kuzmin arrived in Trylisy together with lieutenants Shchepillo, Soloviev and Sukhinov. They found Kuzmin's residence surrounded by guards, but, somewhat unexpectedly, managed to free the prisoners. At this point Sergei Muraviev-Apostol determined that it was time to raise the Chernigov/Chernihiv regiment in revolt. He instructed Kuzmin to gather his troops and march to the village of Kovalivka, 15 kilometres (9 mi.) away, where the 2nd Grenadier Company was stationed. Next, Sergei and Matvei set out to Kovalivka to speak to the officers of the

Grenadier Company. When the officers proved favourable to the uprising, Sergei ordered them to assemble their troops. Later, together with their commander, Lieutenant Petin, he addressed the soldiers. According to witness statements, he told them they were to perform a great deed – to free the people from slavery – and asked if they were ready. The soldiers answered in the affirmative.[16] Sergei then ordered them to prepare for the campaign. However, for the uprising to succeed, the assistance of all members of the secret society was needed. For this reason, Muraviev-Apostol sent out several additional orders. Flegont Bashmakov, a demoted colonel in the Chernigov/Chernihiv regiment who shared quarters with Muraviev-Apostol, was dispatched to notify the members of the 8th Artillery Brigade of the uprising. He was also instructed to call on Captain Andrei Furman and send him to notify the 8th Infantry Division. A non-commissioned officer, Kakaurov, was told to call on lieutenants Aleksandr Vadkovskii and Dmitrii Molchanov of the 17th Jaeger regiment to request that they come to Vasylkiv. Yet, despite their importance, Muraviev-Apostol's orders were not carried out properly.

The members of the Southern Society were spread over a large area, making communication difficult. After taking leave of Sergei in Lyubar, Bestuzhev realized that he should take the opportunity to notify the United Slavs, stationed in Zhytomyr, of the events and tell them to prepare their soldiers. It was only about 80 kilometres (50 mi.) from Lyubar to Zhytomyr, and in any case Zhytomyr was on the way to Vasylkiv. So, while Sergei made his way east from his cousin in Lyubar to Trylisy and Kovalivka, Mikhail had been trying to reach the members of the United Slavs in Zhytomyr. However, he had to turn back when he learned that the area was full of gendarmes looking for him. Now he turned up in Kovalivka on his way back to Vasylkiv. Shortly after Bestuzhev, Kuzmin arrived with most of his company. Some of them were on leave, but his sergeant had promised to bring them to Vasylkiv.

On 30 December, early in the morning, Sergei Muraviev-Apostol marched out from Kovalivka with the 2nd Grenadier Company and most of the 5th Musketeer Company. At three o'clock in the afternoon the vanguard entered Vasylkiv and occupied the city without meeting any resistance. Military banners and the army's coffers were seized. All gendarmes were arrested and their prisoners released from military custody (including Soloviev and Shchepillo, who had been arrested on their return to Vasylkiv after freeing the Muraviev brothers). The soldiers already in the city (two companies of the first battalion) joined the uprising, as did the

4th Musketeer Company, which was on guard duty, and the 6th Musketeer Company, when it came to report for guard duty. Vadkovskii's arrival enhanced the hopes of the insurgents. With the help of Dmitrii Molchanov, Vadkovskii promised to raise if not the whole Jaeger regiment, at least a battalion. Unfortunately for the conspirators, he was arrested on his return to Bila Tserkva, about 40 kilometres (25 mi.) south of Vasylkiv, where the regiment was stationed.

Sergei and Matvei Muraviev-Apostol and Mikhail Bestuzhev-Riumin planned their next steps together with the four officers from the United Slavs. They debated whether to attack Kyiv, or proceed to Bila Tserkva, where they hoped to win over the 17th Jaeger regiment with the help of Vadkovskii and Molchanov. The third option was to go to Zhytomyr, where they could join forces with the United Slavs. Also in Zhytomyr were the headquarters of the 8th Infantry Division, in which many members of the Southern Society were serving. The officers of the United Slavs favoured a surprise attack against Kyiv, where they had some support. Muraviev-Apostol appreciated the strategic value of this plan but found it too dangerous given the small number of troops at their disposal. He preferred to wait until they had gathered more support. Instead, he sent Ensign Aleksandr Mozalevskii to Kyiv with letters to the Society's members in the city, along with copies of a political statement to be circulated among the people. But, as Mozalevskii was distributing the letters in Kyiv, someone raised the alarm. He tried to leave the city unnoticed but was discovered and arrested.

When Mozalevskii did not return, the rebels decided to march to Brusyliv, where they could unite with the Aleksopol regiment. Brusyliv was also considered a strategic assembly point between Kyiv and Zhytomyr. This was probably a mistake. They could have taken advantage of the element of surprise and moved on Kyiv directly. Several members serving in the Artillery were stationed in the city and would have joined the uprising, and the rebels could have seized the Kyiv arsenal. From there, they could have marched to Zhytomyr, where they had strong support from the United Slavs and could have contacted the Polish Society.

The next day, before leaving Vasylkiv, Sergei Muraviev-Apostol had a conversation with the regimental chaplain, Daniil Keizer, in which he outlined the purpose of the rebellion and asked for the priest's support. Keizer agreed to help, provided his family would be taken care of should the rebellion fail. Muraviev-Apostol then gathered the soldiers on the wintry square of the small garrison town. At noon he and Keizer addressed the thousand-strong column of soldiers. In a stirring speech, Muraviev-Apostol told them they were to fight for freedom, and that nothing nobler existed than to sacrifice one's life for liberty. He then asked the priest to read aloud from 'An Orthodox Catechism', a document he had written with Bestuzhev-Riumin. This political statement couched in religious language was inspired by the political catechisms that had been produced by European revolutionaries ever since the French Revolution to reach the masses, in particular those catechisms used in the Spanish War of Independence (1808–13) and the Spanish Revolution of 1820.[17] Being the son of the Russian ambassador to Spain, Muraviev-Apostol was a fervent supporter of the Spanish liberal movement.

Political catechisms employed religious language to convey political messages, and often took the form of short dialogues to be read aloud, but they could also be public speeches.[18] Several such documents were written in Russia. Nikita Muraviev of the Northern Society (and Sergei's second cousin) began work on a catechism called 'A Curious Conversation' or 'Catechism of a Free Person', about princes who enslaved the people against the will of God.[19] Sergei owned a copy of his cousin's unfinished catechism.[20] The main message of 'An Orthodox Catechism' that the assembled troops heard was that any monarch acted against the will of God when he took away the people's freedom. The Russian tsar had brought suffering to the people by enslaving them, and it was time for the suffering people and the suffering country to be liberated. This sacred duty had to be performed by the army. It was left to them to fight against tyranny to restore faith and liberty in Russia. The soldiers had to overthrow the tsar in the name of God.[21] The extent to which the soldiers fully understood either the meaning of the catechism or the reasons for the revolt, and whether or not they took it to heart, is impossible to know. Muraviev-Apostol himself was unsure. He later backtracked and told his soldiers that they were fighting in the name of the legitimate tsar, Constantine.[22]

As they were about to march from Vasylkiv, Sergei's nineteen-year-old brother Ippolit arrived bearing a message from Trubetskoi of the Northern Society, with information about the uprising in the capital. Overjoyed at the unexpected meeting with his brothers in Vasylkiv, Ippolit refused Sergei's attempts to send him back home. Instead, he joined the troops marching towards Brusyliv.

On the evening of 31 December the troops arrived in the village of Motovylivka (Motovilovka), about 20 kilometres (12 mi.) west of Vasylkiv. There they were joined by the 1st and 2nd Musketeer companies, but then events turned against them. The Aleksopol regiment refused to join the uprising. As a result, Sergei made a change of plan and decided to go to Bila Tserkva instead of Brusyliv. This created a sense of insecurity among the troops; a number of officers deserted and there was some disorder among the soldiers. In an injudicious move, Sergei allowed the soldiers a day of rest on New Year's Day. This fatal decision gave the regime time to organize its defence. The troops stationed in the vicinity of Motovylivka, suspected of being unreliable, were withdrawn and replaced with loyal units. The new units were told to search for bandit soldiers who were allegedly plundering the population, and were ordered to give no quarter and to use canister shots.

Early on 2 January the rebels left Motovylivka for Bila Tserkva, hoping to occupy this city as a staging point for their attack on Kyiv. With the support of the 17th Jaeger regiment, stationed close to Bila Tserkva and led by Vadkovskii, it should have been possible to seize Kyiv. Yet fate once more turned against the Decembrists. Bivouacked in the town of Polohy, just north of Bila Tserkva, Sergei learned that the Jaeger regiment had been transferred and Vadkovskii arrested. Meanwhile, the morale of the soldiers was declining. In light of this new situation, he decided that it would be too dangerous to enter Bila Tserkva. Instead, they would proceed towards Pavoloch, from where he hoped to win over the 5th Artillery Company, which was commanded by Society members. From there, he planned to march to Zhytomyr and join up with the United Slavs and perhaps with the Poles.

Yet again Sergei's plans were thwarted by circumstance. On the morning of 3 January the rebels left Polohy and turned back north. In fields near the villages of Kovalivka and Ustymivka they came face to face with a detachment of government hussars and artillery led by one General Geismar. Strength and numbers were on the side of the government. The rebels had about 1,000 infantrymen, but the government had both cavalry and artillery. Rather than taking the road through the villages, where they could have taken up a defensive position, the rebels chose to push ahead across the steppe, where they were on open, wintry ground without means of entrenchment. It was the perfect battleground for cavalry and artillery. For a moment, the rebels believed the government detachment was the artillery unit of Captain Pykhachev, a member of the Southern Society. But they soon realized their mistake; Pykhachev had been arrested the night before.

It was more a slaughter than a battle. According to Horbachevskii's account, many rebel troops were killed by the first volley of grapeshot. The second volley wounded Sergei and killed Shchepillo. Bleeding profusely from a head wound, 'Muraviev-Apostol mustered all his strength . . . to make the necessary orders, but the soldiers, seeing him bloody, hesitated.' Several threw down their guns and ran away across the field. Many were run down and killed by pursuing hussars. Kuzmin, Ippolit and Lieutenant Andrei Bystritskii were wounded. One squadron of hussars pursued the fugitives, another surrounded the officers. Ippolit put a gun to his head and fell dead to the ground.[23] At 5 p.m. the captured soldiers and officers were escorted to the village of Trylisy, where the officers were locked up at an inn and the soldiers in peasant cabins. Kuzmin shot himself, having hidden a pistol in the sleeve of his coat. The next day the survivors were brought to Bila Tserkva, where an investigation began.

Sergei Volkonskii, leader of the Kamianka branch of the Southern Society, learned of the disaster at Kovalivka when on a visit to his wife, who had given birth at her parents' house on 2 January. Before dawn on 7 January, a messenger delivered a letter from Sergei's division chief, Piotr Kornilov, explaining (falsely) that his brigade had moved against the Chernigov/ Chernihiv regiment and that Volkonskii had to return home. Volkonskii left immediately. On the way he met a secret envoy sent from his Uman house, telling him that it had been put under guard. His later recollections speak of how his heart was plunged into sadness at the thought of what this meant not for his own life, but for that of his wife.[24] Entering the courtyard, he found a sleigh with two waiting police officers, and a government emissary stepped forwards bearing the order for his arrest.

Meanwhile, the members of the Society who were in Kyiv were intent on carrying out an uprising there. On hearing of the defeat of the Chernigov/ Chernihiv regiment, they immediately decided on a plan to free Sergei Muraviev-Apostol and Bestuzhev-Riumin. They found a man who was willing to bring the captives from Bila Tserkva to Kyiv for 2,000 roubles, but before they managed to raise the funds, Yakiv Andriyevych and one of the Borisov brothers were arrested.

The last attempt at an uprising was made as late as early February 1826 by two officers of the United Slavs. During an inspection, they tried to persuade the soldiers of the Poltava regiment to revolt against 'the tyrant Nicholas' and win Russia's freedom. They were both arrested. February 1826 was also the month when the authorities finally found *Russian Justice*. It had been buried near the village of Kirsanovka by the brothers Nikolai and Pavel Bobrishchev-Pushkin, and Lieutenant Nikolai Zaikin of the Second Army admitted when questioned that he knew its whereabouts. However, when sent to dig up the manuscript, Zaikin failed to locate the spot. Instead, it was left to his younger brother to point to the place where, shortly before his arrest, Nikolai Bobrishchev-Pushkin had indicated that the manuscript was buried.

# PART III
# DECEMBRIST VISIONS
# AND IDEAS

# 5

# Liberty, Rule of Law and Representative Government

> I have become addicted to politics, and how could you not love it in
> our age, this science of the rights of the people and nations, this great,
> unchanging measure of yours and mine, this sacred flame of truth in the
> darkness of ignorance and in the dungeon of autocracy?[1]

The Decembrists were well aware of the danger they faced when planning an uprising against the autocracy, yet they were prepared to risk everything for the dream of freedom. Part I discussed various explanations for their commitment to liberal reform. This part will explore what such reform entailed. What were the Decembrists' political visions and on which conceptions were these based; what did they hope to achieve and what kind of future Russian society did they imagine? The purpose here is not to cover all their ideas – which were many and sometimes diverging – but to present the key ideas they had in common.

One goal on which the Decembrists could all agree was the transformation of the Russian autocratic empire into a modern representative state. However, they had different ideas about the pace and degree of this transformation, as well as the form of state that would best suit Russia. Some of them preferred a federative state structure modelled on the United States of America, while others wished to establish a unitary state, as in France.

The Decembrists were influenced by four related and overlapping intellectual currents that dominated Western thinking in the age of revolutions, which they adapted to the Russian context: liberalism, republicanism, nationalism and Romanticism.[2] Liberalism and modern republicanism shared many basic assumptions at the time, such as political liberty, the rule of law and representative government, but differed somewhat in the values they emphasized. While liberal thinking gave prominence to individual autonomy, private property and freedom from state interference, central to republican thought were civic virtue, active political participation, the common good and independence from arbitrary power. The modern idea of the civic nation that emerged at the end of the eighteenth century was related to ideas of republican citizenship and popular sovereignty, but also to notions of political representation, the rule of law, equality and individual rights. This did not prevent civic nationalism from being ethnocentric, as can be seen in the formation of both the American and French civic nations. Romanticism interacted with each of these tendencies in various ways.[3] The influence of Romanticism on the Decembrists is seen most clearly in their aversion to conventions and rules, their celebration of freedom and rebellion against tyrannical control, their cult of heroic sacrifice, and the importance they attached to friendship and genuine feeling.[4]

Students of the Decembrist movement have found it difficult to reconcile the political message conveyed in their literature with that expressed in their political documents. However, when viewed in the light of the interwoven discourses of republicanism, liberalism and nationalism, it becomes easier to see how these different texts express a cohesive vision based on a desire for freedom. This freedom was wished for in both a positive and a negative sense. Decembrists sought freedom for people to communicate and associate; to develop their abilities and to realize themselves; to be involved in politics and make change. But they also sought freedom from an oppressive state and bureaucracy. Given their view of freedom, serfdom was of course unacceptable. The emancipation of the Russian peasants was a fundamental goal of the Decembrist movement, but they had different opinions about how best to reach this end.

Decembrists also had different and changing opinions regarding the pace and extent of the required social transformation. Some wanted to establish a republic, while others were more conservative and wished to preserve the monarchy for the time being. Some wanted a more thorough form of democracy, promoting equality in both the political and the economic sphere, while others feared radical change and supported a classical liberal state focused on the protection of private property and limited suffrage. Yet they all agreed that for freedom to be realized at all, autocracy had to be restricted. The absolute power of the tsar had to be limited by means of a constitution and a representative government. Over time, more Decembrists became convinced that the monarchy had to be abolished. Hence there was a general trend towards radicalization in their thinking.[5]

The Decembrist societies produced political documents that outlined the future Russian state and government. Nikita Muraviev of the

Northern Society was the author of *Konstitutsionnyi ustav* (A Project for a Constitution), proposing the establishment of a constitutional monarchy in Russia.[6] This document was never approved by all members of the Northern Society – some of whom, such as Kondratii Ryleev and Evgenii Obolenskii, preferred a republic – but it represents the view of the more moderate members. The leader of the Southern Society, Pavel Pestel, wrote the ambitious document *Russkaia Pravda* (Russian Justice), which was intended as an instruction for a transitional government.[7] It presented a project for the political and economic reform of Russia, inspired by Western liberal and republican thought and adapted to the Russian context in quite an original way. Both *A Project for a Constitution* and *Russian Justice* were radical proposals in the context of Russia's autocratic government; Pestel's even more so since he promoted a republican form of government, radical agrarian reform and universal suffrage. Muraviev started out as a republican, but later embraced constitutional monarchism. However, as a prisoner in the Peter and Paul Fortress, he returned to his republican beliefs.[8]

## Civil liberties

The Decembrists' perception of liberty included freedom both in the classical liberal sense of non-interference and in the republican sense of self-government. However, their political documents primarily expressed freedom in the former sense. Their principal objective was freedom from the sovereign's interference in private life, in the form of civil rights. Their main concern was with freedom of expression, freedom of the press and the abolition of censorship, and they emphasized the right to write, print and publish political ideas. As stated in the constitution of the Northern Society, everyone had 'the right to freely express his ideas and feelings and communicate them by way of print to his countrymen'.[9] Other important rights were those related to personal liberty, which was regarded as 'the first and most important right of any citizen'.[10] Freedom from arbitrary arrest had to be guaranteed and the principle of habeas corpus upheld. There had to be strict rules for the treatment of suspects and for making arrests. House search and detention had to be enforced according to the law, and people could not be imprisoned without it being known what offence they had committed. Thus within 24 hours prisoners had to be acquainted with the cause of confinement and the name of their accuser. Moreover, no person could be imprisoned who offered bail, and the confiscation of property should never be imposed. Prisoners could be incarcerated only in public prisons, and civil and criminal offences tried only in established courts.[11]

Freedom of religion was another important civil liberty. In the Decembrist manifesto drawn up on the eve of 14 December 1825, religious tolerance of all faiths was proclaimed.[12] In Chapter IX of the Northern Society's constitution, it was stated explicitly that freedom of conscience and opinion was not subject to the power of the People's Assembly: 'No one may be disturbed in the exercise of his religion in accordance with his conscience and feelings, as long as he does not violate the natural laws and morality.'[13] There was a similar formulation in Pestel's *Russian Justice*, but Pestel proclaimed the Christian Orthodox Graeco-Russian religion as the ruling faith of the Russian state. This statement might seem contrary to the concept of freedom of conscience central to liberal ideology, but it was common at the time. Several constitutions in the West – including many of the American states – spoke of a state religion. The Spanish Constitution of 1812, which was seen as one of the most liberal of all contemporary constitutions and an inspiration to the Decembrists, declared that the Catholic apostolic Roman faith was the only true faith. Furthermore, it stated explicitly that the state should prevent the exercise of any other religion. In contrast, *Russian Justice* ruled that all other Christian and non-Christian beliefs should be accepted, provided they were not contrary to 'the Russian spiritual and political laws [and] the rules of morality[,] and do not violate the natural obligations of man'.[14]

Contemporary liberals commonly equated religious tolerance with respect for the beliefs of foreigners, something they regarded as a prerequisite for economic progress. They did not see the paradox in defending religious tolerance while also wishing to protect the specific religious nature of the nation. Another example of this is the Portuguese Constitution of 1822, which defended the practice of other religions by non-nationals, but at the same time contained the basic assumption that the nation should remain religiously homogeneous.[15]

Another inconsistency in Decembrist thought is the apparent contradiction between the emphasis on civil rights and Pestel's plans for a provisional government. That government would be made up of appointed liberals of high morals, who would rule Russia until a Constituent Assembly could be formed. Pestel argued that to avoid both anarchy and attempts at counter-revolution, this transitional regime needed stability, and suggested that this would require the support of a large police force.[16] If we place this in the context of similar revolts during the age of revolutions, it becomes

clear that the fear of anarchy and counter-revolution was evident in them all. Some scholars argue that Pestel's provisional government was tantamount to an authoritarian dictatorship.[17] It may well be that this was what he had in mind, but we cannot be sure. He was clearly influenced by the French Jacobins and their unorthodox efforts to protect the gains of the revolution against aristocratic reaction. Still, the available evidence is scarce and unreliable, mainly based on testimonies by other Decembrists given to the investigating committee under duress. Pestel's own vision is vague and fragmentary.

Nevertheless, it does appear that Pestel considered using certain authoritarian means to ensure the transformation of Russia into a democratic republic. He was well aware that the Decembrists were fighting a repressive state, as well as strong conservative forces, and he was convinced that their opponents would not give up power and privilege easily. How to uphold civil liberties and the stability of the state simultaneously is a dilemma faced by many transitional regimes. But it is also, it seems, a dilemma for contemporary democratic states, which make use of various surveillance systems while claiming to uphold civil rights, or delegate security and military matters to private corporations without any mechanism for transparency or accountability.

## Liberty and serfdom

Emancipation of the serfs was one of the most important issues for the Decembrists, if not *the* most important. They employed moral, political and economic arguments to advocate for the abolition of serfdom in Russia. The peasant question was particularly important in this country where agriculture dominated the economy and where the landed nobility depended on serf labour. In the sense that the majority of Decembrists belonged to the landowning nobility, they worked against the interests of their own class. Instead of seeking to preserve the nobility's property rights (in serfs), they tried to limit their rights over their serfs. In the eyes of most Decembrists, serfdom was the main obstacle to their goal of drawing together all social classes to form a nation of citizens.

The debate about the emancipation of the serfs gained momentum after the Napoleonic Wars and the abolition of serfdom in the Baltic provinces in 1816–19. At first these discussions were encouraged by Alexander I, but after the Semionovskii revolt in 1820, the subject was banned from public debate. This did not prevent serfdom from being discussed at unofficial gatherings and in private correspondence, however. The emancipation debate in Russia coincided with the growing interest in the new subject of political economy. Such French thinkers as François Quesnay and Anne Robert Jacques Turgot were already well known in Russia in the late eighteenth century. The publication in 1802 of Germain Garnier's French translation of *The Wealth of Nations* popularized Adam Smith's ideas, and Jean-Baptiste Say's treatise on political economy, published the following year, also became very influential. Although political economy was taught at all universities after 1801, Moscow and St Petersburg were among the first places in Europe where lectures in the subject were delivered. Christian von Schlözer, who joined the faculty of Moscow University that year from Göttingen in Germany, wrote a textbook on political economy in 1805. However, the most prominent interpreter of Smith's ideas in Russia was the Riga-born economist Heinrich Storch, who published his magnum opus, *Cours d'économie politique*, in 1815.[18]

Criticism of serfdom had been expressed in the eighteenth century by such Russian writers as Aleksandr Radishchev, Fedor Krechetov, Denis Fonvizin, Nikolai Ivanovich Novikov and Ivan Pnin. But they had primarily relied on ethical arguments. Political economy stimulated ideas about the cost of serfdom. Now, such economists as Storch and Aleksandr Kunitsyn (the liberal teacher at the Alexander Lyceum) took part in the debate, arguing that serfdom prevented economic growth and national prosperity.[19] Progress and economic development could be achieved only if labour were free. Russian industry depended on the labour of serfs and social outcasts, who lacked the purchasing power to meet industrial output. As long as serfdom existed, capital could not be used optimally.

Future Decembrists who participated in the debate over serfdom also made use of concepts and arguments from political economy. Nikolai Turgenev was the most prominent of these.[20] He had studied with Smith's disciple Georg Friedrich Sartorius at Göttingen University, then worked for Baron von Stein in the Prussian government during von Stein's efforts to emancipate serfs. Returning to Russia, he pursued a career in the Russian government. In 1818 he published *Essay on a Theory of Taxation*, based largely on *The Wealth of Nations*. Turgenev argued that it was difficult to see the usefulness of serfdom considering the financial difficulties of the regime and the indebtedness and bankruptcies of the landlords. Serfdom also furthered dependence on foreign trade.

However, although Turgenev used economic arguments for emancipation, he also felt – in common with his fellow Decembrists – that serfdom was unethical and unjustified. In a diary entry from 7 August 1818, he wrote, 'I now loathe more than ever before the baseness of slavery, having seen closely how it degrades people.'[21] This 'baseness of slavery' was felt even more strongly after the Napoleonic Wars, when the peasants had fought bravely for the liberation of their country. The Decembrists often used the term 'slavery' to emphasize the immorality of serfdom. To them, the distinction between serfs bound to the land and enslaved people owned by their master by law was immaterial. In the early 1820s Vladimir Raevskii, a leading member of the Southern Society, wrote a pamphlet in which he criticized serfdom on ethical grounds:

> Who gave one man the right to label another man his own property? By what right can the body, the property and even the soul of one man, belong to another? Whence the law permitting a man to trade in, exchange, gamble with, give away or tyrannize other men like himself?

It was degrading for Russia to allow the sale of serfs that divided families, Raevskii wrote. So was 'the despicable and infamous institution of harems which has become a custom among base Russian nobles, when neither wives nor daughters are safe'. The law did not provide protection through court proceedings. Instead, it rested solely in the hands of the landowners, and they would always use it to defend themselves.[22]

Sergei Trubetskoi used more pragmatic arguments for emancipation. In order to convince landowners that such reforms were necessary, he played on their well-known fear of peasant uprisings. Thus he told them it would be better for the landowners if they freed the serfs themselves so that they could conclude favourable conditions with them. If they did not voluntarily agree to liberation, Trubetskoi warned, the peasants could wrest it from them by force. Peasant uprisings would inevitably lead to fearsome horrors, and the state would become a victim of strife and perhaps the prey of ambitious people using civic disturbance to set themselves up as tyrants.[23]

The need to abolish serfdom is reflected in the Decembrists' political documents. Freedom, they maintained, implied that all people had a fundamental right to their own body. Therefore, no one could own another person. The Decembrist manifesto stated explicitly that the right to own men should be eliminated.[24] 'Serfdom and slavery are abolished,' proclaimed Muraviev in *A Project for a Constitution*.[25] *Russian Justice* declared that the destruction of slavery was the most sacred duty of the provisional government. Pestel next developed the argument against serfdom on ethical grounds:

> To own other men in property, to sell, pawn, give away, inherit men like things, to use them according to one's own caprice without their prior consent and exclusively for one's own profit, advantage, and at times whim, is shameful, contrary to humanity, contrary to the laws of nature, contrary to the Holy Christian Faith ... There can no longer be in Russia the right for one man to possess and call another his serf. Slavery must be definitely abolished and the nobility must forever ... renounce the vile privilege of owning other men.[26]

State peasants and free agriculturalists were less problematic. They could easily be freed and given civil rights. The difficult question was how the emancipation of the serfs of the nobility should be implemented. One of the most fundamental liberties was the right to private property. It was defended in the Decembrist documents as a sacred right. This position made it complicated to argue that the emancipation of serfs be accompanied by land redistribution, which many believed was the only viable solution. To justify the redistribution of land, Pestel made use of the classic liberal argument that those who worked the soil had earned the right to it. Land was the property of the entire human race; toil and labour were the sources of property. In addition, in Pestel's scheme, the landowners would be compensated for the loss of their land. Muraviev's *Project for a Constitution* suggested that the land should remain the landowners' property, while the houses, tools, cattle and gardens were to be the property of the peasants.[27]

In the first draft of *Russian Justice*, written in 1822, Pestel proposed a process of gradual transition, inviting provincial assemblies of the nobility to take part. The freeing of peasants from slavery should not deprive the nobility of the revenue they received from their estates, he stated, and it must not give rise to disorder in the state. Yet the freeing of peasants must lead to actual improvement in their condition and not merely give the appearance of freedom. The second draft was more radical. Talk of a gradual process had been removed and the serfs were now to be freed immediately. Emancipated serfs were to be granted a landholding of around 10 *desiatina* (just under 11 hectares/just over 27 acres), which would be obtained by halving the landowners' land. Pestel suggested that the land of the rural township, in which the former serfs would continue to live, should be split into two holdings: one half in communal ownership and the other in private ownership. His idea was that communal land would prevent poverty because it provided a minimum level of subsistence for everyone in the village. Private land, which would be freely alienable, was for the creation of an agricultural surplus to be sold in the marketplace. Regional banking infrastructure would be developed to facilitate transactions of land as well as the financing of reforms. In contrast to the private land, the land in communal possession could not be sold. Every peasant was to be granted a plot of this land. Landowners, meanwhile, were to be compensated by cash payments or landholdings in other places.

To Pestel, the redistribution of land was a logical consequence of the concept of equal rights. All Russian citizens must have equal enjoyment of private, civil and political rights, but they also had a right to subsistence. A minimum livelihood should therefore be guaranteed not out of charity, but as a right. The right to subsistence was a radical idea at the time, long before the development of welfare states, which were largely premised on this basic right. Pestel envisioned a future Russia where every citizen was a landowner and where poverty would be eliminated, not unlike the American revolutionary Thomas Jefferson's image of the United States as a community of small, self-sufficient family farms. In fact, Jefferson included the right to subsistence in his draft for Virginia's constitution of 1776, but it was not accepted by the legislators.[28]

## Economic freedom

The economic policies of the Russian regime had oscillated between free trade and protectionism, and this uncertainty had led to great distress among merchants. The Decembrists were concerned about this situation. In common with Smith and the French physiocrats, they were critical of the mercantile system and promoted laissez-faire in the economy and the elimination of corporate privilege. They were convinced that guilds and professional corporations hampered economic development. In the draft constitution of the Northern Society, Muraviev underlined the importance of abolishing existing merchant and trade guilds and corporations: 'Everyone has the right to engage in whatever trade that seems to him the most profitable: agriculture, cattle, hunting, fishing, craftwork, factory work, trade, etc.'[29] The Decembrist manifesto echoed these views, stating that every citizen had the right to choose whatever occupation he wished, to acquire every kind of property and make every kind of contract. Poll tax and arrears should be cancelled and monopolies on salt and alcohol abolished.[30]

Pestel concurred with this economic liberalism. He criticized all the injustices, contradictions, impediments and difficulties that in his opinion ruined trade. The best means to foster national prosperity was to grant people freedom. This freedom consisted of three elements: 1) That every citizen should have the right to engage in any branch of the economy; 2) That everyone should be free to engage in any economic enterprise wherever he might wish; and 3) That economic enterprise itself should be freed from all difficulties and impediments. Government decisions should not be obstacles to the success of economic enterprise, but should serve as its protection and support. Townspeople should have the same civil rights as other citizens and the liberty to live and work wherever they wished.[31]

In this context, Pestel presents a classic liberal view of the state, based on the idea that the welfare of the state depends on two goals: security and prosperity. Security, he argued, was the primary goal because it could be reached only through the common action of united forces and wills. Prosperity, on the other hand, had to be the second goal for government; there were so many definitions of this concept that it had to be left to the individual to realize it. While private individuals could gain prosperity by their own means, they could not safeguard their security by private means. The role of the state was to provide protection and to eliminate obstacles that individuals did not have the power or ability to overcome. This understanding can be contrasted with Pestel's view of land reform, in which the state had an obligation to protect its citizens against poverty through policies of redistribution.

Just as on the subject of serfdom, in this the Decembrists worked against the interests of their own class, seeking to form a modern liberal nation with a capitalist orientation.[32] The statutes of the Union of Welfare already promoted the liberal idea that national wealth through trade and industry would bind together not only the different estates, but the different regions of the empire, through equalization.[33] Acting against noble privileges, the Decembrists spoke of the important role of the middle class in building a citizen-nation. They lamented the fact that 'the middle class is respected and important in all other countries; in our country this class is miserable, poor, burdened with duties, deprived of the means of subsistence.'[34] Such leading Decembrists as Pestel, Kakhovskii and Aleksandr Bestuzhev complained that the burgesses were overburdened by duties and taxes and that the time had come for them to be freed from the old guilds, which only hampered industry.[35]

## The rule of law and equality before the law

Liberty was the most fundamental Decembrist idea, but if it were to be assured there had to be checks on power that limited the prerogatives of the ruler. The most effective means of limiting absolute power was the rule of law, according to which all citizens were subject to the same laws, and the establishment of a liberal constitution. The Decembrists were very aware of the need for the rule of law in Russia. In Baron Andrei Rozen's stark critique of the prevailing legal order, 'only officers passed sentence and the plaintiffs served as judges,' which was 'the customary method in Russia when important cases were to be decided'.[36] Pestel believed that in order to establish constitutional rule, the entire political order in Russia had to be transformed and replaced by an organization based solely on precise and just laws, leaving nothing to personal arbitrariness. For this reason, a provisional government had to be established. It was also necessary to issue a supreme Russian charter in the form of instructions to this institution as a pledge that it acted exclusively for the good of Russia.[37] The drafting of a complete legal code would take a long time. What is more, such a code should contain the positive laws that established the future government, rather than the transitional measures or theoretical considerations on which the edifice of the government would be erected. This is why Pestel wrote *Russian Justice*. That document was needed to set forth the basic rules and principles that would serve as guidelines in establishing the new order and in drafting the new constitution.

In the introduction to *A Project for a Constitution*, Muraviev criticizes autocratic arbitrariness and extols the merits of equality before the law: 'It is impossible to accept that all rights belong to one side and all duties to the other ... By putting themselves above the laws, the sovereigns have forgotten that they are thereby putting themselves outside the law, outside humanity!' The Decembrists saw a direct link between autocratic arbitrary power and corruption. To prevent the corruption of power, they argued, transparency in public transactions was needed. Therefore, sessions in parliament should be open to the public and closed only in special circumstances.[38] Minutes of the proceedings should be kept and published periodically. It was also important that each chamber keep minutes and publish them from time to time. Furthermore, Muraviev pointed out that on occasion parliament should publish for the information of the whole nation a detailed account of all public receipts and expenditures.

Equality before the law pertained not only to the ruler, but to the aristocracy. The new Russian nation was to be constructed in opposition not only to the absolute power of the monarch, but to corporate and noble privilege. In this the Decembrists were inspired by the French Revolution, which contrasted the nation both to the monarch and to the privileged orders and corporations of the *ancien régime*.[39] In the words of the French political writer and revolutionary-era politician Abbé Sieyès, 'the nobility possesses privileges and exemptions which it brazenly calls its rights and which stand distinct from the rights of the great body of citizens.' Because of these special rights, the nobility did not belong to the common order, nor was it subject to common laws. Its private rights thus made it 'a people apart in the great nation'.[40] Following French revolutionary thinking, Pestel justified removing noble rights and privileges, because all members of the nation were entitled to the same universal rights. He argued that the advantages enjoyed by the Russian nobility were not based on any corresponding obligations. On the contrary, these advantages served to excuse those who enjoyed them from all obligations; so, Pestel held, they must be recognized as privileges rather than rights. Hence the nobility should no longer enjoy the exclusive right to public office. This right should be equal to all Russians. Whoever deserved public office by virtue of his knowledge, capabilities and qualities should be entitled to it, regardless of his background or class. Talent, knowledge and virtue could be found in all estates, so entry to the governmental bureaucracy should be based on merit rather than social status. It should be noted that this meritocracy did not extend to women, however.

Pestel criticized the existing criminal law in Russia on the same grounds: that it meted out different punishments according to the social status of the perpetrator. The nobility, he argued, should be subject to the same punishments as other Russians for the same crimes. To Pestel, the nature of the punishment should correspond to the nature of the crime and not to the social class of the criminal, 'for crime is the product of a person's moral qualities and not a mark of his belonging to a particular class'.[41] Consequently, all appointments to government office should be made on the basis of talent and virtue alone, and the same offence should be punished in the same way, regardless of the status of the perpetrator.

In the spirit of the egalitarian idea of the nation expressed by the American and French revolutionaries, both Decembrist constitutions removed all titles and ranks and, in that sense, did away with the nobility as a separate estate, creating one class of individuals enjoying common rights, bound by common obligations, formally equal before the law. In Pestel's words, 'any statute which violates this equality is an intolerable abuse which must be eradicated.'[42] Because they were all created by God, all people were born for the good. It was thus unjust to reserve the term 'well-born' only for the nobility, and the nobility's privileged use of this term should be abolished. Similarly, Muraviev declared that 'the distinction between nobleman and commoner is not recognized in that it is contrary to our faith, whereby all men are *brothers*, all are *well-born* in that they are born by the will of God, all are born *for the good* and are *simply men*.'[43] The titles of prince, duke, count, baron and so on derived from the time when such titles indicated different positions in the power structure. Such titles could not exist in a state based on reason, justice, morality and good sense. For that reason, noble status and all titles and ranks should be abolished.[44] In *A Project for a Constitution*, Muraviev stated specifically that the imperial family should not enjoy any special rights or privileges. He also argued against the division of men into grades: 'Civil ranks adopted from the Germans are to be abolished in accordance with ancient resolutions of the Russian people.' The titles and classes of smallholder (*odnodvorets*), petit bourgeois (*meshchanin*), nobleman (*dvorianin*) and distinguished citizen (*imenityi grazhdanin*) should all be replaced by the title 'Citizen' or 'Russian'.[45]

As stated by Pestel, the aim of society was the gratification of common needs, which, arising as they did from common and identical properties in human nature, were the same for all men.[46] However, distinctions between classes prevented this aim from being fulfilled. They ruined the bonds between citizens so that separate factions were formed. They aimed exclusively at granting greater privileges to some people and oppressing the masses for the selfish interest of a minority. It followed from this that

> in the state all men without exception must be completely equal before the law . . . the estates [the aristocracy based on both wealth and hereditary rights] must be eliminated . . . all men must form but a single estate which may be called a civic estate, and all citizens of the state must have one and the same rights and be equal before the law.[47]

The Northern and Southern societies both agreed that privileges and special rights had to be removed, but Pestel put more thought into the matter and analysed it from both a philosophical and a sociological perspective. One good reason to abolish social distinctions and the division of people into classes or estates, he wrote, was that social inequality was rejected completely by political economists, who had shown that every man must have full freedom to engage in the type of enterprise from which he might expect the greatest advantage and profit for himself. Pestel feared what he called the 'aristocracy of wealth'. This group was much more harmful than the old feudal aristocracy. The latter would always be influenced by public opinion, while the former found in its wealth the means for its own designs, against which public opinion was completely helpless, and by these means it would subject the entire nation. England, he said, was a cautionary example of a country in which the aristocracy of wealth had become stronger than the monarch.[48]

Civic rights were linked to civic duties. The Decembrists held that civil society was created for the greatest possible good of all citizens and not for the good of the few at the expense of the majority. Consequently, not only did all the people in a state have an equal right to enjoy the benefits afforded by that state, but everyone was equally obliged to bear the burdens associated with state organization. To achieve the aim of the greatest possible good, the state had to collect revenues, and because all citizens had equal rights to enjoy society's benefits, they also had equal obligations to contribute to the creation of those benefits. Muraviev stressed that 'every citizen is obliged to carry out his social duties.' Therefore, the Decembrists argued, it was not right that only a part of the people carried the entire burden of taxation, while others did not contribute. The nobility could not be exempt from the payment of taxes on an equal basis with others. Nor should they be exempted from military service. Since all members of society benefited equally from military power, all social classes should contribute to maintaining this power. The nobility, therefore, should not be exempt from personal obligation to serve, and its present privilege not to do so should be abolished.[49]

## Popular sovereignty and representative government

The concept of equal citizenship also underpinned the form of government the Decembrists proposed. They made use of the idea of popular sovereignty, expressed in the American and French revolutions, whereby 'the people' was considered to be sovereign and the source of the authority of the state.[50] Because the nation, or people, was essentially the source of all sovereignty, no individual or faction could be entitled to any authority that was not derived expressly from it. Most importantly, the people should themselves write the laws that would govern them. Obedience to a law that the people had imposed upon themselves was what constituted self-government, or liberty.[51]

This idea of popular sovereignty is reflected in *A Project for a Constitution* when Muraviev writes that 'The people is the source of sovereign power; to whom belongs the exclusive right to make fundamental statutes for itself.'[52] This new concept also applied to the organization of government. The People's Assembly was to be composed of men elected by the Russian people, that is, the segments of the population that constituted 'the people', representing them and assuming 'the character of Majesty'.[53] The People's Assembly, consisting of the Sovereign Duma and the Chamber of the People's Representatives, would be invested with all legislative power.[54] The Sovereign Duma was to be composed of three citizens from every state, two from the Moscow region and one from the Don region. The delegates were to be elected by the governing institutions of the states and regions. The Chamber of the People's Representatives was to be composed of 450 members elected for two years by the citizens of the states. There would be one representative for every 50,000 voters. Electoral assemblies were to be held every two years. However, just as Indigenous Americans were disregarded by the U.S. constitution, so nomadic peoples living in Russia were ignored in Muraviev's constitution.

Conditions for eligibility to the Sovereign Duma included having been a citizen for at least nine years and owning property worth 1,500 lb

(680 kg) of silver in real estate or 3,000 lb (1,360 kg) of silver in movables. The People's Assembly had the power to make laws, set up institutions of public welfare, establish judicial procedures and dissolve the government assemblies of the states if they exceeded their rights. In case of invasion or rebellion, it had the power to place an affected region under martial law. It published laws of amnesty and declared war. Furthermore, it established common taxes and expenditures, leaving particular ones to the State Assemblies.

In *A Project for a Constitution*, executive power would remain with the emperor, who had the right to compel the legislative branch to reconsider a bill. He was commander-in-chief of the armed forces and supreme head of any militia unit. He negotiated with foreign powers and concluded peace treaties with the advice and consent of the Sovereign Duma. The emperor appointed judges to superior courts, again with the advice and consent of the Sovereign Duma. He appointed the heads of all branches of the government and of all government departments. For the emperor to depart from the empire was considered tantamount to abdication, and in such a case the People's Assembly would immediately proclaim the tsesarevich (the eldest son of the emperor) the new emperor. In line with common European practice at the time, women were excluded from the throne. Court officials received no salaries from public funds. They also lost their rights as citizens, meaning that they could not be electors or be elected to official posts.

*A Project for a Constitution* was a federal constitution that outlined the form of government for both the central government and the states. The government of each state would consist of three separate and mutually independent branches: the legislature, the executive and the judiciary. The governing assembly of each state would consist of two chambers and mirror that of the central government. The state assemblies had the right to make laws for the internal administration of the state; to establish electoral centres; to raise taxes for expenditure necessary to the administration and welfare of the state; to set up the necessary public institutions; and to maintain means of transportation. The executive power in every state was entrusted to a state governor, his lieutenant and a council. Every three years the People's Assembly elected the governors from among a list of candidates submitted by the governing assemblies of the states. Each governor faced the same criteria of eligibility in terms of citizenship and property as for the Sovereign Duma.

When it came to central executive power, the constitution of the Northern Society was even more liberal than the Spanish Constitution of 1812, which was itself regarded as strikingly liberal. The latter declared that the Cortes (parliament) had the power of making laws, albeit 'with the King'. The power of the executive was greater in the Spanish Constitution.[55] For instance, the Spanish king had a more extensive veto power. In *Project for a Constitution*, Muraviev wrote that if the Russian tsar disapproved of a bill (which he could do only once), but two-thirds of the first chamber and a majority of the second voted in favour, the legislature would overrule the executive veto and the bill would become law.[56] In contrast, the Spanish king had the power to delay lawmaking for several years. Another difference was that in the proposal for a new Russian government, the parliament had the power to declare war, while in Spain this was the prerogative of the king.[57] In other respects the various obligations of the legislative and executive branches were largely the same; the legislature was to approve treaties and alliances, determine expenditure for public services, borrow money, establish customhouses and rates of duty, promote industry, establish public education and protect the liberty of the press.[58] The executive in both *A Project for a Constitution* and the Spanish Constitution of 1812 appointed high officials, nominated judges and received an annual payment from parliament. In both cases, the sovereign was prohibited from leaving the kingdom without parliament's consent, and likewise from making alliances or treaties or taking over national property without that consent.

In contrast to Muraviev, Pestel was opposed to the institution of monarchy altogether. Thus, in *Russian Justice*, the Duma (council) of the state, elected by the National Assembly, would be vested with executive power.[59] However, the exact function of the executive branch remains obscure. Unfortunately, the sixth chapter of *Russian Justice*, dedicated to the organization of the new state, was never completed, or it was destroyed at the time of Pestel's arrest.

Muraviev, who like most members of the Northern Society wanted to replace unlimited autocracy with constitutional monarchy, held that the people were free and independent and thus could not belong to any family or individual. One cannot allow the arbitrary rule of one man to become a principle of government, he declared in the constitution of the Northern Society, 'not only because the experience of all nations and all epochs has shown that autocratic power is equally ruinous for both rulers and society, but because the Russian people is free and independent'. Therefore, he continued, 'it is not and cannot be the property of any single person or family.'[60] Pestel concurred, using the very same phrase: 'The Russian people is not the possession or property of any individual or family.' Making the argument even clearer, he stated that the government belonged to the people:

'It exists for the good of the people, and has no other grounds for its existence, whereas the people exists for its own sake and not for the good of the government.'[61] The power by means of which the government carried out its obligations of procuring happiness for the people was the sovereign power (*verkhovnaia vlast*). In a letter addressed to General Levashev of the investigating committee, Piotr Kakhovskii of the Northern Society later emphasized the significance of this idea: 'the people have conceived a sacred truth – that they do not exist for governments, but that governments must be organized for them. This is the cause of the struggle in all countries.'[62]

Pestel was particularly inspired by Antoine Destutt de Tracy's critical *Commentaire sur l'esprit des lois de Montesquieu*, a text that was hugely influential among Russian constitutionalists and republicans and which Decembrists referred to as 'the epitome of wisdom'.[63] Pestel read the *Commentary* in the winter of 1819–20.[64] It was a radical criticism of Montesquieu's liberalism and his insistence on the superiority of constitutional monarchies. Destutt de Tracy held that 'every system, where the state is headed by just one person, particularly where the office is hereditary, will inevitably end in despotism.' In his view, all governments could be divided into national or special regimes. A national regime was founded on 'the principle, that all rights and power originate in, reside in, and belong to, the entire body of the people or nation; and that none exists, but what is derived from, and exercised for the nation'. A special regime, in contrast, recognizes particular or unequal rights. In a special government, the legitimate source of power does not belong to the general will of the nation. However, Destutt de Tracy argued that the modern concept of representation, whereby a nation delegated the effective power to functionaries elected by the people for a limited period, enabled special regimes to become national. In 1811 he predicted that this transformation of regimes would spread across the world, stimulated by republican revolutions. In his view, this development indicated the progress of civilization – the old world giving way to the new.[65]

The Decembrists felt that the time was ripe for Russia to take part in this process and establish a 'national' regime. They all agreed that a representative system had to be installed and the aristocratic order eliminated.[66] To be a citizen, Muraviev asserted, meant to have 'the right to participate in the government of society, either *indirectly*, that is, by choosing officials or electors – or *directly*, by standing oneself for election to public office in the *legislature, executive* or *judiciary*'.[67] Pestel's provisional government was charged with the duty to introduce a representative system. The idea was that this government would eventually be replaced by a unicameral legislative body, the National Assembly (*narodnoe veche*). Annually convened local People's Assemblies were to elect deputies directly to the next level of representative political institution. These People's Assemblies were to be divided into two kinds: the Land Assembly and the Assembly of the Vicegerency. There would be a popular Land Assembly in every township, consisting of all citizens in that township. They would be exclusively concerned with electing citizens to the popular Assemblies of the Vicegerencies. These would be established in every town, district and province. Executive power would be vested in the Sovereign Duma, whereas judicial power would be assumed by the Supreme Council. The members of this body were to be elected for life.[68]

Pestel emphasized the fact that an immediate implementation of these changes would generate disorder and turmoil that would lead to the downfall of the state rather than to its improvement. The transformations that had taken place in Europe over the previous fifty years showed that people who rejected gradual government reform had soon been subjected anew to the yoke of despotism and lawlessness. Hence transition to a republican government required a gradual approach with an interim government at its head. For this reason, when *Russian Justice* was accepted by the Southern Society at the Kyiv meeting in 1823, it was agreed that a provisional government would implement it. Pestel presented *Russian Justice* as an instruction to the provisional government on how to organize the transformation of the political order and the establishment of a government based on precise and just laws. The Northern Society also saw the need for a transitional government. However, while Pestel envisioned a long period of transition, the Northern Society believed three months would be sufficient. During this time, elections to a Constituent Assembly would be held.[69] Seen in the light of many modern 'democratic' revolutions, Pestel's proposal was probably more realistic. At the same time, a long-lasting provisional government was of course problematic in other ways, not least from a democratic viewpoint.

While the Northern and Southern societies agreed on the advantages of representative government, they had different ideas about who should have the right to vote. Pestel advocated universal suffrage for men; all Russian males would be enfranchised from the age of twenty without any property requirements. Women, in contrast, were not welcome to participate in politics. According to Muraviev's constitution, women did not even have admission to the visitors' gallery during parliamentary sessions. In *Russian Justice* Pestel declared proudly that when electing their representatives, citizens would need take into account neither class nor wealth; talent and merit alone (in addition, of course, to gender and settled status) would matter.

A common argument among republican thinkers at the time was that a republic could not function with too much socioeconomic inequality and concentration of power among the citizenry. This view is reflected in Pestel's opinion of the so-called aristocracy of wealth, and his belief that the privileges of this moneyed elite had to be abolished. He could not understand why some people were afraid of granting the people the right to vote. Such fear was completely unfounded, he felt. The people created disorder only when faced with oppression or when the rich bribed and agitated the masses for their own ends.[70]

Muraviev's *A Project for a Constitution* was more conservative than Pestel's *Russian Justice*. Muraviev agreed with several contemporary Western republicans and liberals who believed that only men who had a stake in public affairs through property ownership could be trusted with responsibility for the common good. According to this view, voters also had to be personally and economically independent, to avoid the possibility of bribery or corruption. In *A Project for a Constitution* all citizens of the Russian empire had the right to participate in its public administration, but citizenship was limited to residents who were personally independent and owned real estate worth 500 roubles or movables (objects or capital) worth 1,000 roubles.[71] The propertyless were thus excluded. Those who tilled land in public ownership were not landowners and therefore did not have the right to elect officials or the people's representatives, unless they had capital of their own. Yet the whole community of common owners had the right to choose one elector for every five hundred male residents.

## Turning an empire into a nation

The civic or liberal idea of the nation that the Decembrists imported to Russia was beset by certain built-in problems. First, not all residents were regarded as citizens of the nation, and therefore some did not enjoy civil rights. Another problem was that civic nationalism did not take cultural difference into account. The civic idea of the nation was defined as a political community in which subjects became citizens who all enjoyed equal individual rights. However, in order to be treated equally, minorities often need special rights.

The political definition of the nation, according to which it was defined by laws and institutions, was evident in both Decembrist constitutions.

*Russian Justice* states that the experience of all periods and all states has proved that nations are everywhere what their governments and their laws have made them.[72] Consequently,

> political laws are the nation's most effective teachers: they form and, so to speak, educate the people and it is from them that the customs, habits and conceptions receive their characteristic traits and forms of action ... it is political and civil laws which make the nations what they are.[73]

The political dimension of civic nationalism can hardly be more clearly manifested than this.

Since political institutions formed the nation, allegiance to these institutions became the essential criterion for nationhood in civic nationalism. The nation was seen as a free association into which individuals entered voluntarily. The notion of voluntary membership is manifest in Muraviev's constitution, which states that a foreigner not born in Russia but having lived there for seven consecutive years had the right to request Russian citizenship through the courts, provided he renounced on oath all allegiance to the government to which he was previously subject. All native inhabitants of Russia and the children of foreigners born in Russia were considered to be Russian citizens, unless they declared that they did not *wish* 'to enjoy this privilege'.[74] It was therefore in terms of adherence to shared political principles, rather than culture, ethnicity or language, that membership of the civic nation was conceived. On the other hand, nomadic peoples living in Russia were not entitled to any civil rights, with the exception of the right to elect township elders. *Russian Justice* declared that foreigners who wished to become Russian citizens would immediately be granted citizenship status, but nomads would be incorporated into the general state system only once they had settled and formed townships. Today this is seen as a blatantly illiberal trait in Decembrist constitutionalism, and rightly so. However, it should be noted that nomadic peoples were often excluded from citizenship in so-called liberal nations at the time. One flagrant example is, of course, the Indigenous Americans in the USA.

The supremacy of political over ethnocultural considerations in civic nationalism presumes that the state is neutral, whereas in fact it usually represents the dominant culture. Hence there is a conflict between the concept of a political nation based on equal rights and the presence of cultural diversity in society, which has often turned civic nationalism into an imperialist force. In fact, civic nationalism often demands, 'as the price for receiving citizenship and its benefits, the surrender of ethnic community and individuality, the privatization and marginalization of ethnic culture and religion of minorities within the borders of the national state'.[75]

In countries that believed themselves to be homogeneous, ethnocultural discrimination was easier to conceal than it was in a multi-ethnic empire of the Russian type, but it did not affect minorities any less. In Russia, both Decembrist constitutions treated this issue at length. Even though Muraviev's constitution was less explicitly assimilationist, a disregard for cultural difference was manifested in both documents. Pestel and Muraviev expected the minority peoples in the empire to be satisfied with individual rights within the old borders of the imperial state. Pestel maintained that all peoples must be formed into one single nation, dissolving all differences into one common mass so that all inhabitants of the entire territory of the Russian state would be Russians. This nation should be realized politically, by applying the same laws and system of administration in all parts of Russia, using the same (Russian) language.[76] For this project to work, the state was to attend to the economic development of the different peoples, particularly those in the borderlands.

Pestel envisioned a Russian nation modelled on the French concept of an indivisible nation. In this nation, special rights, or laws that in any way come into conflict with national ones, could not be accepted. In *Russian Justice*, he stressed the importance of subordinating religion to the state. He declared that the 'the laws of religion' must be combined with 'unitary political laws', and that religious laws were not to influence political laws in any way. But he accepted that 'variety in religious laws may be combined with uniformity in political laws.' Such religious tolerance had to conform to the basic tenets of Christianity, however, and 'the acts of all non-Christian faiths which are contrary to the spirit of the Christian law must be prohibited, but everything that is not contrary to its spirit, even though different from it, may be permitted according to circumstances.'[77] The Tatars, who professed Islam, were thus 'allowed to keep this faith[,] and any persecution of it is forbidden'.[78] The Decembrists believed that freedom of religion was significant to the formation of a modern nation, but that it should be accepted only as long as religious rules were not in conflict with the laws of the nation.

Freedom of religion was central to liberal theory, but in reality few countries implemented it. In 1791 all Jewish people living in France attained civil equality, but in most Western countries they did not receive civil rights until long after the Decembrist revolt. The Russian empire had a large population of Jews, who suffered from the regime's discriminatory policies. However, they did not fit into Pestel's idea of a unitary nation. He disapproved of the Jewish rejection of Christianity and what he saw as their unwillingness to accept assimilation. He was also critical of their exemption from certain laws. He proposed some form of acculturation of the Russian Jews with the help of the most learned rabbis. If this did not work, he proposed rather draconically to resettle them in a state of their own in Asia Minor.[79]

Linguistic diversity was treated in a similar way to religious differences. Pestel insisted on the primacy of Russian over all other languages of the empire. In this regard, Muraviev's views were not very different. He stated that twenty years from the promulgation of his constitution, only those who had become literate in the Russian language would be recognized as citizens.[80] Again, this was in line with the ideas of Western thinkers. The Spanish Constitution had a similar wording. To the French revolutionaries it was a matter of political pragmatism that a nation based on the common will of the people should share the same language. Only when all citizens spoke the same tongue could they 'communicate their thoughts without hindrance' and enjoy equal access to state office.[81] To participate in the republic, the population had to understand the language in which political debates were held and administrative documents written. Moreover, it was believed that a high culture could not prosper without a common language. Linguistic diversity was denounced as conducive to reaction. It held the peasant masses in ignorance.[82]

Contemporary thought was divided regarding how a free republic should be organized to avoid tyranny and promote the general will. French revolutionaries like Abbé Sieyès and Destutt de Tracy advocated a unitary state with a centralized government, where political representatives represented the nation as a whole. American revolutionary thinkers like James Madison and Alexander Hamilton preferred a federation. Destutt de Tracy argued that 'the confederate system' might work well in America, 'because they have no powerful neighbours'. But if 'France had adopted this form, it is doubtful whether it could have resisted all Europe, as it did by remaining one and indivisible'.[83] This was probably one reason why Pestel advocated the French model. He feared that a federal system would weaken the link between the regions, leading to less support for the union, or even secession. In either case, the new Russian nation would be destroyed.

In a federal system, Pestel argued, each regional government would hold that it could arrange the public affairs of its own region better without the interference of the supreme authority. Each region, forming a small separate state within the federal state, would be connected only tenuously to the whole.

> The particular wellbeing of the region might in the short term have a more decisive influence on the imagination of its rulers and people than the general wellbeing of the whole state, the benefits of which for the region may not be readily apparent. The word 'state' will in such a system be an empty word, since nowhere will people be aware of the state, only of their region.

The consequence of such a system would be that the 'love of the fatherland' would turn into allegiance to a region. As far as Russia was concerned, Pestel believed that the federal system would be ruinous. Not only were its regions governed by different institutions and judged by different civil laws, but they spoke different languages and professed different faiths. Their inhabitants were of different origins and at times belonged to different powers. So, 'if this heterogeneity were to be reinforced through a federal system, it is easy to predict just how quickly these diverse regions would secede from the Russian core.'[84] Hence Pestel regarded this as a geopolitical rather than a cultural issue.

As specified in *Russian Justice*, Russia was to be divided into fifty-three provinces, fifty of which were called areas and three districts. The three districts were Nizhnii-Novgorod, Don and Aral. Don was the lands of the Don Cossacks and Aral the land of the Kazakhs; Nizhnii-Novgorod was the new capital. The fifty areas would form ten regions, each of which was to be divided into a number of districts, and each district into townships. Democratic townships constituted a cornerstone of Pestel's future Russian republic. The idea was that they would form political families in which citizens were protected. It was important that these townships were not overcrowded. Large towns were considered detrimental to the morality of the population, and the state of morality was important for the survival of all nations.[85] The decision to place the capital in Nizhnii-Novgorod was made mainly for economic reasons and because of its central location, which allowed easy communications and trade, but there were also political reasons given its patriotic history.[86]

Muraviev, who had in-depth knowledge of both the U.S. federal Constitution and the state constitutions, advocated a federal system for Russia modelled on the United States of America.[87] In the introduction to

*A Project for a Constitution*, he discusses the best form of government for large states, such as Russia. He subscribed to the view, promulgated by Montesquieu, that only a federal or union form of government could solve the problem of populous nations, which often suffered from domestic oppression. Federalism was the best system for harmonizing the expanse of such a nation with the freedom of its citizens. Muraviev proposed a legislative assembly in the capital that would make decisions affecting the whole state, while regional assemblies made decisions on particular issues that affected specific regions. However, as in the American Constitution (and even more so in the legislation regulating the creation of new territories and states in the American union), the autonomous states that were to be created in Russia would not reflect the ethnic make-up of their population.[88] The country was to be divided into 13 states, 2 regions and 569 districts. The states were Bothnia, Volkhov, the Baltic State, Western State, State of the Dnieper, Black Sea State, State of the Caucasus, Ukrainian State, Transvolga State, State of the Kama, State of the Lower Steppe, State of the Ob' and State of the Lena. The regions were the regions of Moscow and Don. The 569 districts were to be subdivided into rural municipalities between 500 and 1,500 male inhabitants.

A common belief among Western thinkers at the time was that the welfare of the nation was dependent on its prosperity, security and progress. Moreover, a nation had to be of sufficient size. In the words of the German-American liberal nationalist Friedrich List,

> a nation restricted in the number of its population and in territory, especially if it has a separate language, can only possess a crippled literature, crippled institutions for promoting art and science. A small state can never bring to complete perfection within its territory the various branches of production.[89]

In Pestel's view, federalism would weaken the Russian state in exactly these respects. As we have seen, he believed that federalism would lead to the secession of regions. Then Russia would lose not only its power, greatness and strength, but perhaps its very existence (as one of the principal great states): 'Russia would once again experience all the harm inflicted in ancient times by the appanage system, which was nothing more than a kind of federal state structure.'[90] The problem was that in large nations of many different peoples, security became difficult to maintain without strong central power. Here, Pestel echoed the prevalent French view that, because of the competitive international states system, strong central governments were necessary to the survival of European nations. He was aware that people of other origins than the dominant nation wanted political autonomy, based on the right to nationhood. But he believed that the state's right to security, to protecting its borders, the right of convenience, often took precedence.[91]

Pestel also believed that for the sake of national security it was necessary for Russia to annex some land at its border. This applied to 1) Moldavia; 2) The lands of the peoples of the Caucasus not subject to Russia and situated to the north of the Turkish and Persian borders, including the Western coastal part belonging to Turkey; 3) The lands of the Kirghiz-Kaisak nomads north of the mountain ridge, extending from the fortress of Bukhtarmin to the Sea of Aral; and 4) A part of Mongolia, so that the entire course of the Amur River would belong to Russia.

Liberal nationalist thinkers in the West argued that small – and especially small and backward – nationalities had everything to gain by merging into greater nations and making their contribution to humanity through these. This, they believed, was simply a consequence of the laws of progress.[92] Destutt de Tracy, who greatly influenced Pestel's thinking, asserted that a people often gained a great deal by being conquered: 'this is particularly true, of those whose fortune it is to be conquered by a representative government, for they thereby gain both liberty and economy . . . To be thus conquered is in truth more like a rescue from bondage, than a subjection.'[93] The case for the establishment of a nation state depended on whether it could fit in with or advance historical evolution and progress. Hence the defence of small (or 'backward') cultures became an expression of conservative resistance to the inevitable advance of history. The measure of a nation's greatness was the freedom its people generally enjoyed in pursuing their *individual* interests, and thus in promoting the wealth and welfare of the community as a whole.[94]

This thinking is reflected in both Decembrist constitutions, but it is stated more plainly in that of the Southern Society. Here, the nomadic peoples are described as

> half savages, and some are even complete savages; they live in ignorance and degradation. Consequently, even out of Christian duty one should endeavour to improve their condition, the more so [considering] that they live in our state, in our fatherland. The goal is that they will become our brethren. It may be reached by settling them permanently and turning them to agriculture.[95]

Furthermore, Pestel held that the right to nationhood must prevail in the case of those peoples who can enjoy their own political independence and have the ability to maintain it, whereas the right of convenience must prevail over those peoples who cannot themselves make use of their political independence and must of necessity come under the power of some stronger state. Otherwise, they would serve as staging areas for military action and destruction. In Pestel's opinion, most people within the borders of the Russian state had never enjoyed and would never enjoy their own independence. They had always belonged to different countries. For that reason, they were subject to the right of convenience. Poland was an exception. It had the right to nationhood, but the final determination of the borders between Russia and Poland should be left to Russia's right of convenience to ensure its own security. Another condition for Poland's independence was the introduction of a representative government there.[96]

The Decembrists clearly expressed the fact that the principle of self-determination, characteristic of civic nationalism, was not promoted in order to encourage the realization of cultural identities.[97] On the contrary, imperialist notions were integrated into the original Western civic idea of the nation and were expressed in various forms of liberal imperialism. Just as the building of a nation state was a fundamental tenet of liberalism, so the assertion of an imperialist foreign policy was a crucial part of this nationalist discourse. Neither the Northern nor the Southern Society was prepared to grant ethnic or cultural minorities the right to secede.

# 6

# Republican Thought

While the Decembrists articulated liberal ideas of the rule of law, representative government and civil liberties, they also voiced republican concerns about arbitrary power and the need for power to be restrained by law for the good of the community.[1] In this they were influenced by the revival of republican thought, popularized in the American and French revolutions. In common with American and French patriots, the Decembrists were greatly inspired by classical antiquity.[2] Homer, Plutarch, Livy, Cicero, Horace and Tacitus were essential reading to many of them, and Decembrist writers translated works that articulated classical republican themes, such as patriotism and hostility to tyranny. In his testimony to the investigating committee, Piotr Kakhovskii announced that he was 'inflamed by ancient heroes', while Piotr Borisov testified that a love of freedom and popular sovereignty had been implanted in him by ancient heroes from Greek and Roman history.[3]

The Decembrists also drew on a Russian tradition of republicanism. They studied Russian eighteenth-century thinkers, such as Aleksandr Radishchev and Nikolai Ivanovich Novikov, who criticized serfdom and argued for restricting absolute monarchy. Plays highlighting the struggle against tyranny had been popular in eighteenth-century Russia; they were suppressed during the French Revolution but revived in the reign of Alexander.[4]

A rejection of unlimited monarchy was an important element of republican thought. Citizens should never allow themselves to become slaves of inhuman tyranny, because the essence of being a citizen was to be free. Arbitrary power should therefore be banished, and representation assured. A free state was a state in which the citizens were moved to act solely by their own will, that is, by the citizen body as a whole. However, if tyranny were to be avoided, there had to be checks on power, and a constitution served this purpose. In a real republic, there should be 'no other Majesty than that of the People' and 'no other Sovereignty than that of the Laws' protecting the freedom and the power of the people.[5]

In Decembrist thought, these ideas are most clearly manifested in literature and poetry. The Decembrists not only employed political tracts and constitutions to convey their political message, but used literature and especially poetry in the service of political change. Poetry was in fact an integral part of the Decembrist movement, used as a subtle yet powerful medium for communicating their political opinions to the educated elite and forming political consciousness around central concerns. There is no precise definition of Decembrist poetry. It can be described as a loose body of political poetry, written roughly between 1816 and 1825 and stemming from the aspirations of the movement. Most of the writers were members of the secret societies, and others were friends or sympathizers. The topics they brought forth, the rhetoric they used and the ideas they expressed could be linked to the outlook of the future Decembrists. What distinguishes Decembrist poetry from other poetry written during this period is its dedication to civic themes and political change. Nevertheless, it is important to separate Decembrist poets from Decembrist poems. Aleksandr Pushkin is a case in point. He cannot be characterized as a Decembrist poet, but he wrote poems, such as 'Ode to Liberty' and 'The Dagger', that can be classified as Decembrist.[6] The same may be said of certain poems by Prince Piotr Viazemskii, a Decembrist sympathizer. Vladimir Raevskii, Fedor Glinka, Aleksandr Bestuzhev (Bestuzhev-Marlinskii), Pavel Katenin, Aleksandr Odoevskii and especially Kondratii Ryleev and Vilgelm Kiukhelbeker were the major Decembrist poets.[7]

The extent to which poetry could be used as a political force is seen in the fear it instilled in Nicholas I, who in May 1826 ordered all subversive poems to be deleted from the records of the investigating commission and burned. Ryleev's poem 'The Citizen' was considered so incendiary that when, during his interrogation, Aleksandr Beliaev quoted several lines from memory, Nicholas ordered that these lines be immediately expunged from the records.[8]

The rejection of unlimited monarchy was an important idea for both the Northern and the Southern Society and was reflected in Decembrist literature. One of its recurrent themes was that to be a citizen, even to be human, you had to live in freedom. Glinka's nightingale in a cage can be seen as a metaphor for the slave, living under tyranny. The nightingale, Glinka tells us, sang beautifully when free, but stayed silent when locked in

Unknown artist,
*Kondratii Ryleev*,
first quarter of
19th century,
drawing.

its cage: 'Thus, holy nature, your law and the voice of the heart tell us that freedom is second life for us!'[9] Living in captivity was comparable to living under tyranny, and had similar consequences. Most importantly, it killed all activity, all creativity and all human life. Glinka also used historical tales to depict the destructive effects of tyranny. One example is his story about the forced detention of the Jews in Babylonia, which expressed the notion of liberty as essential to human life. Here, the captives point out that 'the harsh days of captivity do not give life to [our] organs,' because 'slaves, trailing chains, do not sing lofty songs.'[10] In a play allegedly about the liberation of the Netherlands from the Habsburg monarchy, Glinka paints another gloomy picture of a people suffering under the yoke of a tyrant: 'Everywhere the people are in torment! ... upon the shoulders of slaves bent beneath the yoke, he has erected his iron and blood-drenched throne, and watered our soil with rivers of evil – the tyrant!'[11] Here, the power of the tyrant is unlimited. As a consequence, he abuses his power and treats the people as slaves.

In common with republican thinkers before them, the Decembrists believed that arbitrary power had to be checked, since all kings were potential tyrants and despots: 'Only give them power,' Nikolai Lorer warned;

'It is for this reason that . . . people *need* a constitution, a limiting of the prerogatives of individuals who rule.'[12] Viazemskii stressed the importance of
establishing the rule of law in order to avoid tyranny: 'Laws are trampled by
the violence of caprice . . . the sanctuary of justice [I have seen become] the
triumph of perfidy, the laws, the sacred weapons of righteousness [I have
seen become] a shield for the powerful and a yoke for the weak.'[13]

The connection made in republican thought between laws and liberty
is evident in the first scene of Glinka's poetic tragedy *Velzen*, or *Liberated
Holland*. One of the characters, Inslar, exclaims: 'Liberty or death! A
country deprived of laws and liberty is a mournful tomb: in it, the people
are captives.'[14] Pushkin also made this connection between liberty and law.
In 'Ode to Liberty', alluding to Radishchev's political tract from 1783 that
denounced autocratic abuse, Pushkin wrote:

> Alas, where'er my eye may light,
> It falls on ankle chains and scourges,
> Perverted law's pernicious blight
> And tearful serfdom's fruitless surges.[15]

Slavery was a consequence of illegitimate power, that is, arbitrary power
unrestrained by law. Liberty was possible only when it was protected by law
and when this law was firmly implemented in society:

> Unstained by human freedom choked
> A sovereign's brow alone is carried
> Where sacred liberty is married
> With mighty law and firmly yoked;
> Where its stout roof enshelters all,
> And where, by watchful burghers wielded,
> Law's sword impends, and none are shielded
> From its inexorable fall.

Nobody, no matter how powerful, stood above the law. Even kings were
subject to it. Their power was neither natural nor God-given and not theirs
to use at pleasure. Monarchs had to rule according to the law, because only
the law legitimated their power:

> Oh, kings, you owe your crown and writ
> To Law, not nature's dispensation;

While you stand high above the nation,
The changeless Law stands higher yet.[16]

Pushkin expressed similar views on the importance of the rule of law in 'The Dagger', in which he stated that Brutus deservedly killed Julius Caesar because the latter violated his mandate when he crossed the Rubicon River on 10 January 49 BCE, entering Italy proper with a standing army. Pushkin's message was that not even a powerful emperor could avoid the 'supreme tribunal' when breaking the law.[17]

Thus laws protected freedom, but this was not enough. According to republican thinking, it was also the duty of the citizen to protect the liberty of the republic and its people. It was the duty of the patriot to protect the common good.

## Patriotism

Patriotism, or love of country, is another key element of republican thought. It was prominent in the revolutionary vocabulary of the late eighteenth and early nineteenth centuries.[18] In classical Rome, *patria* (fatherland) referred to the republic and denoted the common good and common liberty. In the eighteenth century 'patria' regained its classical meaning as a self-governing community of individuals living together under the rule of law. 'Patriotism' signified love for the republic and common liberty for all citizens.[19] Love of one's fatherland should take precedence over private interests. Civic virtue meant heroic patriotism and public spirit. A patriot was a civic hero under the obligation to defend the liberty of the people (citizens) against tyranny and injustice. The highest good was the good of the community, and a republican government was a government concerned with the public affairs of the nation. The most important civic duty was to maintain the republic and thereby the liberty of the people. Freedom was preserved through the public spirit of the citizens.

Patriotism was central to Decembrist thought and was manifested in political tracts, poetry and personal records. In his memoirs, Nikolai Basargin described the members of the Southern Society as patriots in the republican sense. They were people who loved their country passionately and wished to be useful to it. They were indignant at every injustice, every measure of the government that served a private instead of a common benefit.[20] Many of the Decembrists explicitly cited patriotism as one of the driving forces for joining the Decembrist societies. In his testimony to the investigating committee regarding his reasons for joining the Southern Society, Yakiv Andriyevych of the United Slavs stated that 'Love for my native land, and for freedom as the condition proper to man, pity for my fellow men who found themselves in such cruel misfortune through nothing other than the negligence of the government . . . obliged me to join this Society.'[21]

Patriotism was also the driving force behind Major Vladimir Raevskii's actions. A member of the Union of Welfare and later of the Southern Society as the leader of its Kishinev branch, he was arrested and imprisoned in 1822 for spreading anti-government propaganda among his soldiers. As a patriot, he could not accept the enslavement of the people, his fellow citizens.[22] When Piotr Borisov, co-founder of the Society of United Slavs, gave the reasons for his involvement in the revolt, he declared that love of freedom and of popular sovereignty had been implanted in him. The moral foundation for his actions, however, was that 'the general good is the highest law.'[23]

Nikolai Turgenev, one of the founders of the Union of Welfare, stated in his diary that the true purpose of men is found in love for their fatherland, in the desire for its well-being, in the sacrifice of themselves for its benefit.[24] Striving for the well-being of one's fatherland meant striving for its freedom. This connection between patriotism and liberty is manifested in his private reflections on the Spanish Revolution of 23 March 1820. The day after this event, he wrote in his diary: 'Yesterday I learned that the Spanish king has proclaimed the constitution of the Cortes [Spanish parliament]. All honour to you, army of Spain! All glory to the Spanish people! For the second time Spain is proving what the popular spirit means, what love of the fatherland means.'[25] Here, Turgenev referred to the fact that the Spanish Constitution of 1812 was re-established in the revolution of 1820. No doubt he knew of the events in Spain from the Russian press, which showed a keen interest in the Iberian revolution.[26]

The constitution of the Union of Welfare expressed some of these ideas. It stated that among the members' duties to others, the most important are those concerning the fatherland; to strive for the common good is the concern of every citizen.[27] The nation's common weal absolutely demands the good of the individual, and every man, whatever his estate, has a right to it.[28] Thus the good of the nation was linked to the common good and to equal rights. Pavel Pestel continued this line of thinking in *Russian Justice*, declaring that states, or civil societies, have as their aim the welfare of society in general and of every one of its members in particular. All government statutes must aim exclusively for the welfare of civil society, and the common weal must be valued more highly than private happiness. Aleksei Iushnevskii, a member of the Union of Welfare and the Southern Society, worked to instil these republican values in his younger brother Semion. There are few people who know how 'to be virtuous, love their country and strive for its good', he wrote in a letter to his brother, instructing him to adhere to the rules of honesty, selfless love for one's fellows and attachment to the society in which he was born.[29]

Patriotism, in the sense of civic heroism and public spirit, was a prominent feature of Decembrist literature. As early as the beginning of the nineteenth century, members of the Russian Free Society for Lovers of Literature, the Sciences and the Arts composed political verse in the spirit of republicanism, especially Ivan Pnin and Aleksandr Khristoforovich Vostokov. Their poetry was replete with patriotic and civic themes. However, the Decembrist Ryleev is the most renowned representative of civic poetry in Russia. As noted by one of his friends, he wanted to awaken in his compatriots feelings of love for their country, and to ignite the desire for freedom.[30] He was not concerned with romantic love. 'Love is not to be found in my mind', he wrote. 'Alas! My country is suffering; my soul, troubled by gloomy thoughts, now thirsts only for freedom.'[31] Ryleev admired the poet Gavriil Derzhavin for his civic conscience, saying that Derzhavin lived up to the noble calling of the poet – to be of use to his country: 'He placed higher than all blessings the common good and in his fiery verses praised sacred virtue.'[32] This was the poet's calling: 'Zeal for mighty deeds. Love for your native country. And scorn for the oppressors.'[33]

Love for one's country, the poet Piotr Pletniov wrote, is 'the prime virtue of a citizen'.[34] But love for one's country also implied love for its people. It was in the name of the people that freedom for one's country was served. We have already seen how Glinka drew attention to the predicament of the people and presented their plight as a problem that ought to concern every patriot. Ryleev criticized the Russian regime for encroaching on the freedom of the people and for 'pushing [them] into poverty with heavy taxes'.[35] In his poem 'Volynskii', he portrays Empress Anna Ioannovna's executed cabinet minister, Artemii Petrovich Volynskii (1689–1740), as a civic hero, a symbol of autocratic tyranny. Ryleev's Volynskii realizes 'how glorious it is to die for the people'. The poem expresses wonderfully the civic duty of the patriot:

> Alive with love for his country
> He endures everything for it ...

> May he be a model of honour,
> An iron breastplate for the suffering
> And forever the sworn enemy
> Of shameful injustice.[36]

The poem 'Nalivaiko' conveys similar feelings of selfless patriotism. It tells of Severyn Nalivaiko, the leader of a failed Ukrainian Cossack uprising against the Polish-Lithuanian Commonwealth (1594–6).[37] Here, Ryleev glorifies the struggle for the freedom of the people. Nalivaiko is cast as a brave hero who willingly sacrifices himself for his country and its people:

> I am well aware that ruin awaits
> Him who rises first
> Against the people's oppressors –
> Fate has already condemned me.
> But where, tell me, and when
> Was freedom ever bought without victims?
> I shall perish for my native land, –
> I feel this, I know it
> Yet gladly, Holy Father,
> I bless my fate.[38]

For republicans, the highest duty was to serve one's country, and the greatest hero was the citizen who was willing to sacrifice everything for the common good and the liberty of the republic.[39] In Glinka's words, 'who would not prefer a glorious death to the fate of slaves?'[40] This republican theme is also found in Kiukhelbeker's tragedy *Argiviane* (The Argives), an attempt to produce a classical Greek tragedy rather than make use of the French neoclassical model. In *Argiviane*, the hero sacrifices himself for the restoration of freedom to his enslaved fatherland.[41] Another tragedy, *Andromache* by Pavel Katenin, based on Virgil's *Aeneid* and Euripides' *Trojan Women*, has a similar message. It evokes the civic spirit esteemed by both the ancients and the Decembrists.[42]

The connection between patriotism and liberty is also manifested in Pushkin's poem 'To Chaadaev' (1818), dedicated to his friend and mentor Piotr Chaadaev, who in his youth was considered a free-thinker and was associated with the Decembrist movement. In the poem, Pushkin presents himself and his friend as freedom fighters. Romantic love and private fame are banished in favour of public spirit and patriotic honour. Under the yoke of despotism, only one desire remains – to fight for liberty and save the fatherland from tyranny:

> Yet 'neath the fateful yoke that bows us
> One burning wish will not abate:
> With mutinous soul we still await
> Our Fatherland to call and rouse us,
> In transports of impatient anguish
> For sacred Liberty we thrill.

Pushkin exhorts all virtuous patriots, who yearn for freedom, to act and liberate their fatherland. This will make them true heroes in the service of the nation against despotism:

> While yet with Freedom's spark we burn
> And Honour's generous devotion,
> On our dear country let us turn
> Our fervent spirit's fine emotion!
> Believe, my friend: Russia will rise,
> . . .
> On Tyranny's stark wreck the nation
> Will our names immortalize![43]

Disregarding calls to do one's patriotic duty was dishonourable. In the poem 'Citizen' (Grazhdanin), written on the eve of the revolt, Ryleev warned those who 'cast a cold glance upon the woes of their own native land' that they would be shamed. As a patriot, one could not 'at the fateful hour bring shame upon the citizen's dignity'. The 'citizen' exclaims:

> No, I am not capable in the embraces of voluptuousness
> Of dragging out my young years in shameful idleness,
> Or of languishing with turbulent soul
> Beneath despotism's heavy yoke.[44]

## Civic participation

For the Decembrist poets, political activity was essential, and their poems can be seen as calls to action. Poetry that did not encourage commitment to the pursuit of the common good was meaningless to them. The struggle for liberty was fought in many parts of the world. Now it was time for Russia to wage this battle, and all patriots were called to join the fight. Liberty had already been victorious in the West, in the American and French revolutions. It was now time for her to travel east. The Decembrists had adopted the view, articulated by American and French patriots, that republican revolutions and the idea of the nation would spread around the world. Odoevskii's 'The Maiden of 1610' illustrates this point. Here, the 'Maiden', who is the goddess Liberty, calls to the Russians: 'Why do you tarry? From the western world . . . From my lands, both free and happy, I have flown to you, to your call.' Odoevskii contrasts Russian autocracy with an idealized image of the nations of the West, where the people had been liberated from their tyrants, from the purple robe of monarchy, and were striving for the good of the community. 'From the Western world', Liberty cries,

> Where I breathe, where I reign alone,
> And where long since the bloody purple
> Has been torn from the gods of injustice,
> Where there is no slavery, but brothers, and citizens
> Adore my godhead,
> And the thousands, like the waves in the ocean,
> Are mingled together into a single family.[45]

The struggle between freedom and tyranny was a central theme in Decembrist poetry. Liberty was summoned to fight against oppression. In 'Ode to Liberty', Pushkin calls:

> Where are you, where are you, terror of tsars,
> Proud muse of freedom?
> Come, tear the laurels from me,
> Smash the pampered lyre . . .
> I want to sing to the world of freedom,
> And strike evil on the thrones.[46]

The Decembrists were part of a transnational movement fighting against absolutism and tyranny, and they sympathized with the Spanish *liberales* in particular. As noted above, the Spanish Constitution of 1812 was the key document for the Decembrists, many of whom owned copies of it; its reinstatement after the revolution in 1820 inspired them greatly.[47] They regarded the Spanish Revolution as part of a European wave of revolutions, an expression of the spirit of the times. It confirmed their belief that liberty and constitutions would spread across the world, and suggested that things would change in Russia as well.[48] The fact that Alexander I recognized the Spanish Cortes and the constitution so soon after the revolt could only emphasize their feelings of hope for the future. The events surrounding the Spanish Revolution also led Russians to reflect on the power of patriotism and the strong link between patriotism and liberty. It was the patriotism of the people that had led to victory over Napoleon and to political freedom.

The establishment of a constitutional regime in Spain proved that, since the American Revolution, the days of absolutism were numbered. Liberty would spread across the world and neither monarchs nor their armies could do anything to stop it. Prince Evgenii Obolenskii, a member of the Union of Welfare and of the Northern Society, wrote in his testimony regarding his liberal way of thinking that it was 'strengthened by the spirit of the age and by observation of the events which during the last years had punctuated the history of almost all countries of the world with all kinds of revolutions'.[49] Pestel concurred, pointing out that 'each age has its distinctive characteristic: ours is marked by revolutionary ideas . . . From one end of Europe to the other, everywhere the same thing is observed . . . The same spectacle is displayed in the whole of America.'[50] Before 1820 even the Russian tsar took part in this movement. As a contemporary stated, 'all were singing a constitutional song in which the leader of the choir was Emperor Alexander Pavlovich.'[51]

Liberty and constitutions belonged to the future. There was nothing the tsar could do, because, as Raevskii put it, 'the universal law of change will bring about the tyrant's downfall' and 'the gates of freedom and repose shall be thrown open.'[52] Kiukhelbeker's 'Greek Song' of 1821 conveys the same idea:

> The ages are marching toward a glorious goal;
> I see them! They are moving!
> The codes of authority have grown old;
> People heretofore asleep have awakened,
> Are looking around and rising up.
> O joy! The hour has come, the happy hour of Freedom![53]

Humanity's progress towards freedom was determined by Providence, and for this reason, the fact that the revolutions in Spain, Naples and

Greece had failed did not discourage the Decembrists.[54] They perceived this as no more than a temporary setback. With the collapse of autocracy, these nations would be avenged and liberated once more. It was important to keep fighting, because one could never be sure exactly when the hour of freedom had come, but there was no question that it *would* arrive.[55] The ardent belief that history was on their side did not vanish completely even after the failed Decembrist revolt. In a poem dedicated to the exiled and imprisoned Decembrists written to his friend Ivan Pushchin and brought to Siberia by Aleksandra Muravieva, Pushkin wrote:

> The heavy chains will fall,
> The prison crash – and freedom
> Will greet you joyously at the door,
> And your brothers will give you a sword.[56]

Odoevskii later responded from captivity with the following lines: 'The flaming sounds of the inspired strings have come to our ears; our hands reached for swords – and found only chains.'[57] But, he comforts the reader,

> Our painful labour shall not be lost;
> From the sparks shall flare a flame,
> And our enlightened people
> Will gather beneath the sacred banner.

> We shall forge swords from chains,
> And kindle anew the fire of freedom!
> She [Freedom] will advance against kings,
> And the peoples give a sigh of joy.[58]

The idea that all the peoples of the world would be liberated through democratic-republican revolutions was articulated by such major Western writers as Thomas Jefferson and Antoine Destutt de Tracy, thinkers who inspired Nikita Muraviev and Pestel. In Decembrist literature, it was often expressed in the language of the momentous hour. Decembrist writers were confident that the hour of change had come – a happy hour for Liberty, but not for the tyrannical ruler. 'Tyrants of the world! Tremble!' Pushkin warned. 'And you fallen slaves, be men and hearken, rise up!'[59] 'Near is the hour, near is the struggle, the struggle between liberty and despotism!'[60] When the 'fateful hour' struck, tyrants could expect nothing less than 'dreadful dungeons'.[61] Then the enslaved peoples would have their revenge and become free citizens:

> Terrible is the despotic prince
> But night's darkness will fall
> And the decisive hour will come
> A fateful hour for the citizenry.[62]

Revolution was inevitable and there was no salvation for tyrants.[63] There are many examples in Decembrist literature of the people taking up arms against tyranny and disposing of the tyrant by violent means. Katenin translated a scene from the French dramatist Pierre Corneille's neoclassical tragedy *Cinna*, about the plot to murder Emperor Augustus.[64] In Kiukhelbeker's tragedy *The Argives*, mentioned above, the hero sacrifices himself for the restoration of freedom to his enslaved fatherland. It is an adaptation of Plutarch's account of the conflict between the Corinthian tyrant Timophanes and his republican brother Timoleon. After much hesitation, Timoleon kills his brother out of patriotic duty to free Corinth from tyranny. The same message is conveyed in 'Experiences of Two Tragic Phenomena', in which Glinka tells a story about a loyal son of a fatherland subjected to a tyrant, who exhorts his fellow citizens to take up arms against arbitrary power.[65] This theme reappears in *Velzen*. We hear of 'crowds of slaves, shedding tears and blood', an enslaved people who suffer. But the revolt is inevitable. 'Already is heard a murmur! . . . They are cursing the tyrant.'[66] No mercy is given: 'There is no salvation for the tyrant: His only friend is the dagger!'[67]

The dagger – a classical symbol of tyrannicide, as the weapon used by Brutus – plays a prominent role in Pushkin's poem 'The Dagger'. Here, Pushkin makes use of references to both ancient and contemporary tyrannicides in order to illustrate the inevitable fate of the tyrant, which in this case represents not the Roman emperor, but the Russian tsar.[68] The idolization of Brutus as civic hero and patriot was a common theme in republican rhetoric. Caesar had become a tyrant when he violated his mandate, so Brutus had to kill him for the sake of liberty. Pushkin portrays Brutus as the patriot who 'restored freedom-loving':[69]

> Forbidden, Rubicon has suffered Caesar's tread,
> Majestic Rome succumbed, the law inclined its head;
> But Brutus righted Freedom's damage:

> You struck down Caesar – and he staggered, dead,
> Against great Pompey's haughty image.

In the unfinished and unpublished tenth canto of his novel in verse, *Eugene Onegin*, Pushkin portrays the Decembrist Ivan Iakushkin in the same context. Here he depicts a scenario where Iakushkin 'silently bared a regicidal dagger' in order to kill Alexander I.

Through Nalivaiko, Ryleev also encourages the nation to rise against tyranny:

> There is no reconciliation, there are no conditions
> Between the tyrant and the slave;
> It is not ink which is needed, but blood,
> We must act with the sword.[70]

Every citizen had a duty not to shrink from active participation in this struggle, but educated people, and especially artists, had an important obligation to act as leaders of the revolt. In Kiukhelbeker's 'Prophecy', a poem of biblical themes, God accuses the main character of 'dragging out his days in mortal slumber'. He asks if it was 'for this that I gave you the fire and the power to awaken peoples? – Rise up, singer, prophet of Freedom! Spring up, proclaim what I have decreed.'[71]

> They will repent when the people, having arisen,
> Finds them in idle languor's embrace,
> And, seeking liberty's rights in the stormy revolt,
> Finds among them neither a Brutus nor a Riego.[72]

While Brutus was portrayed as a classical patriot, Rafael del Riego, the leader of the Spanish Revolution of 1820, was seen as a modern version of a civic hero. Kakhovskii described him as a 'holymartyr hero' and friend of the people.[73] Riego was a role model for many Decembrists, and they were outraged by his execution. And yet it was his execution that turned him into a martyr. Basargin of the Southern Society recalled when Alexander I received the news that Riego had been captured (on 15 September 1823). The emperor had completed an inspection of the army and was about to have lunch at the camp of General Rudzevich when a courier appeared with a message from Chateaubriand, the French minister of foreign affairs. Addressing the generals next to him, Alexander I allegedly said, 'Gentlemen, I congratulate you:

Riego has been taken prisoner.' Everyone fell silent and lowered their eyes. Only Count Vorontsov exclaimed: 'What happy news, Sire.'[74]

Pushkin also makes a hero out of the student Karl Ludwig Sand, who killed the reactionary German playwright and tsarist agent August Friedrich von Kotzebue in 1819. His murder resulted in Klemens von Metternich's repressive Karlsbad Decrees and in Sand's execution. The dagger is presented as 'the avenging knife' and 'the secret sentinel of Freedom's threatened life'. Sand is portrayed as the patriotic hero who sacrifices himself for liberty. Brutus, Riego and Sand were used frequently by the Decembrists as examples of civic heroes:[75]

> Oh, righteous youth, the Fates' appointed choice,
> Oh, Sand, you perished on the scaffold;
> But from your martyred dust the voice
> Of holy virtue speaks unmuffled.
>
> In your own Germany a shadow you became
> That grants to lawless force no haven –
> And on your solemn tomb ungraven
> There glows a dagger for a name.[76]

## The construction of a republican past

In their support for republicanism, the Decembrists evoked the traditions of both ancient Greece and Rome and the Russian medieval republics of Novgorod and Pskov. This continued a Russian tradition that had originated in the eighteenth century among exponents of the Russian Enlightenment, who utilized Roman history in a politically radical way. Iakov Kniazhnin's *Vadim from Novgorod* (1789), in which the eponymous hero is depicted as a defender of ancient liberties, is a case in point.[77] By focusing on liberty and the existence of a republican tradition in Russian history, the Decembrists presented a different, modern view of the past from that of the official conservative government historian, Nikolai Karamzin, who praised autocracy as the decisive formative influence in Russian history.[78]

History has often been used to justify changes to a traditional order. Republicans who could not lay claim to the classical inheritance of antiquity looked elsewhere in history. The American revolutionaries used British history to justify their claims to liberty.[79] They argued that their revolt was motivated by an effort to restore ancient English liberties.[80] Hence, in common with French, English and American republicans, the Decembrists tried to justify their present position by an appeal to a constructed legendary past of freedom and equality. This was in fact a common strategy to defend political claims and demands for change.[81] The Decembrists employed the medieval Russian city republics, such as Novgorod and Pskov, to demonstrate that a kind of democracy had existed in Russia before autocracy. In medieval Russia, they argued, the republican spirit reigned and the people were free.[82] It was now time to bring to life again 'the sacred times when our *veche* [medieval Russian assembly] thundered and from afar broke the shoulders of arrogant kings'.[83] The existence of an ancient Russian liberty not only made it possible for the Decembrists to criticize the contemporary lack of freedom in Russia while describing historical events, but established an important historical link between the modern ideas they propagated and the fundamental notions of the ancient Russian city republics, which justified their claims. They were in fact restoring liberty, and the whole nation, not only the nobility, would benefit from this.[84]

Glinka wrote of the need to bring ancient Russian liberty back to life:

> Freedom! Country! Sacred words!
> Will you forever be empty sounds?
> No, we'll bring you to life! Not tears and groaning . . .
> But sword and valour to freedom shall lead:
> We'll die or recover the golden rights,
> That our forefathers bought us with their blood!
> Death is a hundred times better than life in humiliation![85]

The same theme is found in Ryleev's writing. His *Dumy* (Meditations) is a cycle of poems about heroic episodes in Russia's past, intended to motivate the reader to fight against despotism. They were inspired by Ukrainian epic folk poems that revolved around historical events in the sixteenth and seventeenth centuries, when the Cossacks struggled for liberty against their oppressors.[86] In Ryleev's *duma* 'Vadim', the hero sacrifices himself for the people of Novgorod, defending them against the arbitrary rule of the prince. In the final section, Vadim expresses his desire to contribute to the restoration of his people's freedom:

> Oh! If I could restore
> To the enslaved people

The pledge of general bliss
The former freedom of our ancestors.[87]

Odoevskii, too, raised the topic of the historical struggle between the old republics of Novgorod and Pskov and autocratic Muscovy. In 'The Unknown Exile', the exiled patriots from Novgorod are accompanied by an 'unknown woman', who turns out to be the Goddess of Liberty. There is no home for her in Russia any more and she departs for heaven, exiled as are her fellow travellers.[88]

The historical link between modern and ancient republicanism was indicated in other ways as well. In the constitutions drawn up for the Northern and the Southern societies, the representative assembly was to be called the *narodnoe veche*, recalling assemblies of this name that had met in the medieval city republics of Novgorod and Pskov. Moreover, the Sacred Artel, a reformist group of officers on the General Staff founded by the Muraviev brothers, gathered at the sound of a bell that was supposed to evoke the old bell of the republic of Novgorod, once used to gather the city's popular assembly.[89] The title given by Pestel in 1824 to his plan for a constitution was *Russkaia pravda*, which deliberately recalled the law code promulgated by Iaroslav the Wise of Kyivan Rus' in the eleventh century. Kyivan Rus' was used as a 'liberal' contrast to the autocratic Muscovite state. In Kyiv, the Decembrists asserted, decisions about important affairs of the state were made by popular assemblies and the power of the prince was circumscribed.[90] Another historical reference is Pestel's choice of Nizhnii Novgorod as the new capital of Russia because of its free-thinking and patriotic history. The city was associated with Kuzma Minin and Dmitrii Pozharskii, known as the liberators of Russia from Polish invaders in 1613.[91] Pestel further proposed renaming the city to Vladimir, after the prince of Novgorod, Vladimir the Great.

# PART IV
# INCARCERATION
# AND SENTENCING

# 7

# Incarceration

He was made emperor, and right then
Displayed his flair and drive:
Sent to Siberia a hundred-twenty men
And strung up five.[1]

By six o'clock on the evening of 14 December 1825, the revolt in St Petersburg had been crushed. Most of the participants were arrested within forty hours of the regime's attack, some in the street, others at home or at friends' homes. The officers arrested after the second revolt in Ukraine were brought to St Petersburg in January. In total, about seven hundred officers and civilians were arrested, and about the same number of soldiers and sailors.[2] Those of lower rank were sent directly to the Peter and Paul Fortress established by Peter the Great in 1703 on a small island in the Neva River in St Petersburg, which served as a prison. The others were brought to the Winter Palace to be interrogated personally by the new emperor, Nicholas I.

Nicholas made every effort to make the revolutionary officers confess, sometimes by showing them sympathy, sometimes by intimidating them. The officers were struck by the arbitrariness of the procedure. Andrei Rozen was arrested at home on the morning of 15 December. He managed only a hasty farewell to his pregnant wife, Anna Vasilievna, before the regimental adjutant took him away.[3] Rozen was brought to the Winter Palace, where he waited until late in the evening, watching other arrested officers being ushered in through a glass door. When the field officer finally arrived for him, he was searched and escorted by soldiers to the emperor. However, as he waited outside the emperor's room, an adjutant suddenly appeared, telling him that Nicholas would not receive any more officers. Rozen was then brought to the guardhouse of the Horse Guards regiment, where he spent the following eight days.

On 21 December Rozen was taken back to the Winter Palace in a sledge. He was brought to the same place behind the glass doors, where he was again left to wait for several hours. At 10 p.m. he was escorted to the inner part of the palace and brought before Adjutant General Vasilii Levashov, the emperor's right-hand man. Levashov began to question him, writing down his answers to prepared questions. Suddenly a side door opened and the emperor entered. 'He looked me searchingly in the face for a minute and expressed his satisfaction with my former services,' Rozen recalled. 'He added that heavy charges were laid against me and that he expected me to make a full confession and ended by promising to do all that was possible to save me.' The emperor then withdrew. After half an hour he returned to read the paper on which Levashov had recorded Rozen's answers: 'He looked at me kindly and encouraged me to be candid.'[4]

Nikolai Bestuzhev also remembered that the emperor spoke kindly to him, promising to forgive him if he was loyal. Bestuzhev was arrested on 16 December and brought before the emperor, who told him, 'I could forgive you and if I had the assurance that from now on you would become a faithful servant – I would do it.'[5] Yet Bestuzhev, by his own account, did not just listen submissively to the words of the monarch. He immediately saw an opportunity to express his political convictions. He allegedly replied,

Sire, that is precisely what we are complaining about, that the emperor can do anything and that there is no law for him. In the name of God, let justice run its course and let the fate of your subjects in the future cease to depend on your whims and momentary impressions.[6]

Nicholas had a hard time understanding why these young noblemen did not cooperate when they had nothing to gain. Most difficult for him to comprehend was why members of the wealthiest and most venerable aristocratic families had taken part in the revolt. This frightened him, but also made him angry. He was furious that the Decembrists had broken their bonds of loyalty and chosen to serve the nation instead of the tsar, and he hated not having any power over them because they did not seek personal benefit. This explains why he felt such animosity towards people whom he knew personally.[7] Many witnesses noted that he was extremely agitated and found it difficult to contain his anger. Ivan Annenkov, who was arrested on 19 December, recalled how the emperor's face had a strange pallor. He spoke abruptly and Annenkov noticed a terrible excitement and anger, barely restrained. When Evgenii Obolenskii was brought in for questioning, the emperor swore at him. Nikolai Basargin was told in a threatening tone that he must tell the whole truth or he would surely regret it.[8]

Prince Sergei Volkonskii in particular incurred the wrath of the tsar. He belonged to one of the oldest and wealthiest noble families in Russia, and his mother was Mistress of the Robes to the Dowager Empress. Volkonskii was arrested on 7 January in Uman, Ukraine. Having been brought in haste to St Petersburg, he was led into the room in the Winter Palace where Adjutant General Levashov was sitting. Levashov went out for a few minutes and returned with the emperor, who warned Volkonskii that his fate depended on the sincerity of his testimony. 'Be frank and I promise you a pardon,' he said. Because of the special position of the Volkonskii family at court, Nicholas regarded Volkonskii's participation in the revolt not only as a betrayal, but as a personal affront. Worse still was his refusal to collaborate and incriminate his friends. Volkonskii's failure to respect the nobility's traditional duty of service and his disloyalty to the emperor seem to have made Nicholas feel the need to belittle him: 'Volkonskii . . . is a liar and a scoundrel in the fullest sense . . . Without answering anything, standing there like a fool, he presented the most disgusting example of an ungrateful villain and a stupid person.'[9] However, it was not just Prince Volkonskii who was subjected to condescending remarks from Nicholas. Artamon Muraviev was 'nothing but a murderer, an outcast without merits', while Obolenskii had 'a black soul' and 'a bestial and mean expression'.[10] They were all stupid, criminal or just plain evil in the eyes of the emperor.

Nicholas was in fact convinced that all liberals and free thinkers were evil. Nikolai Lorer writes about this. He was taken to the Winter Palace early in the morning of 4 January and brought to the brightly illuminated room, where Levashov was sitting at a table. The general told him to await the arrival of the sovereign behind some screens set in the corner. Lorer found an armchair there and sat down to wait. After a short while, Levashov came to fetch him. From the other end of the hall, the emperor came walking in the uniform coat of the Izmailovskii regiment, fastened with all the hooks and buttons. His face was pale, his hair dishevelled. 'I went to meet him with firm steps,' Lorer recalled,

> but he stopped me . . . with a movement of his hand, and he quietly approached me, measuring me with his eyes. I bowed respectfully. 'Do you know our laws,' he began . . . 'Do you know what fate awaits you? Death!' – And he ran his hand along his neck, as if my head

were separate from the body right there. Then he continued, much softer. 'You must tell me everything, otherwise you will perish.'

As Lorer repeated that he could add nothing more to his testimony, Nicholas listened attentively. Then, suddenly, he took Lorer by the shoulders, turned him towards the light of the lamp and boldly looked into his eyes. Lorer was shocked, but afterwards guessed that the emperor, according to his superstition, was looking for black eyes, assuming that all 'demonic' liberals (либералы) had them.[11] Aleksandr Gangeblov was also subjected to this behaviour on the part of the emperor and felt threatened by it. He described how he was suddenly face to face with the emperor, who was alone in the room in a frock coat without epaulettes. '"Come closer to me," he said. "I did everything I could do for you . . . So you don't want to confess? Look me straight in the eye! So you don't want to confess?"'[12]

The emperor's personal involvement in the case of the Decembrists demonstrates the importance he attached to the whole affair. Not only did he interrogate the suspects personally in the Winter Palace, but he issued orders indicating to the commandant of the Peter and Paul Fortress, General Aleksandr Sukin, how each prisoner should be treated: if he were to be fettered, placed under close supervision or allowed more liberty.[13] The order that Nicholas issued after Kondratii Ryleev's first interrogation in the Winter Palace read: 'to be placed in the Alekseevskii ravelin [that is, out-work], his hands not tied. He shall not be allowed any contact with others, but given paper to write on. Everything he writes is to be delivered personally to me each day.' Sergei Trubetskoi, with whom the emperor was particularly disappointed, was 'to be placed in the Alekseevskii ravelin and treated more severely than the others. In particular, he is not to be allowed out of his cell and is to have no contact with anyone.' Nikolai Bestuzhev and Obolenskii were ordered to be manacled and Ivan Iakushkin, who firmly declared to the tsar that he would not name any names, was to be chained so tightly that he could not move. Pavel Pestel, who also refused to talk, was placed in the Alekseevskii ravelin in chains. Nicholas was furious with him and described him as an 'evil-doer in the fullest sense of the word, showing not the slightest trace of remorse, with a bestial expression'. Furthermore, he had 'the most brazen audacity to deny everything . . . such a monster is rarely to be found'.[14]

Naturally, the emperor was deeply concerned about the threat to his life and his power, but his personal involvement was also part of a deliberate strategy to induce the Decembrists to confess. He played the role of the father who meted out righteous punishments to his children, but forgave them if they showed sincere repentance and confessed everything. To give the impression that he cared about them, Nicholas sent one of his adjutant generals to visit the prisoners once a month. In this way, he hoped they would open up and talk about their political convictions. The fortress priest was charged with calling for confessions. Psychological pressure was also used. The prisoners would receive letters from their unhappy relatives, who, being deceived by superficial politeness, praised the generosity of the tsar. Those prisoners who were reluctant to cooperate were punished in various ways, including by being put in shackles and left on a diet of bread and water.[15] Mikhail Lunin, who was particularly uncooperative, was deprived of food for eight days.

The chaining of noble prisoners was clearly a violation of the law, since the nobility was exempt from corporal punishment. Hence, from the very beginning of the process, the emperor made it clear to the Decembrists that their punishments would be personal and arbitrary and that their case would not receive due process of law. This created a sense of insecurity among the incarcerated officers and made them dependent on the emperor's goodwill.

## Captivity

The prisoners Nicholas detested the most were placed in the Alekseevskii ravelin of the Peter and Paul Fortress, a prison inside the prison, and the place of ultimate confinement. It had its own commandant, rules and procedures. About twenty Decembrists were placed there in single cells. It was in the western part of the fortress, above the moat, a place unknown to most people. To reach the ravelin you had to cross the moat using a little bridge that was guarded day and night at both ends.[16] After it came the entrance to a narrow corridor by a triangular stone building. Inside were twelve dark, damp casemates. In front of the windows was a high wall, which prevented daylight from entering. The inner triangle was enclosed by three walls, with one door and no windows. In the centre of the triangle was a tiny garden with two slim birches, a blackcurrant bush and a few yards of grass. Twice a week, prisoners were permitted to go outside, but they were not allowed to meet anyone.[17]

Once you reached Alekseevskii ravelin, you felt as if 'you could easily spend your whole life [there] without seeing anything but a piece of the sky and the tip of the Peter and Paul spire or just the angel on it.'[18] In his memoirs, Iakushkin recalled how in January he was taken there in shackles

Peter and Paul Fortress, St Petersburg.

weighing 10 kilograms (22 lb). They were not removed until 14 April. His cell was six paces long and four wide. The walls were covered with stains from the flood of 1824; the windows were painted over with white paint, and a firm iron grille was set into the wall in front of them. By the window stood a bed with a mattress and a cotton blanket. A small table was by the bed, with a mug of water on it. There was a stove in one corner and a latrine in another. Two chairs made up the remaining furniture, one with a night light on it. 'Left alone I was perfectly happy,' he recalled. 'Torture had been passed over this time.'[19]

In another part of the fortress, Lorer was brought to his cell. He was told to undress and the Platz-Major subjected him to a strip search, after which he was given a smelly robe and a pair of shoes. The guard lit an earthen bowl (an oil lamp made from clay) and left. The door closed, and he heard a huge iron bolt slam shut. Writing about the experience many years afterwards, Lorer could still vividly recall the sound of the key in the padlock and the deadly silence that ensued. The cell was three steps in length and the same width. Along one wall stood a green hospital bed with a mattress and a soiled pillow. The small window was white with chalk. 'I fell asleep from physical and spiritual exhaustion. So everything ended for me in the 32nd year of my life, January 4, 1826.'[20] Lorer was so exhausted that he hardly noticed the water rats. Huge, reddish and plump, they had grown so bold that they walked right over him. Other prisoners told of cockroaches and woodlice in huge quantities. Aleksandr Poggio's damp, dark cell was full of bedbugs and fleas. There was a wooden bed with a thin mattress stuffed with a coarse washcloth, and a flat pillow covered with a dirty, thick sackcloth. Poggio took his coat of bear fur, which he had been wearing when he was arrested, placed it on the bed and used it as a nest.

The first night in captivity was the worst. Even thirty years afterwards, Basargin remembered the despair he felt when the door was locked from the outside and he was placed in solitary confinement: 'All your relations with the world are severed, all ties are severed. You remain alone before an autocratic, unlimited power, indignant at you, that can do whatever it wants with you.' The memories of the first night in the casemate remained vivid:

> On the one hand, the memories of the past, still so fresh, on the other, all the horror of the present and the hopeless future. Several times at night, I jumped up from my rigid bed and did not understand where I was. There was no sleep, but a kind of painful slumber ... The morning found me completely exhausted.[21]

Recalling his first night in the fortress, Poggio concluded that 'sleep was the most difficult test, because afterwards you wake up in the same dungeon with the same locks, the same hopeless, humiliating situation!'[22]

All the cells in the fortress were cramped, damp, dark and dirty. Basargin was assigned a casemate in the crownwork curtain wall. It was four paces in length and width, and its window, too, was smeared with chalk. There was an infirmary bed, a table and a small iron stove. He was undressed and everything was taken away, even his wedding ring. Instead, he was given two shirts, a pair of trousers, a frock coat and a hospital robe. Rozen was also incarcerated in the crownwork curtain wall. His cell was almost pitch-dark; the window was secured with a thick iron grating through which only a narrow strip of the horizon and part of the glacis could be seen. Against the further wall of the three-cornered cell stood a bed with a blue-grey coverlet; against the other, a table and a bench. The room was dark even at midday because the window was set in a deep embrasure. Towards evening, a lamp was brought in, but there was nothing to read. In the first months of their confinement the prisoners were not allowed any books, or any type of distraction at all. They barely got any exercise. This left too much room for contemplation. 'Alone, confined in a narrow room, there was no exercise for the body, no distraction for the mind; thought alone was free,' Rozen remembered. 'The future stretched before me, uncertain and drear; the present offered nothing; only the past remained to me.'[23]

The fact that the prisoners were under constant surveillance added to their feeling of distress. Set in each cell door was a little window with a linen curtain outside that the sentries could raise at any moment in order to watch the prisoners. Many Decembrist prisoners were annoyed by this window and found the fact that the sentry was constantly peering into their cell very painful. Whether they moved, coughed or prayed, his head would appear in the opening. The worst aspect of imprisonment, however, was the isolation. The prisoners were deprived of all social interaction and were not allowed to talk to one another. This was part of the regime's strategy to break them so that they would confess and reveal everything.

Yet they found other ways of communicating. In the absence of books and conversation, Rozen sang prose and poetry of his own, as well as many traditional songs. Gangeblov sang arias by Rossini and Weber, but he whistled too. When he had whistled his first aria, he heard a timid round of applause from his neighbour and several whistles in return. This type of interaction was essential for solitary prisoners. Sometimes singing was used as a more direct form of communication. Mikhail Pushchin, Ivan's younger brother, communicated with his neighbour, Sergei Krivtsov, by singing. The guards did not seem to object, but this was not always the case. When Mikhail Bestuzhev tried to communicate by whistling, the guard stopped him. Then he developed an elaborate system of knocks to communicate with his neighbours.[24] He was in cell no. 14 in the Alekseevskii ravelin. His brother Nikolai was in the cell next to him, no. 15, while Aleksandr Odoevskii was in no. 16 and Ryleev in no. 17. Nikolai recalled how he gradually re-established relations with his brother by means of the alphabet he had invented by tapping on the wall. 'We conversed freely,' he recalled. Yet all his attempts to explain the alphabet to Odoevskii, who was in the cell next to him on the other side, failed. Thus Nikolai could not communicate with Ryleev, who was on the other side of Odoevskii.[25]

Singing was not only used to communicate with fellow prisoners. Lorer recalled how the incarcerated men conversed with their relatives by singing to them when they passed the fortress in boats. Through the embrasure, he could see the palace embankment. In the evening, having clambered up to the large window with its grille, he could breathe in the light wind from the river. He reckoned that his neighbours were probably family men, for he often managed to catch sight of boats, 'filled with people of different sexes and ages, darting about below our windows . . . Oarsmen looked up at the embrasures and, as it was impossible to talk, sang and so conveyed to their relations what they wished to tell them.' Aleksandra Muravieva and her mother-in-law, Ekaterina Fedorovna, were in one of these boats, although on the other side of the fortress from where Lorer sat. They spent hours sailing past the walls of the fortress, waving their handkerchiefs in the hope that Nikita would notice them.[26]

Ryleev found an unusual means of communication. He was fortunate in that one of his guards agreed to deliver a message to Obolenskii. Obolenskii, who had not realized that Ryleev was also in the Alekseevskii ravelin, was overjoyed when the kind guard brought a message from him, written on the back of two maple leaves. He put them at the back of the room, in the far corner, where the sentry's eyes did not penetrate: 'I received the first message from him on 21 January; when reading the few lines my joy was immeasurable. The warm soul of Ryleev did not cease to love ardently, sincerely.' At first, Obolenskii could not think how to answer his comrade: 'I had no art to preserve pen, ink and paper. There was no place to hide these things ... Everything was so open.' He later found a way to write with a thick needle on a few scraps of grey-brown paper: 'For a long time, in the most concise terms possible, I pricked up everything that asked for the recalcitrant weapon of my writing, and after labouring for about two days my soul was calm and I gave my note to the same kind guard.'[27]

Despite these alternative modes of interaction, the order not to allow the prisoners any contact with other people did fulfil its purpose of weakening their mental faculties. The men felt terribly isolated, and this feeling was reinforced by what was called 'the silent treatment', which meant that the guards did not speak to the prisoners. They only watched them through the little window in the door every fifteen minutes. The guards would not even answer simple questions, such as what day it was. The mute servants and the mute attendants made everything appear to be covered with 'a darkness of obscurity'.[28] 'Whoever has not experienced the misfortune of being imprisoned in a dungeon without books ... without light and the sounds of lively conversation, will not understand its full burden,' Lorer noted later. Left completely to their own thoughts, and with nothing to distract them, some prisoners actually lost their wits; others attempted to take their own lives by beating their head against the wall or swallowing broken glass.[29]

Annenkov was one of those who tried to kill himself. Owing to the large number of rebels imprisoned after the revolt was suppressed, there were not enough casemates in the Peter and Paul Fortress, so the buildings that served as barracks for the garrison were converted into a prison. The windowpanes were covered with chalk and glue so that the sun's rays could not penetrate. Cells were made of logs, arranged to ensure that all communication between them was impossible. These casemates were extremely cramped, measuring only two or three paces diagonally, and an iron pipe ran through some of them, making them unbearably hot. In this way, 140 temporary cells were constructed. Still, despite these efforts, the fortress did not have room for everyone arrested and arrangements were made to transfer prisoners to other fortresses.

Annenkov was brought to Vyborg Fortress, where conditions were not too bad. The officers and soldiers who made up the guards were kind and sensitive people who, learning of his fate, sent him pretzels and other provisions, even socks of their own making. However, in March 1826 Annenkov was brought back to St Petersburg for interrogation, after which he was placed in a cell in the Peter and Paul Fortress. It was a small room with a vault that made it possible to stand up straight only in the middle of the cell. The pipe was dripping, and the cell was full of lice. His first thought was that he had been placed in a grave. He found it unbearable and started a hunger strike. The prison authorities' response was to threaten him with force-feeding by pouring hot broth down his throat, and with isolation in a rat-infested cell. Annenkov held out for three days before giving up. Late that autumn, he tried to hang himself.

Annenkov's regiment friend, Aleksandr Muraviev, had a similar experience. Muraviev spent four months in Reval Fortress in the care of Colonel Sherman, 'an excellent man', who provided him with books, paper, pencils and other things he needed. Sherman's wife even sent him fruit. But on 1 May Muraviev, who had recently turned 24, was sent back to St Petersburg. He was led into a dirty, damp, gloomy, cramped cell. A broken table, a vile bed and an iron chain made up the furnishing. After a journey of 580 kilometres (360 mi.), he was exhausted. When the parade-major left, he rushed to the bed and heard the bolts of the two doors to his cell slam shut. 'Here I am alone, cut off from life! I spent hours lying down, thinking about my mother, about my brother . . . Tears gushed from my eyes.'[30]

## The investigating committee

An investigating committee (in May renamed investigating commission) was appointed days after the revolt on Senate Square. Its purpose was to investigate the uprising and the crimes of which the participants were suspected. However, the committee never intended to make an impartial investigation in accordance with the law. Aleksandr Muraviev called it an inquisitorial tribunal, 'without a shadow of justice', whose members were ignorant of the law. The proceedings were arbitrary and intended solely to extort confessions. An important purpose of the interrogations was to make the Decembrists name other members of the Society and to reveal the whereabouts of significant documents. But the main intention of the committee was to make them admit to plans of regicide.

Pestel's announcement that he considered regicide a prerequisite for the creation of a republic led the committee to focus on this subject. Any plan to assassinate the tsar constituted an immediate threat to the regime and had to be investigated. However, the committee was also aware that presenting the Decembrists as regicides would make them unpopular among the people. It was more than a little ironic that two committee members had been implicated in the assassination of Paul I in 1801, something Lunin was not slow to point out. When asked about the secret society and regicide, he answered, 'Gentlemen, the Secret Society never had the goal of regicide, since its goal is nobler and more lofty. But, as you know, this idea does not represent anything new in Russia.'[31]

During the seven months the committee was in session, it convened 146 times and conducted 2,083 interrogations.[32] The meetings, which were most often held in the house of the commandant of the Peter and Paul Fortress, were long, especially during the first months, and frequently lasted from six in the evening late into the night. The committee was chaired by the minister of war, A. I. Tatishchev, with his assistant A. D. Borovkov serving as secretary. Its members, appointed by Nicholas, included the tsar's younger brother Grand Duke Mikhail Pavlovich, State Secretary Dmitrii Bludov, St Petersburg Governor General Pavel Golenishchev-Kutuzov, the former minister of education and spiritual affairs Prince Aleksandr Golitsyn, Generals A. N. Potapov, Vasilii Levashov, Aleksandr Chernyshev, Alexander von Benckendorff and I. I. Dibich, and Wing Adjutant V. F. Adlerberg, who was present to take notes.

The committee did everything in its power to make the Decembrists cooperate. All means were acceptable: pressure, threats, warnings, exhortations, intimidation, promises, false statements, straight-out lies, psychological torture and corporal punishment in the form of manacles, shackles and the withholding of sleep, light, food and drink. The committee confused the prisoners, intimidated them, made promises it never intended to keep, presented perverted or fictional testimonies, and made threats of direct confrontation.[33] Levashov had already hinted at torture when interrogating the arrested officers in the Winter Palace; several prisoners later recalled him saying that 'there were ways to make them talk.'[34]

The most frequent tactic was to assure a prisoner that his friend had confessed everything. Sometimes the committee showed the prisoner a genuine signature of a friend on a sheet of paper, then read out something other than what was written on the paper above it. The confused prisoner, who believed that everything was already known, was then convinced to sign the paper. Some were persuaded that a full confession would save them. Others were told that only the main culprits would be punished, and everyone else would be pardoned. A few, who tried to confess to everything, were deliberately misunderstood and made to admit to things they had not done or said. Other prisoners, such as Midshipman Vasilii Divov, one of the youngest participants in the revolt and an ardent republican, made up things that the committee believed in. In an attempt to give weight to all the Society's actions and render the revolt meaningful for posterity, Ryleev tried to represent the Society to the committee as much more important than it really was. As a consequence, he often made testimonies about things that never existed.[35] Furthermore, according to Rozen, Ryleev took all the blame, asking the committee to execute him and save the others. During interrogation, he constantly appealed to the tsar, asking him to treat his comrades leniently.

Another strategy for breaking down the prisoners and taking advantage of their weakness was to subject them to constant interrogation. They were often awakened in the middle of the night and taken to the commandant's house. Many had both hands and feet in fetters, and some were blindfolded. The entire procedure was intended to confuse them and make them anxious – and it was often successful. Prisoners worried about their loved ones and about accidentally implicating their friends during interrogation. Some were not able to withstand the psychological pressure and tried to exculpate themselves or, in a few cases, to shift the blame on to others. Prisoners often lost consciousness while being interrogated. A doctor was normally present in an adjoining room in case help was needed. Many of the prisoners were made ill by the interrogations.[36]

Basargin was grateful that he had not been called before the investigating committee during his first two weeks in captivity, when he was morally weak and depressed. In such a state, he could easily have said things that he would come to regret. This happened to Mikhail Bestuzhev-Riumin, who was placed in the cell next to Basargin. Bestuzhev-Riumin, who was very young and impressionable, was continually interrogated and tricked into implicating others. This affected his mental health. He was sometimes unusually cheerful, but at other times terribly gloomy. As the date of the verdict approached, he asked Basargin to explain to his friends that he had been tortured by the committee and never intended to speak about them during the investigation. Basargin's own experiences in the fortress made him realize that solitude, material deprivation and physical suffering affect people in different ways. Some endure them calmly; others give in to them completely and act contrary to their convictions. This understanding prevented him from placing blame on individuals who tried to earn forgiveness by showing repentance.

The emperor and the committee used a number of tricks and elaborate strategies to obtain confessions. One was to take advantage of the prisoners' personal relationships. Many had young wives and children about whom they worried and towards whom they felt obligations. By granting prisoners the right to write letters to their wives, the authorities made use of these feelings. Unbeknown to them, the wives were used to pressurize the prisoners to cooperate. Nicholas also exploited the prisoners' sense of gratitude for being granted this privilege.

Trubetskoi had received permission to write to his wife, Ekaterina, when he was interrogated in the Winter Palace the day after the revolt. He was a colonel from one of the noblest families in the country, so it was especially important to Nicholas that he should confess. During the interrogation, the tsar instructed Trubetskoi to inform his wife that he was alive and well. This is what he wrote to Ekaterina:

> I have ruined you, but not with malicious intent. Do not be angry with me, my angel, you alone are still tying me to life, but I am afraid that you will have to drag out an unhappy life, and perhaps it would be easier for you if I were not there at all. My fate is in the hands of the sovereign, but I have no means to convince him of any sincerity ... God save you, my friend. Forgive me.[37]

The very next day, Ekaterina replied: 'Whatever fate awaits you, be sure that everything will be easy and good for me with you. In my eyes ... and against me you can never be guilty.'[38]

The first days in the fortress were difficult for Trubetskoi. He suffered great remorse and struggled with his different loyalties – to the emperor, to the Society and to his wife. On 23 December he was summoned for questioning, but he refused to provide the answers the emperor wanted. As punishment, Nicholas revoked his permission to write letters, and made it clear to Ekaterina that if Sergei did not confess everything, their right to correspond – their only opportunity to communicate – would be taken from them. Ekaterina could not endure the thought of losing contact with her husband. It bears emphasizing here that the couple were under immense pressure, since they did not know how Sergei would be punished in the end. Execution was a very real possibility. On 25 December Sergei received a letter from his wife urging him to admit to everything: 'Confess, my angel, what is required of you . . . do not deprive me of one consolation that supported me . . . they want you to confess things that they already know without you . . . Oh, have pity on me, for Christ's sake.'[39] It is obvious that the emperor was using her to pressurize her husband to confess. Sergei decided that his loyalty to her was of the most importance and resolved to do what she wanted. He had ruined her life and wished to do everything he could to make amends. Her peace of mind was his only goal.

On 27 December Trubetskoi was granted the tsar's permission to correspond with his wife, on the recommendation of the investigating committee, 'in recognition of the full and frank testimony of Prince Trubetskoi on the membership and purpose of the society'.[40] After a period of 'fear and unspeakable anxiety', the correspondence between the spouses resumed.[41] But the emperor continued to pressurize them. A few days later Nicholas promised to allow them a meeting. 'If you continue sincerely and frankly to confess everything, as you have now begun to do,' Ekaterina wrote to Sergei on 31 December, '. . . they hope to allow us a meeting.'[42] This promise inspired great hopes. 'I look forward to a blissful moment when I hold you to my heart,' Sergei wrote. 'Just like you, my dear friend, I am incomparably calmer since I have this unexpected hope.'[43]

The correspondence with his wife was tremendously important to Trubetskoi. Unlike many other prisoners, he did not have to live in uncertainty regarding his family. Ekaterina's letters gave him comfort and hope and made him trust in God. His letters to her are brimming with love and yearning. 'My friend, my life, my consolation, I kiss and embrace you with all the fervour of my soul,' he wrote on 23 December. Yet he also had strong feelings of remorse: 'The thought of what fate I have prepared for you cannot but be heavy for me'; 'How sad it is for me when I think that I have forever driven away the smile from your sweet face, that tears are all the consolation that I have left you.'[44]

Ekaterina's letters to Sergei reciprocate his feelings of love and show that she is prepared to give up everything for him: 'I really feel that I cannot live without you. I am ready to take everything with you . . . I will calmly say goodbye to all secular blessings. One thing can make me happy: to see you, to share your grief . . . and to devote all the minutes of my life to you.'[45] She is concerned about her husband's health, both physical and mental. Above all, she fears that he will indulge in melancholy, despondency and despair: 'We cannot expect bright happiness . . . but not everything is lost for us. When we are together, we will support each other through mutual love.'[46] Sergei, in turn, is worried about his wife's health; that she will not be able to cope with all the sorrow and anxiety: 'I need you both in this life and for the future; through you only can I have any consolation, and only through you can I be saved. For God's sake preserve yourself . . . do not indulge in so much sadness.'[47]

The meeting that Nicholas had promised them finally took place on 19 April. This encounter filled them with hope and calm and revived their feelings and spiritual strength. Afterwards, Sergei wrote to Ekaterina: 'When after the first tears I saw a joyful smile on your face, when I saw pleasure written on it instead of sadness, then all my sadness was dispersed and I had nothing left in my heart but joy.'[48]

However, the more time passed, the more anxious both Sergei and Ekaterina became about his sentence. They encouraged each other to be prepared for anything. When, at one point, Ekaterina despaired, Sergei wrote that they must trust in God's plan for them; that they must not offend him by despairing but must trust that if they are not allowed to see each other again, he will give them the strength to cope. Otherwise, he warned, they might be punished. Yet Sergei did not trust in God alone. When reading his letters from this period, it is possible to discern a more active strategy. Being aware that all letters are read, presumably even by Nicholas himself, he is providing the emperor with grounds for showing mercy. Sergei flatters Nicholas and talks about how big-hearted he is, what compassion he shows. In his letters, Trubetskoi tells his wife that even though he is guilty and has no right to make demands, he still has hopes, because the greater the sin, the greater the mercy: 'Do not think, my dear friend, that I suppose to have any right to the sovereign's mercy, but everything proves that he wants to be truly merciful to everyone . . . The greatness of transgression cannot stop mercy.'[49] Three weeks later, Sergei wrote, 'I rely in everything on the sovereign's mercy . . . I am absolutely sure that if he could follow the movement of his heart, he would tell me: "Go, I completely forgive you and I forget everything that happened."'[50]

Other prisoners were also granted the right to communicate with their wives as part of an elaborate strategy to exploit their personal relationships and their sense of gratitude. Ryleev, who was showing signs of being accommodating, was given the privilege of corresponding with his wife.[51] He was promised forgiveness from the tsar in return for a full confession; his wife, Natalia, was told the same thing. According to his friend Nikolai Bestuzhev, every means was used to force Ryleev to talk.[52] The emperor even sent money to Natalia, who after his arrest found herself in a financially difficult situation. She was immensely grateful. 'My friend, I do not know with what feelings or words to explain the incomprehensible mercy of our monarch,' she wrote in her first letter to her husband in the fortress. 'The day before yesterday, God made me happy. The emperor sent your note and then 2000 r[oubles].'[53] A couple of days later, on their daughter Anastasia's name day, Empress Aleksandra Fedorovna sent Natalia 1,000 roubles as a gift.[54]

The emperor's strategy worked. Natalia urged Kondratii to atone for his deed and return the mercy and love of the emperor, 'the father of our fatherland'. Kondratii replied that 'the graces shown to them by the Sovereign and Empress' had cut deeply into his heart; 'Perhaps they will let me see you.'[55] No such meeting took place, however, and Natalia was deeply disappointed: 'I hoped from your letters that I would soon see and consult with you, my friend, but to this day there is no date.'[56] In fact, they were not allowed to see each other until June. Still, Kondratii kept his hopes up. Like many inmates, he appears to have become profoundly religious in captivity. On 15 February he told his wife that he had 'completely surrendered to His holy will', and as a result had 'completely calmed down'. Now, he placed all his hopes in 'the Creator'.[57] Ryleev believed in the tsar's mercy to the bitter end. Barely seven weeks before the sentence was pronounced, he told his wife that, 'no matter how great my crime is, to this day they treat me not as a criminal, but as an unfortunate one, therefore do not indulge in despair.'[58]

Like Ekaterina Trubetskaia, Natalia found the opportunity to communicate with her husband precious. 'If it were not for the royal mercy over us, I would no longer be able to bear it. With every letter you write, I receive new strength and hope,' she told Kondratii on 25 January.[59] The awareness of the importance the wives attached to this correspondence affected their husbands in prison. They all expressed strong feelings of guilt. 'My dear friend,' Kondratii wrote, 'I am cruelly guilty before you and her [Anastasia]. Forgive me, for the sake of the Saviour.'[60] Natalia replied that she did not blame him; she knew he never wished to hurt anyone, neither his family nor anyone else. She is quite outspoken in her letters and writes openly about her feelings of love, but in Kondratii's there is very little of the Romantic poet. His letters most often concern practical matters. Perhaps his feelings for his young wife were not that strong, or perhaps he felt a need to hold them back if he were to be able to endure his captivity.

Nikita Muraviev, too, was allowed to write to his wife, Aleksandra Grigorievna. She was only 21 but was expecting her third child.[61] In his first letter to her, dated nine days after his arrest, Nikita's feelings of guilt are evident. He was arrested on 20 December while visiting his wife's estate, where he had been since November. When they parted, Aleksandra told him not to worry, because he had done nothing wrong. He did not reply at the time, but in a letter from the Peter and Paul Fortress, dated 29 December, he confessed:

> Yes, my angel, I am guilty – I am one of the leaders of this newly exposed society. I am guilty before you, who so often asked me not to have any secrets from you. I should have been virtuous. How many times during our marriage did I want to reveal to you the fatal secret? My vow of silence, and above all false shame, hid from my eyes all the cruelty and carelessness of what I did, linking your fate with the fate of a criminal ... My angel, falling at your feet, I beg you for forgiveness.[62]

Unbeknown to Nikita, Aleksandra had followed him to St Petersburg, where she arrived on 30 December. Reading his letter all alone, she was crushed by grief, but did not hesitate to forgive him. In her second letter to him, dated 2 January 1826, she tells him:

> When I wrote to you for the first time, your mother had not yet given me your letter. It came like a bolt from the blue! You are a criminal! You are a guilty one! This does not fit in my poor head ... You ask me for forgiveness. Do not talk to me like that, you break my heart. I have nothing to forgive.[63]

Aleksandra further begs him not to despair, and tells him that he has made her happy. Then she adds: 'Do not lose courage, maybe you can still be useful to your Emperor and correct the past.'[64] Quite possibly this was a call on her husband to confess.

Nikita read his wife's letters and her declarations of love with emotion. He did not mention the emperor in his reply but wrote that his soul had been cleansed. The letter ended with the words: 'You don't need to ask me to love you, you know that I love you with all the strength that my soul is capable of. I hug you a thousand and a thousand times.'[65] That letter was dated 3 January, the very day he was granted permission to receive letters. Two days later he gave a detailed testimony to the investigating committee. That day, he wrote to Aleksandra that he was very happy about the opportunity to hear from her every day – 'a happiness for which we can never be grateful enough'. He then expressed remorse for participating in the preparations for a revolt: 'Every day, with tears, I pray to the Lord to forgive me for participating in this madness and lawlessness and for working on the creation of this new tower of Babel.' Whether this was sincere or a way of feigning submission in the eyes of the tsar is impossible to know, but it is evident that the right to correspondence was of great importance to Nikita. 'Receiving your letters is a great celebration for me,' he told his wife. 'Reading them touches me, makes me cry, but at the same time it is also a consolation that gives me hope.'[66] The fact that Nikita asked Aleksandra to conceal compromising evidence casts doubt on any genuine feelings of remorse. In mid-February he managed to smuggle a letter to her. 'My good friend,' he wrote,

> I ask you to review my letters, which are in the bureau in the large office, and take to yourself those that seem dangerous to you, if there are any . . . Remove from the books that are in the left glass cabinet, all those that are titled 'constitution', the well-bound book of rights of man, the writings of [Jeremy] Bentham, which stand together, as well as commentaries on the spirit of the laws . . . As for my study books in the bureau, put them where the military-related notebooks are. This is a precaution against searches, as these notebooks contain verses that could be compromising.[67]

On 19 January Nikita was unexpectedly allowed to meet Aleksandra briefly in the fortress. 'I still cannot recover from joy and surprise,' he wrote to her afterwards.

> How quickly this moment passed. But, still, this is one of the happiest days of my life – you were hope embodied for me. You appeared before me as a comforting angel . . . I hug you a thousand and a thousand times and kiss your hands with all the tenderness that I have for you. Goodbye, my angel, I love you more than life.[68]

The correspondence between Nikita and Aleksandra exhibits a close, warm and loving relationship. For a father in the early nineteenth century, he took an unusual interest in their two small children. 'I am delighted with what you write to me about the children, which means that Mikhail's teeth suddenly erupted,' he wrote to Aleksandra on 5 January 1826. He craved information about their daily life and development: 'Write to me if Katya has changed – has she kept her sly little face? Has Mikhail changed a lot? How is their day going?'[69] 'Do they play as they once did on the carpet in the large living room upstairs?'[70] 'You cannot imagine how interested I am in all the details that you tell me about the children. I think I can see both of them with their drum. Katya, it seems, will be an Amazon, since already at this age she is so fond of military music.'[71] Although Nikita asked about the children, he was even more concerned about his pregnant wife. He reminded her constantly of the importance of fresh air and exercise. Like Trubetskoi, he worried that too much grief and anxiety would harm his wife, and asked Aleksandra to trust in God and submit to his will: 'Now you and the children will be the only purpose of my existence, if the Lord permits it.'[72] On 15 March, with Nikita still in prison, Aleksandra gave birth to a girl, Liza.

On 3 May Muraviev was transferred from cell no. 4 to cell no. 1 in the Ioannovskii ravelin, the eastern fortification of the Peter and Paul Fortress. It was a vast improvement to his circumstances. In a note sent by messenger to Aleksandra, he told her that he now had 'a pretty room on the second floor with a large window'. Best of all, he was separated from his neighbour by a wooden wall, which gave him the opportunity to talk and even transmit his thoughts through him to the neighbours on the other side: 'My health is very good, and I confess that I feel incomparably more lively here than in the previous place, where I was absolutely deprived of any society.' In the new quarters, Muraviev was even able to play chess with his neighbour. Each man made a board and small pieces of paper for themselves, communicating their moves through the wall. Aleksandra was now allowed to send him things, such as books, oranges, lemons and preserves. Muraviev was happy to be able to provide his neighbours with these little luxuries.[73]

As the date of the sentencing approached, Muraviev became nervous and admonished his wife to be careful. In an uncensored message smuggled out of prison, he explained to her that if his letters were restrained, it was owing to the strict censorship in the fortress:

> Be very careful and restrained in your words if you do not want to cause irreparable harm to me, your brother and everyone. You

know what gossips and talkers are here . . . You can never be sure that a word spoken between two people will not become known to the whole city in a few days, and you should not rely on a person's modesty – this is what is most important.[74]

In a note to his mother, sent at the same time as this message to his wife, Muraviev cautioned her as well: 'Become extremely distrustful. Do not make any hints in letters – this can further increase suspicions.'[75]

Twenty-six-year-old Andrei Rozen, who had married Anna Vasilievna eight months before his arrest, was given permission to write to her once a month. But letters could be only a few lines long. Even if the answers Anna wrote also had to be brief, they were of great comfort to Andrei. On 20 May he was finally allowed to meet his pregnant wife:

> In the Commandant's House, I once more held my wife in my arms. To see her face, to hear her voice, to listen to her words once again filled my heart with joy and comfort, but as the Fortress Commandant was present during the whole interview, we could not converse at ease . . . The time of her confinement was approaching and she wished that we could once more receive each other's blessing.[76]

A son was born on 19 June, but Rozen did not learn the news until three days later. He had been very concerned about his wife, but a few lines from her comforted him. He blessed his son in his thoughts but entertained no hope of ever seeing him.[77] Despite – or perhaps because of – their unfortunate situation, a child meant a lot to the prisoners. When Iakushkin received a letter from his wife telling him that she had successfully given birth to a son (his second), and that she and the children were well, he was blissfully happy, holding himself to be 'the most fortunate fellow in all of St Petersburg'.[78]

Over time, the investigating committee meetings became less frequent. The Decembrists, awaiting trial, were told that they would be tried in the senate with doors open. They therefore expected that they would be able to defend themselves, but in this they turned out to be horribly wrong. The inquiry was biased from the start. Afterwards, Lorer was convinced that if the accused had been given a proper defence, half of them would have been acquitted.[79] Not only were testimonies perverted, enforced or deliberately misunderstood, but everything that was favourable to the accused was omitted in the reports of denunciations.[80] Most of the Decembrists preferred not to talk about the trials in exile, but some, among them Mikhail Fonvizin, continued to be angry long afterwards.[81]

On 30 May 1826 the investigating committee presented its report, after which the cases were transferred to a special supreme criminal court. This court held sessions for nine days, beginning on 3 June. Prisoners were not called before the court but were visited in their cells by a subcommittee. They were asked to confirm whether the statements read before the commission had been correct, and if their signature was authentic. In fact, what they had told the commission played less of a role in the court's decision than the replies they had written to a set of questions.

# 8

# Sentencing

On 9 July 1826 the court passed sentence on the prisoners and forwarded it to the emperor. In total, 579 people were brought to trial, of whom 290 were acquitted. Of the remaining 289, the court singled out 121 as the conspirators most responsible for the revolt, and those were branded state criminals. Of these men, 61 were members of the Northern Society, 37 of the Southern Society and 23 of the United Slavs. The average age of these state criminals was 27.4 years.[1] Most were sentenced to between ten and twenty years of hard labour in Siberia and/or exile for life, but 31 were sentenced to death by decapitation. This sentence was later commuted to penal labour and exile for life, and the loss of rank and property. The court also recommended that one group of five convicts, who 'by the particular character and gravity of their crimes could not be categorized', should be executed by quartering.[2] This group consisted of Pavel Pestel, Kondratii Ryleev, Piotr Kakhovskii, Mikhail Bestuzhev-Riumin and Sergei Muraviev-Apostol. By suggesting such a barbaric sentence, the court allowed the tsar to appear merciful. As expected, Nicholas told the court that he preferred a less cruel punishment. The sentence that was subsequently meted out to the five leaders was execution by hanging.

Still, the members of the educated elite were horrified at the brutal severity of the sentences. The writer Aleksandr Herzen, who was fourteen at the time, later recalled:

> Everyone expected some mitigation of the sentence on the con-demned men . . . Even my father, in spite of his caution and his scepticism, said the death penalty would not be carried out, and that all this was done merely to impress people. But, like everyone else, he knew little of the youthful monarch.[3]

The Russian people had grown unaccustomed to the death penalty since the days of Catherine II, and public opinion had shifted against it. In fact, capital punishment had not been used since the execution of Yemelyan Pugachev, the leader of the Pugachev Rebellion, in 1775. This is probably why Nicholas was careful to point out that it was not he who sentenced the five Decembrist leaders to death, but the court.[4]

The foot soldiers and junior officers who had taken part in the uprising were convicted by military courts and mostly sentenced to transfer to battalions fighting in the Caucasus. Many were punished by having to run the gauntlet, which meant that they were dragged up to twelve times through a line of 1,000 soldiers, each of whom hit them on the back with a rifle. These soldiers thereby received between 10,000 and 12,000 blows, which was tantamount to being beaten to death. A few were also sentenced to hard labour and sent to Siberia with the regular convoy of common criminals.[5]

Nicholas was concerned about the impact the sentences would have on civil society, particularly the hangings – and rightly so. Thus everything was carefully prepared.[6] Neither the reading of the sentences nor the executions was public. Instead, the idea was that they would have an important symbolic value to all the soldiers and civil servants who participated in these actions.[7]

On the morning of 12 July 1826, the criminal court convened in the senate building to sign the sentences that had been approved by the tsar. Escorted by a squadron of cavalry guards, its members were ordered to proceed to the house of the commandant of the Peter and Paul Fortress, to communicate the sentences to the prisoners. The prisoners noticed that there was a lot of activity in the fortress, but they had no idea what was happening. A large number of carriages, cavalry guards and a platoon of gendarmes were moving as in a funeral procession to the commandant's house. First, the five men condemned to death were brought before the criminal court to receive the verdict and their sentence. They were then held together in the crownwork curtain wall. Subsequently, all the other prisoners were ordered to get ready and led through the backyard into the commandant's house. They were grouped in different rooms according to their sentence category. Nikolai Basargin recalled entering a room and finding about twenty of his companions in various outfits: some in full uniform, others in tailcoats and yet others in robes. The meeting of these prisoners, who had been held in solitary confinement for so long, was joyful, as he recalled: 'We were all very cheerful; greeted, embraced, talked to each

Aleksandr Polyakov, *Emperor Nicholas I*, 1829, oil on canvas.

other and completely forgot what fate awaited us. Everyone was happy to meet, even if just for a minute, after six months of solitary confinement.'[8] Nikolai Lorer had a similarly happy experience. He was led into a large room and, to his great surprise, found many of his old acquaintances there, among them Mikhail Fonvizin and Mikhail Naryshkin of the Northern Society. There were about twenty people in the room. No one knew why they were gathered there or had any idea that other prisoners were assembled in adjacent rooms.

According to many accounts, what followed felt to the prisoners like a surreal spectacle. The parade-major told them to leave their rooms in a specific order. They passed through several rooms until they found themselves suddenly in a large hall in front of all the members of the supreme criminal court. The judges were sitting on benches in two tiers, near tables covered with red cloth and arranged in a rectangle. Opposite the court sat the clergy, members of the Holy Synod; to the right were members of the State Council; to the left on benches and chairs sat senators in red uniforms. Everyone was dressed as for a grand gala. On a stand placed in the middle of the room was a book of some kind. At the stand stood the minister of justice, Dmitrii Lobanov-Rostovskii, with the chief secretary of the senate, Ivan Zhuravlev. The hall was hot, stuffy and completely silent. According to several accounts, Zhuravlev suddenly began to read out the sentence in a loud, distinct voice: '"Major General Fonvizin, by his own admission of this and that, is deprived of all rights of state, ranks, decorations and is referred to hard labour for twelve years and then to exile for life," and so on to the end.'[9] No one could recall the judges showing any sign of compassion during the reading. When it was over, Lobanov-Rostovskii said: 'To the right!' and the prisoners went out through another door and through other rooms, accompanied by sentries and police officers. The prisoners were then placed in new casemates.[10]

When Aleksandr Poggio recalls this event in his memoirs, anger shines through. He was outraged by the illegal verdict, by its expression of arbitrariness and lawlessness, by the fact that the prisoners were never heard. More than a hundred young people were sentenced without a trial and with no defence. In common with other Decembrists, Poggio held that the accusations were based more on words than on deeds. As had others, he had rejoiced at being back in 'the world of the living' after six months in solitary confinement, but he was greatly affected by hearing the sentences read out. His hatred of arbitrary power only intensified in prison. As he grew older, he did not change his political opinions. In his memoirs, written more than forty years after the revolt, he still advocates limited government, representative rule and universal suffrage. Moreover, he argues that the emancipation of the peasants along with their own plot of land – a reform that was carried out as he was writing his memoirs in the 1860s – was originally Pestel's idea. The mistake the Decembrists made at the time of the revolt, according to Poggio, was not to involve the people in their struggle to achieve change.[11]

Poggio was not the only Decembrist to maintain his political ideals after being arrested. Lorer, for instance, recalled that captivity strengthened his political beliefs. He became even more convinced that the people needed a constitution, 'a restriction of the prerogatives of the ruling individual'.[12] Aleksandr Muraviev, too, retained his radical ideas. As late as 1852, a couple of months before his death, he described the Peter and Paul Fortress as a 'ghastly monument to autocracy'. It faced the sovereign's palace, he wrote, 'like some fateful sign that the one cannot exist without the other'. Muraviev longed for the day when it would be understood 'that people were not created to be playthings for a few privileged families. When the light of publicity shines upon us, the lawlessness now concealed behind those walls will cause a shudder!'[13]

Mikhail Lunin, one of the founders of the Union of Welfare and a member of the Northern Society, was probably the most extreme in this respect. He was not only loyal to the cause of liberty, but even continued to fight for it in exile. Having gained the right to correspond with his sister Countess Uvarova from his Siberian exile in Urik, Lunin wrote her letters that contained explicit criticism of the government and its politics. Even though the letters were addressed to his sister, they were meant to be spread to a wider public. 'The publicity which my letters enjoy through numerous copies transforms them into a political weapon ... which I must use for the defence of freedom,' he wrote. His sister implored him to be more careful. The government eventually banned him from writing for a year, but he was not in the least deterred. When he was allowed to write again, he continued as before. 'Let them show me the law,' he states in one letter, 'which forbids one to express political ideals in letters to relatives.' He wanted 'to tease the white bear', and he succeeded. But it was only a matter of time before the bear struck back. In 1841 some of Lunin's writings intended for publication in the foreign press were seized. Nicholas ordered him to be transferred to a more isolated location. On 27 March of that year he was arrested and sent to the remote prison in Akatui, where he died in 1845 after four years of isolation.[14]

Not all reacted like Poggio and Lunin to the pronouncement of the criminal court. Rather than anger, some reacted with disbelief, others with feelings of righteousness. When Sergei Muraviev-Apostol realized that he had been sentenced to death by hanging, he wrote down a quotation from the New Testament book of Timothy.[15] The passage reads in full: 'For I am already becoming a victim and the time for my departure has come. I have fought the good fight, I have completed the course, I have kept the faith.'[16] This is not an expression of regret; rather, in the manner of Poggio and Lunin, Muraviev-Apostol presents himself as a civic hero, a victim of arbitrary oppression.

Kondratii Ryleev reacted differently again. Even after the verdict, he was convinced that everything would end well. Perhaps Nikolai Bestuzhev was not altogether unfair when he described him as gullible. This was evident from the note Ryleev sent to his friends in the Peter and Paul Fortress when he learned about the actions of the supreme criminal court. It began with the following words: 'Red caftans [senators] get excited and have awarded us the death penalty, but God, the Sovereign and good-minded people are on our side.'[17] Unfortunately, Ryleev was wrong. The condemned men were not saved, not by God, the emperor or noble-minded people. Less than 24 hours later he was hanged.

The emperor planned the execution of the sentence in the smallest detail. He used the occasion to demonstrate his power and to disgrace the officers who had dared to question his authority. In the early hours of 13 July 1826 some 2,000 soldiers from the guards regiments stationed in St Petersburg were deployed in and around the Peter and Paul Fortress. The execution of Pavel Pestel (who had just turned 33), Kondratii Ryleev (30), Sergei Muraviev-Apostol (29), Piotr Kakhovskii (28 or 29) and Mikhail Bestuzhev-Riumin (25) was scheduled for four o'clock in the morning. At three o'clock a memorial service would be held. This meant that the condemned men did not get many hours of sleep. Before leaving his cell, Ryleev wrote a final letter to his young wife. He had finally realized that things might not end happily:

> God and the Sovereign have decided my fate. I must die and die a shameful death. May his holy will be done! My dear friend, surrender yourself to the will of the Almighty and He will comfort you. Pray to God for my soul ... you, my dear, my kind and invaluable friend, have made me happy for eight years ... God will reward you for everything.[18]

The letter ends with the words: 'They have told me to dress. His holy will be done ... I have 530 roubles left here. Maybe they will give it to you.'[19]

Just before 3 a.m., the five condemned men were brought to the memorial service in the cathedral church of the fortress, where they received communion. Pestel had already been given his last communion by the Lutheran pastor Theodore Reinbot. After the service the fortress priest, Piotr Myslovskii, accompanied them from the church to the scaffold on the eastern rampart of the fortress. They were surrounded by soldiers from the Pavlovskii Life Guards regiment. According to Myslovskii's account, those sentenced to death wore white shrouds with black strings, belted with leather belts.[20] The quarterly assistant's records state that the prisoners' arms and legs were tied, so that they could take only the smallest steps. When they crossed the bridge to the crownwork, a towering gallows was visible on a scaffold. Five ropes with long loops were swaying from the crossbeam. The condemned men were taken to the side, where they had to wait their turn. They sat on the grass, talking quietly. The Pavlovskii regiment musicians were playing on the crownwork. The weather was lovely.[21]

The other prisoners, who had been sentenced to civil execution, that is, deprivation of civil rights, as well as to hard labour and exile, were also to be publicly humiliated. They were awakened before dawn and ordered to dress. Evgenii Obolenskii recalled that a door was opened on the opposite side of the corridor, accompanied by the sound of chains: 'I heard the drawn-out voice of my unchanging friend, Kondratii Fedorovich Ryleev. "Forgive me, forgive me, brothers!" he called and measured steps withdrew to the far end of the corridor.'[22] Shortly afterwards all the other prisoners were taken out of their casemates. They were parted into four groups, surrounded by soldiers and led through the fortress gates on to the glacis behind the crownwork curtain wall, where bonfires had been lit. Outside the fortress gates, soldiers of the Guards formed a large semicircle. Several generals on horseback could be seen in the background. Aleksandr Chernyshev, one of Nicholas's most trusted officers, rode about with a troubled expression; the other adjutant generals also moved about. There, on the glacis, the prisoners met their friends and acquaintances. Many of the incarcerated Decembrists later remembered this as a happy moment: 'Faces came to life, tongues loosened'; people 'started to shake hands and embrace. There was a general [atmosphere of] enthusiasm.'[23]

Decembrist officers who had served in the Imperial Guard were separated from the others. Then they were all lined up and brought to blazing bonfires, where they were ordered to take off their uniforms. Underofficers produced swords that had been sawn through. After the sentence was repeated, each prisoner was ordered to fall to his knees while the executioner broke a sword over his head, tore up his uniform, and cast the clothes and swords into the fires. Symbolically, these men were thereby stripped of noble status, privileges and rights, declared civilly dead, officially expelled from society. After the ceremony, the convicts were handed grey prison gowns and taken back to the fortress. Decembrists who had been naval officers endured a similar ceremony. They were dispatched in closed boats to the naval base in Kronstadt, where the civil execution was carried out before a group of admirals, and their uniforms were cast into the sea. On his return to the prison, Nikolai Basargin was convinced that all his relations with the world were now at an end.[24]

According to several witnesses, the five men awaiting execution remained calm and composed during this time, despite having to wait for more than an hour because of a delay in the construction of the scaffold.[25] Executioners in red shirts walked around on the wooden platform. Couriers were constantly galloping off with reports to Nicholas, who had left for his residence in Tsarskoe Selo, 24 kilometres (15 mi.) south of St Petersburg. Myslovskii later told Lorer that it was believed that Aleksandr Benkendorf (Alexander von Benckendorff), Chief of Gendarmes, delayed the execution deliberately in the expectation of a pardon. However, clemency was never part of the emperor's plan, and no such order was sent to the fortress. When the time came, Myslovskii led the condemned five in a final prayer. Slate boards stating their names and their crime were hung around their necks, and sacks were placed over their heads. The soldiers pushed the men forwards and directed their steps. The men calmly ascended the platform. Nooses were put around their necks. Only a handful of civilian witnesses were present, because the police had spread false information about the time and place of the execution.[26]

Owing to the inexperience of the executioners, the ropes broke and three prisoners plummeted to the ground: Ryleev, Kakhovskii and Muraviev-Apostol.[27] Ryleev's hood fell off; he was bleeding from his eyebrow and ear. Muraviev-Apostol broke both legs. There are numerous accounts of what these men said after they fell. Their friends embellished the stories they heard, invariably emphasizing the courage of the executed and their contempt for the regime. According to several reports, Muraviev-Apostol exclaimed, 'Oh Lord, they can't even hang people properly in Russia!'[28] Ryleev supposedly declared: 'I am happy to die twice for my fatherland.'[29] At this point Governor General Golenishchev-Kutuzov rushed forwards, shouting furiously, 'Hang them up, hang them up immediately.' Ryleev reportedly cried back: 'Vile *oprichnik* of the tyrant! Give the executioner your aiguillettes so that we don't die a third time.'[30] According to Nikolai Bestuzhev, Ryleev then added, 'Our execution is not enough for them – they still need tyranny!'[31] Many of those present believed that the fact that the executed had fallen down was a sign, and that they would be pardoned. But, after a brief interlude, the ropes were fixed and they were hanged a second time.[32] By 6 a.m., all were dead. The bodies were kept for a day in the

Fortress and buried secretly after dark on Golodai Island (now Decembrists' Island (Ostrov dekabristov)), a little downriver of the fortress.

## Aftermath

Further examples of the importance Nicholas attached to the execution of the sentence as a cautionary example are provided by the two decrees he issued after the event. The first was aimed at the troops, informing them that the sentence and execution of the 'instigators of villainous intentions' had been carried out and their 'faithful regiments' had 'been cleansed of the infection that threatened you and all of Russia'. On behalf of Russia, he thanked them for saving the throne and the Orthodox faith and 'delivering the fatherland from the horrors of the rebellion'. The second decree was the manifesto announcing the sentence. It was written in the same spirit, portraying the ideas behind the revolt as alien to the Russian people.[33] The emperor also organized public ceremonies to demonstrate his power and instil the idea of the importance of loyalty in his subjects' minds.

On the day after the execution of the sentence, a thanksgiving prayer was held on Senate Square to commemorate the fallen soldiers, but also, in Benckendorff's words, to cleanse 'this place of its shameful crimes'. A field chapel was set up on the square beside the monument of Peter the Great, with soldiers stationed around it. The high nobility gathered in the Admiralty Church, from where they all went on foot to the square, following the clergy. After the service, the metropolitan sprinkled holy water on the troops. Nicholas followed the service on horseback, with the empress in her carriage.[34]

Similar prayer services were then held all over Russia. That in Moscow was held on 19 July, on Cathedral Square in the Kremlin. The Moscow Postmaster, Aleksandr Bulgakov, described it as a glorious ceremony. In the middle of the square, a round pavilion with columns was constructed and the army deployed around it. The empress and Grand Duchess Elena Pavlovna went on foot with all the clergy and court staff to this pavilion. The ceremony began with a requiem for the innocent victims of 14 December. Then the army said a prayer. In Bulgakov's words, 'the empress, the army, the people – they all knelt down and thanked God for saving Russia from the intrigues of malefactors. This picture was very moving. Metropolitan Philaret walked through all the ranks of the troops and sprinkled the soldiers. The weather was good without the [scorching] sun.'[35] Fourteen-year-old Aleksandr Herzen, who was present on Cathedral Square, perceived the service very differently. He later recalled that this was the moment when he swore 'to avenge the executed' and dedicated himself 'to the struggle with this throne, with this altar, with these cannon'.[36]

These carefully staged public ceremonies can be seen as examples of what the historian Richard Wortman calls 'scenarios of power', that is to say, events used as instruments to demonstrate or exercise absolute power in the empire.[37] They were also part of a process of constructing a myth about the Decembrists. This myth was shaped to fit into a new political narrative formed around a conservative-Romantic notion of the nation, which in 1832 would be expressed in the doctrine of Official Nationality.[38] The new conception of the nation as a unique people was employed as a substitute for the radical idea of the nation as a sovereign people advocated by the Decembrists. It allowed the regime to create a narrative in which the Russian autocracy was tied organically to the Russian nation, intrinsic to Russian nationality and rooted in Russian traditions. Love for the monarch was a native characteristic. By contrast, the Decembrists' ideas were portrayed as alien to the Russian national character and way of life. Their ideas were symptoms of an infection imported from the West, one that threatened national unity. According to the official narrative, all Russians, regardless of rank, were united in the fight against the conspirators and their dangerous ideas. It was 'us against them'; true Russians against alien Decembrists. In support of this narrative, Nicholas highlighted the devotion shown by those Decembrist families who renounced their 'criminal children'.[39] The fact that some people whose daughters were married to Decembrists sought to have the marriages annulled shows how frightened people were of the emperor's revenge.

The aftermath of the revolt was a defining moment for Russian conservative nationalism, which subsequently developed in two directions: on the one hand, into a state-sanctioned and -controlled doctrine linking the idea of the nation to absolute power and to Orthodoxy (Official Nationality); on the other, into a Romantic quasi-liberal philosophy of cultural nationalism, formulated by the so-called Slavophiles. At the same time, the revolt and its aftermath constituted a defining moment for the Russian opposition movement. Members of the educated elite would never again believe they could cooperate with the autocratic regime. It was a watershed in Russian history, a parting of ways, as Nicholas Riasanovsky once described it, between those who served the regime and those who served the nation or people.[40] A new relationship was forming between the educated elite and the tsar.

As the rumour of the execution reached the convicts in the Peter and Paul Fortress, they listened in disbelief. Apparently, Myslovskii had convinced several of them not to believe any stories about executions. The priest himself was genuinely shocked by what he had witnessed.[41]

Nevertheless, even when faced with this reality, many prisoners remained convinced that they would be set free. When Nicholas I returned from Moscow for his coronation on 3 September 1826, the sentence of penal servitude was reduced by five years. This led many Decembrists to believe that their exile to Siberia would be cancelled, that they would be imprisoned for two years and that the emperor would gradually commute the period of hard labour so that, finally, they would be allowed to return to their families. Hope dies last.

Supervision in the fortress was relaxed after the sentences had been read. The prisoners were allowed fresh air and exercise. Every day they were taken out for a walk around the yard under the supervision of a junior officer. In bad weather, they walked in the hallway. During these walks, they sometimes met friends occupying distant cells and were able to exchange a few words.[42] They also obtained permission to receive books. According to his own accounts, Nikita Muraviev devoured books in both English and French.[43] Rozen could manage only light fiction, and he read all the novels of Sir Walter Scott with great pleasure: 'The hours passed so quickly that I often did not hear the sound of the fortress clock.'[44] Basargin and Aleksandr Beliaev were also reading light fiction, including the works of Scott and James Fenimore Cooper. Relatives were now allowed to visit them every week in the commandant's house, in the presence of the parade-de-camp, and to deliver things to them, such as linen, clothing, books and food.[45] At visiting time, there were crowds of people. The vast fortress yard was usually filled with carriages, and in the halls of the commandant's house it was difficult to get through the crowd of relatives.

One fine evening, as Lorer was sitting by the window watching the little boats on the River Neva, the non-commissioned officer Sokolov arrived and asked him to come for a walk. He was quite persistent and Lorer agreed. As they approached the fortress gate, he caught sight of a group of soldiers in greatcoats and caps. To his great surprise, as he came closer he recognized the privates of his own company of the Moscow regiment. 'We wish you good health, your honour,' they said.

> The company sent us to say goodbye to you ... They ask that you be strong, and they themselves are praying God to give you strength to

endure your misfortune and safely reach Siberia. We have an icon lamp burning in front of the image of St Nicholas, and we ... pray for you every day.[46]

Deeply touched, Lorer thanked them with tears in his eyes. He would need all the strength he could muster in the hard years to come.

# PART V
# EXILE

# 9

# To Siberia

The transport of the incarcerated Decembrists to Siberia began immediately after the sentence was confirmed. In 1822 a new charter on exiles and transports had been approved, but the new legislation was not applied to the Decembrists. Nicholas considered them so dangerous that special precautions were taken. All the Decembrists were transported in shackles, which, according to the Charter to the Nobility of 1785, should not have been used on nobles. The use of shackles also contravened the rules for escorting convicts, whereby only those who had been given a new sentence, or had tried to escape, had to wear them.

Furthermore, rather than being sent on foot in regular prison convoys, which changed guards at every stage, the Decembrists were sent to Siberia by post-horses in groups of between two and four every other day, accompanied by one courier and a guard of gendarmes. The prisoners travelled day and night, stopping for rest every third day. Generally, the groups of prisoners were dispatched secretly at night, so as not to attract attention. The courier was instructed to take them along the Yaroslavl route only, bypassing Moscow, and to prevent them from communicating with anyone.[1] Many of the Decembrists believed that they were given such a fast passage so that there would be no opportunity for spreading revolutionary ideas.[2] That may have been the case, but it was probably also because of the emperor's fear of negative public reaction to the sentences.

Evgenii Obolenskii, Aleksandr Iakubovich, Artamon Muraviev and Vasilii Davydov were the first to leave. Obolenskii recalled that the guards came to his cell in the middle of the night, telling him to put on a grey jacket and trousers of the same coarse soldier's cloth and ordering him to get ready to set out on a voyage. Soon after midnight on 22 July, he was taken to the commandant's house, where he met Iakubovich dressed in the same way. 'If I look like Stenka Razin, you look like Van'ka Kain,' Iakubovich exclaimed.

Razin was a Cossack leader who led an uprising against the Russian nobility and bureaucracy, whereas Kain was a famous Moscow thief, provocateur and swindler. Both were heroes in their own way.[3]

In August the transfer of Decembrists to Siberia was halted temporarily because the Siberian authorities were not able to receive such a large number of convicts. As a result, some prisoners were instead sent to forts belonging to the South-Eastern Finland fortification system.[4] Most prisoners were not told where they were going and were extremely disappointed to find themselves locked up in a fort again. Mikhail Lunin was sent to Suomenlinna (Finnish) or Sveaborg (Swedish), together with Piotr Gromnitskii, Ivan Kireev, Mikhail Mitkov, Vasilii Norov and Piotr Mukhanov, whereas Ivan Pushchin, Aleksei Iushnevskii, and Mikhail and Nikolai Bestuzhev were dispatched to Shlisselburg Fortress on Lake Ladoga.[5] Vladimir Shteingel, who left St Petersburg on 25 July 1826, was shocked when he realized that he was going not to Siberia, but to Svartholman (Finnish) or Svartholm (Swedish) Fortress in Finland. It was known as a particularly horrific place. He was placed in a low casemate eight paces long and six wide, with two iron doors and a small window with an iron grille: '"This is your place," said the warden callously and noisily locked the doors with bolts and a key.' Shteingel remembered this as the worst moment of his life.[6]

After the sentence was handed down, the families of the Decembrists, especially their wives, were terribly worried about the future and tried to get in touch with the prisoners as they left St Petersburg. Many of the wives did not learn that their husbands were being transferred until it was too late, but sometimes they managed to get the information in time. Anastasia Iakushkina succeeded in meeting her husband, Ivan, when he was on his way to Fort Slava, an isolated section of the Ruotsinsalmi (Finnish) or Svensksund (Swedish) Fortress in Finland. He was transferred on 5 August 1826, with Matvei Muraviev-Apostol, Aleksandr Bestuzhev, A. P. Arbuzov and A. I. Tiutchev. Iakushkin was pleasantly surprised when he encountered his wife, who was waiting for him with her mother and their two children at the first posting station. They spent several hours together and agreed that Anastasia, who was only eighteen, would follow him to Siberia with the children, accompanied by her mother.[7] 'After all the anxieties that we had lived through, such a future smiled on us,' he recalled.[8]

Ivan spent about fourteen months in his dark, damp cell in Fort Slava. Then, suddenly, an order came for him to be transferred to Siberia. Anastasia knew that the transport would go via Yaroslavl, but she did not know when they would arrive, so she travelled to Yaroslavl several times before she finally managed to meet her husband. She was miserable. Her mother had not received permission to accompany her to Siberia, and, worse, she had not been allowed to bring their children. Despite these severe setbacks, she had decided to follow her husband anyway. Ivan was now facing an extremely difficult decision. He did not want to be separated from his wife: 'That a life for us together . . . would always be marvellous I could not doubt.' At the same time, he was sure the children needed her. He finally decided to ask her never, in any circumstance, to part with them: 'She resisted my request at length, but finally gave me her word to carry out my wish.'[9] The husband's will prevailed.

In December 1826 the transport of exiled Decembrists to Siberia resumed. The first group to leave were Nikita and Aleksandr Muraviev, Ivan Annenkov and Konstantin Torson. Annenkov's fiancée, Pauline Geuble, had tried to go to St Petersburg to see him in the autumn. She had been bedridden for several months after giving birth and had no money. When she finally received 600 roubles from Ivan's mother, she travelled to St Petersburg, where she obtained a note from her fiancé via a non-commissioned officer. The note contained only a few words: 'Where are you, what have you done, my child? My God, not a single sharp object to destroy my existence.' Yet she was not allowed to see Ivan because they were not yet married. However, on 9 December, when she heard that Ivan had tried to hang himself, Pauline managed to arrange a short meeting.[10] None of them knew at the time that Ivan would be sent to Siberia the following day. As soon as Pauline was informed that he had left, she travelled to the first staging post, but she was too late, and the prison convoy had left.

Aleksandra Muravieva, Nikita's young wife, was more fortunate and made it to the post in time. She had received the news earlier and was waiting with her sister and her mother-in-law in the stationmaster's house. But it was a sad farewell. According to Aleksandr Muraviev, they were never allowed to meet properly because the carriage drove past and they had time only to run out and call goodbye.[11]

Almost two months later, at the beginning of February, Andrei Rozen was dispatched to Siberia. Like Iakushkin, he had concluded that his wife should stay with their child, but only to begin with. After the sentence was carried out, Anna Rozen had received permission to let her husband see their newborn son in the house of the commandant. 'Although in tears, she was composed and firm,' Andrei commented afterwards. Their son, Eugene, was six months old and had blue eyes. When Anna asked when and where they would meet again, Andrei begged her not to follow him at once to Siberia, but to wait until Eugene was old enough to run without assistance. In the end Anna, like the other wives, was forbidden to bring him with her and had to leave him with her sister. Before she left, Anna managed secretly to give Andrei 1,000 roubles. On 3 February 1827 the couple met for the last time. He was 27 and she had recently turned 29. Anna gave him a wooden cross from Jerusalem, which first she and then their baby boy had been wearing. She had made him a coat of reindeer skin lined with silk for his journey to Siberia. Two days later the transport started. Mikhail Kiukhelbeker, Nikolai Repin and Mikhail Glebov went with Rozen to the commandant shortly before midnight, where fetters were put on them.[12]

Natalia Fonvizina managed to see her husband before he left for Siberia. Mikhail Fonvizin left the Peter and Paul Fortress one evening at the end of January, together with Nikolai Basargin, Ferdinand Volf and Aleksandr Frolov. The group of exiles arrived at the first posting station in the middle of the night and went to warm up in the caretaker's room. According to Basargin's account, as they were sitting down at the table and the courier went out to change horses, the caretaker signalled to Fonvizin. To his great surprise, his wife was waiting for him in another room, and they managed to spend a few minutes together. Despite being heavily pregnant, Natalia had travelled to St Petersburg at the time of the arrests in the hope of meeting Mikhail but had to return to Moscow to give birth to their second child on 4 February. Now she informed him that they were being sent to Irkutsk in Eastern Siberia, and secretly handed him 1,000 roubles.

The road to Siberia went over the Ural Mountains. This is where the exiles left Europe behind, never to see it again – or so they feared. Crossing the border into Asia had a symbolic meaning for the Decembrists, who identified very strongly with Europe and saw Asia as foreign in every way. Nikolai Lorer recalled his feelings as he was about to cross the frontier:

> In the morning we silently ascended 21 km [13 mi.] to the waystation, which stood alone, dejectedly on the very peak of the mountain. From the summit, a boundless sea of forests, blue and violet and a road twisting through them, stretched out before us. The coach driver pointed ahead with his whip and said, 'That's Siberia!' And so, we were no longer in Europe! Separated from the entire civilized world![13]

In the Russian imagination, Siberia was a prison house for exiles: gloomy, wild, 'a kingdom of frost, inhabited by bears and bandits'.[14] The convicts were filled with dread at the prospect of spending the rest of their lives in such a godforsaken place. But the further into Siberia they travelled, the more their perception of the place changed. Despite their chains, they were warmly welcomed everywhere.

The Decembrists' encounter with Siberia altered their outlook fundamentally. Rather than an uncultured and isolated space, it came to represent an alternative to authoritarian, hierarchical European Russia with its enslaved peasantry. The Decembrists also changed the negative view of Siberia among the educated Russian elite, promoting a vision of a more egalitarian, democratic land, full of potential, not unlike an idealized image of the American West.[15] Rozen remembered the charity of the Siberians fondly: 'Everywhere from Tobolsk to Chita, they received us kindly; warm wraps were fastened over our open sledges, our feet carefully packed with hay, and blessings were showered on our heads.' It was the custom for the villagers living near the Great Highway to gather and wait for the exiles to pass by, in order to sell them food and other supplies. Poor prisoners were supplied free of charge. This took place twice a week, when the prisoners were going from one military station to another. Rozen recalled that the villagers brought pies, rolls and other edibles, as well as warm shoes, to sell to the rich and give to the poor.[16] Basargin also recalled that people crowded around the carriages and often threw copper coins into them. After staying in Siberia for some time, he found the common people 'much freer, sharper, even better educated than our Russian peasants, especially more so than the estate serfs ... They better understood the dignity of man and valued their rights more [highly].' In fact, Basargin held, Siberians had many similarities to Americans.[17]

## The Decembrists' wives

Because many of the Decembrists were so young, only a few of them were married or betrothed. But, to many people's surprise, a significant number of these women decided to follow their husbands to Siberia. There were also those, such as Sofia Briggen (who had four children) and Pelageia Shteingel (eight children), who wanted to go, but had no one to look after their children, or could not bear to leave them.[18] Anastasia Iakushkina never received permission to travel. When, in 1829, she appealed yet again to the government to allow her and her two sons to join her husband, her request was turned down. The main reason given was that the boys would not be able to receive a proper education in Siberia. By 1832, desperate, she was ready to go without the two boys and asked her husband to send her the necessary papers for the journey. But on 3 April 1832 Nicholas I wrote: 'Turn down the request on some plausible excuse.'[19] Another woman who would have followed her husband had it been possible was Natalia Ryleeva. In May, before her husband's death sentence was pronounced, she wrote to him, 'Can you really think that I can exist without you? Wherever fate brings you, I follow you. Death alone can sever the sacred bond of marriage.'[20] Iosif Poggio's wife, Maria, also wanted to join her husband, but was prevented by her father, who had been strongly against the marriage.

The women who did follow their husbands to Siberia had to make great sacrifices. Many had to leave children behind – perhaps the greatest sacrifice of all – but most also had to give up a safe environment and comfortable material conditions. Maria Volkonskaia later recalled that Nicholas had warned her not to travel beyond Irkutsk, implying that she would not be allowed to return home if she did. Yet it is unclear whether she really understood the meaning of his words, or if she believed him. Her son Nikolai was eleven months old and had started to talk. 'Am teaching him how to say "Papa",' she wrote to her husband.[21] Maria left Nikolai in the Volkonskii Palace with her mother-in-law and never saw him again. 'My son is fortunate,' she reasoned, but 'my husband is unfortunate, hence my place is to be with my husband.'[22]

The decision of these women to join their husbands or fiancés in exile became a symbol of feminine loyalty in Russian culture. It was not just a matter of marital duty, however. Notions about marriage among the Russian nobility had started to change in the second half of the seventeenth century, when marriage began to be perceived as something more than a prosperous alliance. Physical attraction and emotional affection assumed new significance, and, as reading increased among noble women, they were influenced by the ideal of marriage promoted in sentimental literature. Romanticism later contributed to this change, providing a language that encouraged the expression of feelings. By the 1820s there was an emphasis on the emotional importance of marriage. Noble women were supposed to feel love.[23]

Aleksandra Muravieva and Ekaterina Trubetskaia were both motivated by feelings of romantic love to follow their husbands to Siberia. Judging by her letters, Aleksandra adored her husband. The fact that her love was reciprocated is evident in Nikita's many letters to his wife. Aleksandra left Tagin, her family estate in Oriol province, only days after her husband's arrest, arriving in St Petersburg on the evening of 30 December. When she received

Pyotr Sokolov, *Maria Volkonskaia with Her Son*,
1826, drawing, pencil on paper.

a letter from Nikita in the Peter and Paul Fortress, asking for her forgiveness, she told him she had nothing to forgive: 'For almost three years that
I have been married, I have not lived in this world – I was in paradise . . .
I am the happiest of women . . . The letter you wrote to me shows all the
greatness of your soul.'[24] Ekaterina loved her husband, too. 'I really feel that
I cannot live without you,' she wrote to him after his arrest. 'One thing can
make me happy: to see you, to share your grief . . . and to devote all the
minutes of my life to you.'[25]

    Scholars have argued that Sergei Trubetskoi put pressure on his wife
to follow him to Siberia. It is certainly true that she was made aware of his

need for her: 'Except you, dear friend,' he wrote in a letter in early May, 'no one needs my life.'[26] Two months later, when he had received his sentence, he wrote: 'Without you, my dear angel, I do not see and cannot see anything in life except sorrow . . . for you alone, I wish the continuation of my life; you alone bind me to this world; life without you is nothing but a heavy burden.'[27] However, there is no doubt that Ekaterina loved Sergei deeply and could not imagine a life without him.

Sometimes a combination of duty and love prompted these women to follow their husbands or fiancés to Siberia. It could be difficult to separate these feelings, especially since a wife's life at this time was tied so strongly to that of her husband. Maria Iushnevskaia was a case in point. She described herself as 'an unhappy orphan' without her husband, who was the only one for whom she still existed. Without him, she was nobody. She stated explicitly that she wished to follow her husband because she wanted to fulfil her most sacred (marital) duty and share his plight. Yet she did not do so simply out of a sense of duty. It was not a great sacrifice for her. For the fourteen years they had been married, she had been 'the happiest wife in the world'. For the well-being of her life, she wrote, she needed 'nothing more than to have the happiness of seeing him and to share with him everything that cruel fate intended'.[28] Anna Rozen was motivated to follow her husband by a combination of love and religious duty. She was devoted to him but could not have managed to leave her son had it not been for her faith and the strong sense of duty it brought.

In Maria Volkonskaia's case, neither love nor marital duty appears to have led to her decision to go to Siberia. She was very young and fascinated by Lord Byron and the Romantic cult of heroic sacrifice. Her father was convinced that she followed her husband because she saw herself as a Romantic heroine.[29] We should also bear in mind that the Decembrist wives, or at least some of them, were familiar with the Decembrist writers' civic poetry, which idealized the image of the selfless hero who sacrificed himself for the people.[30] To Volkonskaia, her husband was the archetype of a civic hero. There was no sacrifice she would not make for him. In sharing his suffering, she herself became a heroic martyr, just like Nataliia Dolgorukova in Ryleev's poem, the young princess who followed her husband, Prince Ivan Dolgorukov, to Siberia when he was banished in 1730.[31] On 5 March Maria wrote to her husband: 'My beloved Sergei, two days ago I learned of your arrest. I will not allow my soul to be shattered by it. I put my hope in the mercy of our greathearted Emperor. I can assure you of one thing, whatever your fate, I will share it.'[32]

Although political conviction was not the reason why these women followed their husbands into exile, they did not lack interest in and were not ignorant of political ideas. In fact, several women, among them Anna Rozen, Ekaterina Trubetskaia, Maria Basargina, Praskovia Muravieva (the wife of Aleksandr N. Muraviev) and Pauline Geuble, were aware of the Society. In the days leading up to the revolt, Andrei Rozen often discussed 'the forthcoming dangers' with his wife. 'I was able to be completely frank with her,' he recalled. 'Her mind and heart understood everything.'[33] Basargin revealed to his future wife in 1824 that he belonged to a secret society, telling her that although his role in it was not significant, a disaster might still happen that would be difficult for her to endure. She replied that she had not chosen him because he was a nobleman, adjutant or future general, but that she had instead followed her heart, and, 'no matter what situation [he] was in, in wards or in huts, in Petersburg at court, or in Siberia, fate would be exactly the same.'[34]

Maria Volkonskaia was not aware of her husband's involvement in a secret society but would have liked to be. Had he confided in her, she explained in her memoirs, 'it would have brought us together. I would have helped him to share the burden.' Realizing the nature of the 'crime' of which the Decembrists were accused, she sympathized with their cause. She believed that justice required recognition of the fact that those who sacrificed their life for their convictions could not but earn the respect of their compatriots. He who laid his head on the block for his beliefs truly loved the fatherland, 'although, perhaps, he had started his work prematurely'. Volkonskaia was convinced that posterity would pronounce its verdict on the government's trial of this 'outburst of pure and disinterested patriotism'. Previously, she held, the history of Russia had provided examples only of palace conspiracies, which had taken place for personal gain. Another example of Volkonskaia's political consciousness is found in a note referring to Governor Ivan Zeidler's attempt in Irkutsk to persuade her to return home. 'His Majesty did not approve of the idea of young wives following their husbands into exile,' she wrote. 'This aroused too much interest in the poor exiles,' whereas the tsar hoped they would soon be forgotten.[35]

According to her own account, Pauline Geuble was politically aware at an early stage. She understood from conversations her fiancé had with friends that they were involved in some kind of conspiracy. When she asked him about it, he confessed that he was a member of a secret society. After the revolt, when Geuble met Prince Lobanov-Rostovskii, a favourite of the tsar, they talked about the sentence of the Decembrists. Lobanov allegedly told her, 'Actually, madam, in your country [France], these gentlemen would be sentenced to death,' to which Geuble replied, 'Yes, prince, but they would have lawyers for the defence.'[36] She also mentioned an encounter with an old peasant on her way to Moscow, who told her that he knew what the Decembrists wanted. They wanted our freedom, he said, according to Geuble: the freedom of the peasants.

There is also much to suggest that Aleksandra Muravieva had some political awareness. When Nikita was arrested, as we have seen, he asked her to review his letters and notebooks and to hide those that seemed 'dangerous' to her. Clearly, he considered her capable of making this decision herself. She was to remove all the books about constitutions, including those by Bentham, Montesquieu and Destutt de Tracy. In doing so, she became his accomplice. He also expected her to understand references written in uncensored messages, such as '[the parade ground major] found the culprits of this whole case, which are: Luther (!) and Voltaire, who turned the heads of the young, convincing them to play the role that Julius Caesar played in the French Revolution (!!!)', or 'Among [my letters], I think, are two concerning the Greeks. Do not burn them, but put them among your rags.'[37]

Another woman who appears to have been politically conscious was Sofia Kiseleva, the wife of General Pavel Kiselev, chief of staff of the 2nd Army in Tulchyn. At the time of the arrests of members of the Southern Society, she told Basargin that she had been present during General Aleksandr Chernyshev's conversation with her husband and could assure Basargin that those who wanted to be saved had to confess to their crimes. When Basargin told Kiseleva that he could not obey her advice because it was contrary to his conscience, she replied that he would perish, but as an honest man, and that her respect for him would only increase because of it.[38]

## Arrival in Siberia

Most of the Decembrists travelled first to Irkutsk, the centre of Eastern Siberia and a hub for trade with China. From there, the exiles were sent on to their final destination. Irkutsk stands in a curve of the Angara River, at the western edge of a plain. Wooded hills stretch to the east and northeast, as well as along the west bank of the river. Maria Volkonskaia was surprised at how beautifully situated the town was. 'Its position is lovely and the Angara River magnificent, even when covered with ice,' she wrote.[39] At the time, Irkutsk had about 15,000 inhabitants; there were several fine public buildings and merchant houses on its wide streets, as well as a dozen churches and two monasteries. It was also the seat of the Governor General of Eastern Siberia, who lived in an imposing stone mansion by the river. Twenty years later an English traveller described how the numerous towers, domes and spires rising far above the dwellings gave the appearance of a large city. There were few shops, he wrote, but they were large and surprisingly well supplied with both European and Chinese articles; the markets were well equipped with provisions of all kinds.[40]

When the first groups of Decembrists arrived in Irkutsk at the end of August, there was no clear instruction as to exactly where they were to be sent. Irkutsk's governor, Ivan Zeidler (Tseidler), dispatched them temporarily to various places in the vicinity. Evgenii Obolenskii and Aleksandr Iakubovich were dispatched to a salt mine at Usolie, about 80 kilometres (50 mi.) north of the town. Artamon Muraviev, Vasilii Davydov, and Piotr and Andrei Borisov were sent to the Aleksandrovskii distillery on the other side of the Angara River from Usolie. Trubetskoi and Volkonskii were sent to the Nikolaevskii salt works, close to Irkutsk. Contrary to what these men had expected, they were quite comfortable.[41] However, after little more than a month, on 5 October they received orders to get ready for a journey and were informed that they were being sent to the Nerchinsk mines.

The Nerchinsk mining district consisted of several prisons and mines scattered across the Transbaikal, from the eastern shores of Lake Baikal to the Chinese border. This was the principal place of penal labour in Siberia, and the most dreaded.[42] The Decembrists were assigned to the Blagodatsk mine outside the administrative town of Nerchinsk. Just as they were about to set off, Trubetskoi received a note from his wife, informing him of her arrival in Irkutsk. He instantly replied that he would try to meet her when stopping in the city.[43] Trubetskaia had journeyed to Irkutsk, a distance of some 6,500 kilometres (4,000 mi.), by horse-drawn coach, travelling day and night. Speed was vital because autumn came early in Siberia and with it rain and floods. In Krasnoiarsk her carriage broke down and there was no one to fix it, so she continued her journey in a four-wheel peasant cart without springs, reaching Irkutsk by the end of September.[44]

The unfortunate Decembrists remained in Irkutsk for two days before continuing their journey to the mines. Shortly before leaving, Obolenskii encountered Princess Varvara Shakhovskaia, who had arrived there with her sister Praskovia Muravieva. Aleksandr Muraviev was also in Irkutsk, waiting to be transferred to his place of exile in Verkhneudinsk on the other side of Lake Baikal. Princess Shakhovskaia had accompanied her sister to Siberia in the hope of meeting Piotr Mukhanov, her fiancé, but in a cruel and ironic twist of events, he had been sent in the other direction, to be imprisoned in Finland.[45] Now she asked Obolenskii if Trubetskoi was there, because his wife was on her way and wanted to see him before he left. The prisoners tried to delay their departure as long as possible, but in the end, they had to leave. Just as the horses started moving, Obolenskii recalled, Trubetskaia approached in a carriage. She jumped down and called out to her husband, at which, 'In the twinkling of an eye, Sergei Petrovich leapt out of the vehicle and was in the arms of his wife; for a long time was this warm embrace prolonged, and tears flowed from the eyes of them both.' The chief of city police asked them to separate, but his requests were in vain; 'At last, however, the final "farewell" was said, and the troikas whisked us off again with redoubled speed.'[46]

The prisoners travelled via Verkheneudinsk and Nerchinsk to Blagodatsk, where they arrived on 26 October. The journey was both dangerous and demanding: bad, stone-strewn roads, severely cold weather and nowhere to warm up, precarious rivers to traverse, high mountains to cross and difficulty finding food. All these circumstances made Trubetskoi bless Providence for stopping his beloved wife in Irkutsk, 'no matter how difficult it is for me to be without her'. In the winter, when the rivers and the sea were frozen, travel was easier, but because of the conditions every possible precaution was required to defend against hunger and the cold. The temperature was usually below -30°C (-22°F).[47]

Reading Sergei's letters to his wife, it is evident that her support was crucial to him. Four weeks after their brief encounter in Irkutsk, he wrote to her from Blagodatsk, telling her that her love gave him incredible strength: 'The Lord gave you to me as a visible guardian angel of mine. We are separated by bodies, but our souls are inseparable; your soul protects mine, and my warm prayers will not cease to accompany you until the merciful Creator deigns to let us unite.' He informed Ekaterina that the regime in the new prison was stricter than in the fortress. Not only did they take away everything sharp, but also they removed paper, pens, ink, pencils and all books, including the Bible. The letter ends with a declaration of love: 'My angel, I kiss you a thousand times from the depths of my soul and press you to my heart, filled with the most lively love for you, and it alone is burning and beating.'[48]

When Ekaterina realized that her husband was going to Nerchinsk, she applied for permission to follow him. But Zeidler had received instructions to use every means to prevent the wives of the Decembrists from going further than Irkutsk. He pointed out that she would not enjoy the privileges and comforts granted to her in Irkutsk if she removed to Nerchinsk. When she refused to bend, she was informed that she would have to sign a document in which she relinquished all privileges to which she had formerly been entitled by virtue of her noble rank. She would also have to give up all claims to property rights, as well as her right to return. Without hesitation, she accepted the conditions and signed the document.[49]

At the beginning of January 1827 another group of distinguished Decembrists arrived in Irkutsk: Nikita Muraviev, his younger brother Aleksandr Mikhailovich, Ivan Annenkov and Konstantin Torson. The young, romantic Aleksandr (24 years old) was proud to share the destiny of his 'noble-hearted' older brother. There was, he thought, something poetic about being sent into exile; they suffered for a good cause. Naturally, he was also glad to leave his dark, damp cell behind.

The exiles had travelled at great speed, covering more than 6,900 kilometres (4,300 mi.) in 24 days (640 kilometres/400 mi. in post-wagons, and the rest in sleighs). They rested only twice for a few hours during the entire journey, and had neither food nor shelter from the cold.[50] On arriving at the prison of Irkutsk, they were locked in a gloomy, dirty, empty room in which they had to stay for several weeks, suffering from cold and hunger.[51] Still, it was a relief to be sent to Siberia rather than be imprisoned in another grim fortress somewhere in Finland.

Maria Volkonskaia travelled to Siberia via Moscow, where she stayed for a few days with her sister-in-law, the writer Zinaida Volkonskaia. Zinaida was famous for her literary and musical salon in Tverskaia Street, and before Maria left, she threw her a farewell party. Aleksandr Pushkin, who had become acquainted with Maria in 1820, when he spent the summer with her family, was present. He had been enchanted by Maria and wrote several poems inspired by her. The passage 'How I envied the waves' in *Eugene Onegin* is supposed to have been written with her in mind:

> I recall some storm-brewing ocean:
> Jealous, I watched its waves that beat
> A path straight toward her in devotion,
> To swirl in sequence at her feet.
> To join those waves my soul was burning,
> To touch those limbs with lips so yearning.[52]

On the third day after leaving Moscow, Volkonskaia reached Kazan, on the banks of the Volga, where she stopped for a few hours. It was New Year's

Eve, but she did not want to take part in the festivities. Just before midnight she left the city once more. It had started to snow heavily, and after about an hour the coachman told her that they could go no further. The horses were exhausted, and he was lost. Fortunately, they found an abandoned woodsman's hut in which they could spend the night. The rest of the journey went at breakneck speed, day and night, making only brief stops to drink tea and eat bread. Volkonskaia arrived in Irkutsk only three weeks after setting off from Moscow and moved into the room Trubetskaia had just vacated. Unpacking her things, she was overjoyed to find the clavichord that Zinaida had secretly stowed among her belongings before Maria left Moscow.[53]

Wives who left Irkutsk were forced to relinquish their rights and sign papers listing the terms they were forced to accept. One such condition was that they were allowed to meet their husbands only twice a week, in the presence of a duty officer, and that the couples must converse in Russian. This was especially difficult for the two French women, but Russian women, too, found it problematic, since Russian aristocratic families typically spoke French. Furthermore, the wives had to deposit money and valuables with the local treasury, and their belongings had to be registered with the commandant. Neither the Decembrists nor their wives were allowed to receive large sums of money. No drinks of any kind were allowed, letters were accepted only if authorized, and the prisoners could not receive money or writing materials. The wives were also obliged to keep the prison authorities informed of their place of residence at all times. One of the hardest conditions to accept was that children born in Siberia were considered state peasants. This meant that the convicts' loss of privilege would be passed on to the next generation.[54]

By far the toughest condition was the ban on returning home. It is unclear at which point the women understood that they were not allowed to return west. Maria Volkonskaia appears not to have realized this until she was in Irkutsk. In a letter to Sergei written a couple of days before her departure from St Petersburg, she wrote, 'without you I am as without life; only my love and duty to Nikolenka prevented me from sharing your fate earlier. I am leaving him without worry; he is surrounded by guardians and will not feel his mother's absence; his dear beaming face seems to tell me: "Go, go and return to take me with you."' Shortly before leaving Irkutsk, Maria seems to have understood that she would not be allowed to return. 'I am glad I did not know what awaited me here,' she wrote to her sister. 'It would have made the decision to leave Nikolenka and the family much harder.'[55] But perhaps she still did not comprehend the full meaning, or else she did not want her mother-in-law to know. As late as 28 May 1827, she told her mother-in-law that she had come to understand that once you had passed Irkutsk you could no longer return: 'I thank God a thousand times that I did not understand it before. This would only have increased the suffering that was tearing my heart apart.'[56]

Volkonskaia stayed for ten days in Irkutsk fighting the governor's attempts to prevent her from travelling further. Like Trubetskaia, she signed all the necessary papers without looking at them. Before leaving the town, Maria managed to see Aleksandra Muravieva, who had arrived a week after her. Aleksandra was just 22 but already had three children, Ekaterina, Mikhail and Elizaveta. The eldest was only two years old and the youngest not even ten months when she departed for Siberia, leaving the children with her mother-in-law. Aleksandra brought Maria greetings from Pushkin and a poem, 'Message to Siberia', to his friends in exile.[57] She also brought a poem to Pushkin's old Lyceum friend, Ivan Pushchin:

> My dearest friend from long ago!
> I too have blessed and thanked my fate
> When my secluded portico,
> Half buried in the mournful snow
> Announced your sleigh bell at the gate.
>
> Now holy Providence, I plead:
> Allow my distant voice to send
> Your soul a like relief in need,
> And to your prison may it speed
> Our glowing lycée days, my friend.[58]

When Aleksandra arrived in Irkutsk on 29 January, she was greeted by two letters: one from her mother, the other from her husband. Her mother was worried about her. Aleksandra immediately sat down to write to her, calming her and informing her that she was in good health. Physical suffering was not a problem, but she was devastated to have left her children behind. 'The journey was quite painful for me,' she wrote, 'but not because of fatigue – for moral reasons. Sadness weakened me: I have no news of my children since I left them. It has been six weeks since I heard anything about them.' Aleksandra also missed her mother and sisters. 'I embrace you and kiss your hands a million times with all the boundless tenderness that I feel and will feel for you until my last breath,' she wrote to her mother. 'I hug my sisters tenderly,' she added.[59]

Nikita's letter was to tell Aleksandra that he had arrived in Chita in good health, and to ask her not to worry:

My angel, be calm and pray to God in whom I place all my trust. I do not know how you will travel; there is almost no snow, especially at the last stations. In the name of Heaven, do not drive across Lake Baikal at night because of the slopes in the ice. Goodbye my angel, I kiss your hands and embrace you with all my love for you. I look forward to hearing from you, waiting for the happiness to hold you.[60]

While Aleksandra was preparing for her journey to Chita, Maria left for Blagodatsk. On the way she stopped in Verkhneudinsk to see her cousin Aleksandr Nikolaevich Muraviev and his wife, Praskovia, who lived there in exile. She then continued her journey in the biting cold. There was very little to eat at the post stations run by Buryats, and she lived on dried or salted beef and brick tea with melted fat.[61] When she arrived at Nerchinsk, she met Ekaterina, who had left Irkutsk eight days earlier, and they soon became friends. Maria found out that her husband was 19 kilometres (12 mi.) away at the Blagodatsk mine, and early the next day the two women left for the mine; they were followed by Burnashev, the head of the mines – a rude and cruel man, according to Geuble – in his sleigh. It was a difficult journey. On the last stretch, it was not possible to go by sledge because there was no snow, despite the cold. Maria recalled her things being loaded on to a *telega*, a rough four-wheeled springless wagon. It was not the most comfortable means of transportation, and hardly suitable for a piano.[62]

## Blagodatsk Mine, Nerchinsk

Volkonskaia and Trubetskaia arrived in Blagodatsk on 11 February 1827. The place consisted of a number of Buriat and Mongol settlements, a Cossack village, a few officials' houses and, by the Shilka River, a prison stockade. Maria described it in her memoirs:

It was a village consisting of a single road, surrounded by mountains ... The location would have been beautiful, except that the forest had been felled 50 *versts* [about 50 kilometres/30 mi.] all around for fear that fugitive prisoners would hide in them; even the bushes were cut down; in winter the view was depressing. The prison stood at the foot of a high mountain; it was the former barracks, confined, dirty and repulsive.[63]

The prisoners lived in a barrack formed of two huts, one for them and one for their guards. In the prisoners' hut, a massive Russian stove stood to the left, and to the right, along the wall, three storerooms had been built. In the wall facing the door there was a third storeroom. Volkonskaia described these as cages made of planks: 'One had to climb up two steps in order to enter them.' Trubetskoi and Obolenskii lived in one of these rooms. Trubetskoi had his plank bed lengthwise, while Obolenskii's was arranged so that half of his body lay under Trubetskoi's bed. The ceiling was so low that it was impossible to stand up straight. Three soldiers were watching them, and whenever they went outside, a sentry followed. The prisoners were not allowed to communicate privately with anyone.[64]

According to Volkonskaia, her husband shared the small cell with Trubetskoi and Obolenskii. When she first entered the room, she could not see anything. It was almost completely dark. Then Sergei came forwards. The rattle of his chain shocked her: 'I did not know that he was in shackles ... the sight of his shackles inflamed and moved me so much that I threw myself on my knees in front of him, kissed his shackles and then kissed him.'[65]

Conditions in the prison were unsanitary, to say the least. The air was stuffy and there were millions of insects. Trubetskoi had begun to spit blood; Volkonskii had chest pains and suffered from an acute liver condition; Obolenskii had scurvy. Maria was very concerned about Sergei's health. She asked her mother-in-law, Aleksandra Volkonskaia, to send medical instruments ('une ventouse') for chest inflammations, as well as fine wine that she could mix with water, and told her that she would not leave Sergei until he had shown some improvement. It was important to Maria that she had not left her son in vain. 'I will not give my son a regret,' she wrote. 'I will only return to him with a perfectly calm soul, even if I have to wait fourteen years.'[66] Once more, it appears that Maria had not accepted that she could never see her son again.

In her letters from Blagodatsk, Maria often returned to the idea that it was her goal in life to support Sergei and alleviate his suffering. 'The loss of titles or wealth, for me, is no loss at all. What would I have done with it all without Sergei?'[67] What would life be like for her away from him? Her only consolation on Earth was to share the fate of her husband. However, in Blagodatsk, she was allowed to meet Sergei only once every three days. In the days between, with nothing to distract her, she felt abandoned by the whole universe. Only letters from relatives could provide comfort.[68] Yet communications were slow and letters greatly delayed. This made her anxious. She begged her mother-in-law to send news about her son. With no future for herself, all her wishes were for him. Finally, letters arrived. Over time, Maria became used to the way of life at the mines. She started to feel that she had not really existed before Blagodatsk. It was only there that she felt the full value of life.

Volkonskaia and Trubetskaia rented a peasant hut from a local Cossack. 'It was so cramped that when I lay on the floor on my mattress, my head touched the wall and my legs rested on the door,' Maria recalled. The stove emitted a lot of smoke and could not be used when it was windy, so the cottage was very cold. It was also dark, because mica instead of glass was used for windowpanes. Ekaterina was well aware that she could not expect any comforts at the mine; Sergei had told her in early November to prepare for hardship: 'you have never seen such cramped, low and poor huts as are here. In addition, you will truly have to be in poverty, for many of the simplest necessities in life cannot be obtained here for any money, and if something can be obtained, then at such a price that you would rather do without them.' He advised her to bring only what was needed, such as kitchen utensils, an iron, warm clothes and shoes.[69]

Without servants, Maria and Ekaterina had to do everything themselves. Being unaccustomed to practical household tasks, they found this hard, but they did not lose heart. They started cooking for the prisoners on the wood-burning stove with the help of a cookbook Trubetskaia had brought. Obolenskii remembered the improvised dishes the women brought to their barracks: 'We were delighted, and everything appeared so delicious to us that bread baked by Princess Trubetskaia almost seemed tastier to us than the best work of the first Petersburg baker.'[70] Food was expensive, however, and most of their funds were deposited in Irkutsk. Furthermore, the prison manager controlled their money and they had to report daily expenses to him. Volkonskaia had saved the money she had sewn into her travel clothes, but it did not last long, so they decided to limit their own food to soup and porridge. When the prisoners realized that Ekaterina and Maria were starving themselves so that they could afford to buy food for them, they refused to accept this. Instead, they paid the prison guards to supply them with food. Maria and Ekaterina helped as best they could with supplies.

The Decembrists took dinner, tea and supper together, and this was a great comfort to them. 'We drew closer and yet closer to each other,' Obolenskii reported, 'and our common grief still further reinforced the ties of friendship that united us.' He also emphasized the comfort the two women provided. 'It is hard to express what the ladies ... were for us,' he wrote. 'One might justly call them sisters of mercy. They cared for us like close relations, and always and everywhere their presence instilled in us courage and inner strength.'[71] The arrival of the two women brought other benefits to the Decembrists. Since the prisoners were deprived of all means of communication as well as financial assistance, Volkonskaia and Trubetskaia helped to re-establish contact with the prisoners' families. They wrote letters and requested packages for them, and soon letters and parcels began to arrive.

When they were not writing letters or doing housework, Maria and Ekaterina spent most of their time sitting on stones under the prison window, talking to their husbands. Sometimes, they went on excursions. Maria especially enjoyed visiting China, which was only about 20 kilometres (12 mi.) away. She was fascinated by anything she found exotic, foreign or different, and this included native peoples, foreigners and common people. A robber was incarcerated in the vicinity, and she regarded him as a sort of Robin Hood figure because he never stole from poor people. Apparently, he had a fantastic voice and organized a choir. Maria helped them and was struck by 'the feeling of gratitude and devotion in these people'.[72]

Nicholas I continued to be personally involved in the destiny of the Decembrists. When considering the best choice of incarceration for them, he followed the advice of Aleksandr Lavinskii, governor of Eastern Siberia, who maintained that the political prisoners should stay together as a group to prevent them from spreading liberal ideas among the exiled population. Concentrating them in a single location would make them easier to monitor, he argued. For this reason, Major General Leparskii, who had been appointed commandant of Nerchinsk mining district in August 1826, was ordered to find a place that was suitable for a temporary prison. In the meantime, the transportation of prisoners to Siberia was halted. Finally, at Leparskii's recommendation, the governor decided to place them temporarily in the fortress of Chita in the Ingoda Valley, while constructing special quarters in another part of the Nerchinsk Mining District. The first Decembrists arrived in Chita at the beginning of 1827. When the building of the larger prison was complete in August, Decembrists were gathered from all the assigned places and removed to Chita.[73]

# 10

# Prison Life

Chita, on the great road between Lake Baikal and Nerchinsk, was a small frontier settlement set on an elevation with high mountains on two sides. It had three hundred inhabitants, who lived by agriculture and fishing. There were 26 cabins, an old wooden church and three houses, occupied by the commandant, the mining superintendent and the town major. Nearby was a waterfall where the River Chita fell into the great River Ingoda, forming a delightful valley. 'Chita stands at a great altitude, and consequently enjoys clear, unclouded skies,' Andrei Rozen recounted. 'If snow occasionally falls, the wind carries it down at once into the valleys. The thermometer stands at forty degrees of frost (Réaumur) [-50°C/-58°F], so that quicksilver freezes.'[1]

The first Decembrists to arrive in Chita were Ivan Annenkov, Konstantin Torson and the Muraviev brothers (Aleksandr and Nikita). Not long afterwards, another group of four arrived: Piotr Svistunov, Dmitrii Zavalishin and the Kriukov brothers (Nikolai and Aleksandr). All were placed in a single room in an abandoned Cossack fortress, a wooden building subdivided into two small rooms and a tiny one by the entrance. When Nikolai Basargin and his fellow travellers Ferdinand Volf, Mikhail Fonvizin and A. F. Frolov arrived in February, they were placed in the second of the two rooms. Accustomed to solitary confinement and strict rules, the newly arrived prisoners were happily surprised the next morning when the eight men from the other room came into their quarters, greeted them and invited them to their room for tea. At first, they had neither linen nor beds. However, unexpected help came from Felitsata Osipovna Smolianinova, the wife of the Chita mining engineer, who sent bed-linen and provisions. Often, when they were working, she would provide them with breakfast.

As more Decembrists arrived, the old fortress became overcrowded. Sixteen people lived in each of the small rooms and four in the minuscule vestibule. There was so little space that it was difficult to move, and the noise from the ironworks was so loud that it was hard to hear what people were saying. Each man had a sleeping space less than 55 centimetres (22 in.) wide, so it was impossible not to bump into your neighbour during the night.[2] The shackles were very heavy and painful to wear, especially for those who were tall, such as Annenkov and Sergei Trubetskoi, whose chains were too short. 'Our rooms were so small that we could not keep them as clean as we wished,' Rozen recalled. They had board beds covered with felt rugs or fur coats; under the bunks lay suitcases and boots. 'In the night, when doors and windows were closed, the air was intolerably oppressive.'[3] As soon as the doors were opened in the morning, Rozen went outside to get some fresh air.

In August 1827 most prisoners were moved to a larger, newly built wooden stockade prison, where each man had a bed and a bedside table. Still, over time this prison also became full. 'We lived there like herrings in a barrel,' wrote Mikhail Bestuzhev, who arrived in Chita with his brother Nikolai on 14 December, and there was a constant din of chains and voices. Mikhail needed rest; he had almost been killed during the journey to Chita when he was hurled out of the coach and his chains caught in the wheels.[4]

Eventually, all the Decembrists who had been sentenced to hard labour arrived, except G. S. Batenkov, Vilgelm Kiukhelbeker and Iosif Poggio, who had been left in fortresses in the western parts of the empire. Batenkov spent about twenty years in confinement, the other two about ten. When Ivan Iakushkin came to Chita from Finland on Christmas Eve 1827, he noticed that everyone was in chains: 'Everything rattled and moved, but no one was depressed.' Only Nikita Muraviev was ill and suffered badly. He had recently learned that his son had died in Moscow. Three days later Ivan Pushchin, Aleksandr Poggio and Piotr Mukhanov arrived, and after two more days came Fedor Vadkovskii. They all ended up in the same room, and 'when the seven of us went to sleep on the plank beds, each had less than an *arshin*'s [about 30 centimetres/1 ft] width; but this did not concern us then at all.'[5] They were so happy to meet their friends and acquaintances.

By the middle of September 1827 the Decembrists from Blagodatsk, and shortly afterwards their wives, were on the road to Chita. Maria Volkonskaia was happy to go. She was concerned about her husband's health. The summer had been extremely hot and the high humidity in the mine was bad for his lungs. In fact, Sergei Volkonskii was spitting blood on the day of their departure, and Maria feared that travel would tire him. The journey to Chita took about two weeks and during that time it would be impossible to receive any news of him. It was at least a comfort to Maria that she was accompanied by Ekaterina Trubetskaia. The journey was very tiring. The cold was insufferable, the roads terrible and often hazardous, the food inadequate and unsavoury. When the two women finally arrived in Chita, their husbands were still on the road and they waited anxiously for them. Maria was so exhausted from the trip that she could not write for several days, but Sergei had managed the journey better than she feared.[6]

When Maria and Ekaterina arrived in Chita, 'tired [and] broken', they first met Aleksandra Muravieva, who had lived there since February.[7] Aleksandra, or Aleksandrina, lived in a rented house with a balcony and a large window in the side of the attic from which the prisoners could be seen when they were in the garden. Elizaveta Naryshkina, the wife of Mikhail Naryshkin of the Northern Society, had moved in with her when she arrived in early summer. Before that, Muravieva had lived alone in Chita for more than four months, seeing her husband only for an hour twice a week in the company of an officer. 'Such incomparable monotony,' she wrote to her mother-in-law in May. 'Fifteen years of this existence is a sad future . . . I have been here only three months, but it seems like ten years. Time has never seemed so long to me.'[8]

Aleksandra missed her children immensely but tried to hide her feelings from her husband. Other prisoners noticed her misery, however.[9] In order not to worry her husband, she was cheerful and positive in his presence, but as soon as she was alone, she suffered from longing for her absent children.[10] These feelings never abated. In her letters, it appears Aleksandra was trying to come to terms with her fate but could not help becoming involved in her children's life. For example, she was delighted to learn that her daughter Katia could already play the piano and told her mother-in-law that she would be very pleased if Katia put her effort into it, because she had a taste for music.[11] Against all odds, Aleksandra seems to have believed that she would see them again.

Maria was very attached to Aleksandra, who had 'a warm heart and nobility in her every act', and would have preferred to stay with her. But Elizaveta was already living with her. Twenty-three-year-old Elizaveta did not leave any children behind; her daughter had died some time ago in Moscow. Elizaveta was a well-educated, proud woman. Pauline Annenkova (née Geuble) later wrote about the contrast between Aleksandra and Elizaveta. In Pauline's opinion, Alexandrina was sweet, young and beautiful, but terribly fretful. She took everything too much to heart. Elizaveta, on the other hand, was not so attractive. When you first met her, said Pauline, she appeared arrogant and made an unpleasant impression. However, as you

N. P. Repin, *Decembrists in Chita*, 1829, drawing, paper on cardboard.

came to know her, you noticed her boundless kindness and unusually noble character.[12]

Elizaveta arrived in Chita in the early summer, together with Aleksandra Ientaltseva, who was 44 years old and childless. Maria described Aleksandra as beautiful, intelligent, well-read and devoted to her husband.[13] She was invited to come and live with Ekaterina and Maria in one room in the house of a local deacon. The room was divided by a partition, and Aleksandra took the smaller part for herself. The three women slept on mattresses laid out on the floor. The heating was primitive and the hut usually smoky, but their living quarters were 'far more comfortable than the one in Blagodatsk', as Maria wrote; 'at least here I have a place for a table to write, an embroidering frame and the clavichord.'[14]

Judging by Maria's correspondence, she was a proud young woman who did not want people to feel sorry for her. In her letters, she emphasized that she was doing well and so was Sergei. She was proud of the way her husband 'exemplified humility and firmness'. The image she conveyed was that she led an active and hard-working life. Her main duty, however, was to be with Sergei, to support him and look after his health. 'I feel myself unfortunate only at times when Sergei becomes ill,' she told her sister-in-law. 'If they would only allow me to share with him the cell and devote my life to him, I would consider myself a fortunate woman.'[15] But things were not as simple as Maria made them seem. She felt she had no right to complain about her situation because of her 'poor little boy' at home. Nikolenka was constantly on her mind and she worried a lot about him. Sergei did too. When they did not receive any news or were told that he was ill, they did not even dare say his name. On the other hand, when they received positive news, they were delighted. In a letter to her sister-in-law, Maria expressed her longing for her little Nikolenka. 'Will he always be deprived of the blessings of his father?' she wondered. If she could only 'live with them both in some corner of Siberia'.[16]

Ekaterina made a strong impression on Maria. She was undemanding, never complained and appeared content with everything. In a letter to her sister Zinaida, Ekaterina wrote that 'you cannot imagine, but since the time I am able to see Sergei, I am calm and contented. I am no more in need of commiseration; I do not think of the past, nor of the present.' She told her sister that she sought no earthly happiness and was prepared to accept everything according to God's will, although she confessed that, if there were anything in the world she might envy, it would be people who lived in a moderate climate.[17] Whether Ekaterina was truthful or not is hard to tell, but many people described her as cheerful, selfless and kind. Moreover, she did not suffer from having to leave a child behind.

Money worries were recurring in the letters from Chita. It was difficult to get hold of things in Siberia, and everything was expensive. Moreover, local people tended to avoid the Decembrists. 'They fear to lend me the smallest item,' Maria complained.[18] The women in Chita asked relatives to send food, cloth, linen and tobacco, as well as books. 'All these things are most unavailable here or are too expensive for us, considering the allowance they issue us,' Maria informed her mother-in-law.[19] Maria was very pleased when she received a package of provisions from home and found bouillon among them. Now she could finally make better-tasting soup for her husband.[20]

Nevertheless, there was a positive mood among the prisoners in Chita. One reason was the healthy climate. The winters were admittedly long and sometimes extremely cold, and the summers hot, but it was not humid. The climate was dry and sunny, fresh and bracing. Summer came late, in early June, when nature exploded in an abundance of flowers. The valley of Chita was renowned for its flora and the region was called the Garden of Siberia.

Even more important to the prisoners' state of mind was the fact that they were now together. The decision to put all the Decembrists in the same place allowed them to draw strength from one another and, with the help of the wives, to rejoin the world, from which they had been cut off by their civil execution. In Bestuzhev's words, they were given 'political existence beyond political death'.[21] After isolation in the fortress, it was a relief for them to meet like-minded people who had suffered the same fate. They had dinner together, usually cabbage soup and porridge with butter but also vegetables from the garden. Wooden trestles were carried into the room; planks were laid across and some sort of cloth was placed on top; the food arrived; they served themselves and sat around the table or on the bunks. Sometimes they had supper standing or walking. Such disorder was strange to them, but exciting at the same time. They took turns to be on duty, to prepare dinner and tea, to clean up and do the dishes.

In concentrating the Decembrists in a single place, the government made it possible for them to preserve their notions of egalitarianism and moral dignity. Basargin held that 'the government gave us the means not only to maintain our moral dignity but also to raise it still higher.'[22] In this spirit, the Decembrists formed a cooperative, an artel to which everyone with money contributed.[23] This community gave them a sense of freedom and at the same time chimed with their Romantic view of loyalty and comradeship. It was also a form of life they recognized from the military, where junior officers sometimes pooled their resources to make ends meet.[24] Every three months a senior, responsible for supplies, was chosen, his bills of exchange to be issued from the commandant's office. After each election a piece of paper was sent around, on which everyone wrote down their contribution to the common cost. The senior used the money for food and household products. Two prisoners were responsible for the vegetable garden. The land was extremely fertile, so that vegetables ripened within five weeks of the frost's ending. Everything grew with amazing speed. The women added things from their own resources. When they received parcels from relatives containing such provisions as sugar, coffee, chocolate, rice, olive oil and wine, everything was distributed among the prisoners. It was at first difficult to transfer wine to the prison, but later, when the men were allowed to visit their wives at home, they were able to put bottles in their pockets, which no one bothered to check.

With the organization of the artel, the prisoners' life improved. Despite the fact that many of the prisoners were quite poor and completely ignored by their relatives, no one lacked anything or became dependent on anybody else. Ekaterina Muravieva, the generous mother of Nikita and Aleksandr Muraviev, provided her sons with supplies that were then distributed to those who needed them. Among other things, she sent an excellent pharmacy, as well as surgical instruments. Former staff-surgeon Volf helped the sick. He had access to the best Russian and foreign medical journals through the

Decembrist wives. Artamon Muraviev, who had some knowledge of surgery, acted as a medical assistant. Volf was considered very skilled, and even the commandant turned to him in the event of illness.[25]

In Chita, the prisoners engaged in intellectual and artistic activities. They created 'a tolerable library' from the books that each individual had brought. Muraviev and Trubetskoi had their private collections sent for and lent books to everyone. The wives ordered books and subscribed to journals and newspapers in various languages. The prisoners had a reading list, and everyone was allowed two hours for reading a newspaper and two or three days for a journal. They formed an informal academy in one of the huts, where they gathered for literary talks and gave lectures on various topics in which they were knowledgeable.[26] Some prisoners busied themselves with translations, while others started learning foreign languages.

There was also artistic talent among the imprisoned Decembrists. Some of them, such as Aleksandr Odoevskii, wrote poetry. Nikolai Bestuzhev, who was a gifted artist, made portraits and drawings of the prison and its surroundings. Others played instruments and sang in a choir. They held concerts and musical evenings. Fedor Vadkovskii was a skilled violinist, Svistunov and Nikolai Kriukov played the cello, and Aleksei Iushnevskii, a skilled pianist, also played the violin. Together 'they made an excellent quartet, which on 30 August 1828, when we celebrated sixteen birthday people, played for the first time for all of us in the large prison.'[27]

The actual labour required of the prisoners at Chita was not excessive. They worked five hours a day in two shifts. Their wives believed the work was good for them, because it allowed them to exercise. There were no mines in Chita; instead, the prisoners cleaned barns and stables, swept the streets, did roadwork, tended the prison garden or worked the hand mills at the local flourmill. In the summer the prisoners spent time outside, each working on his own patch of land.

In the spring, three additional women reached Chita. Natalia Fonvizina arrived in March. She had been only 22 at the time of the arrests, and had to leave behind two infant sons, Dmitrii and Mikhail. This affected her health badly. Maria Volkonskaia described her (in a way that may seem unfavourable) as having 'a typical Russian face, white, fresh, with bulging eyes; small and plump'. By contrast, Nikolai Lorer found her especially charming, with beautiful blue eyes. Svistunov remembered her as 'free from all vanity' and gave her praise typical of the gender roles of his time: 'She never sought to expose her intelligence or that she was well read. People who met her knew only by chance that she was clever.'[28]

Aleksandra Davydova also arrived in early spring. She was only a year older than Fonvizina, but already had six children and had to leave them with relatives to follow her husband. She was described as a sweet, charming woman, deeply devoted, with a mild temper.[29] She arrived in Irkutsk at the same time as Pauline Geuble, the French fiancée of Ivan Annenkov, but was allowed to continue to Chita before her. To Volkonskaia's delight, her maid Masha arrived with Davydova. Masha stayed with Maria for many years.

Geuble's journey from Moscow to Irkutsk took only eighteen days. It was an adventurous voyage; she was almost killed by horses, had an accident with the carriage, was at risk of frostbite and narrowly escaped from robbers. Yet when she later called this journey to mind, what she remembered most clearly was the hospitality of the Siberian people. She arrived in Irkutsk on 10 January but was not allowed to continue her journey until 28 February. As soon as she received the permit, she bought provisions and utensils, sewed her money into black taffeta and tied it up in her hair. Having reached her destination, it was several days before she was allowed to meet Annenkov. On the third day he arrived in shackles guarded by a sentry and an officer. The officer left them for two hours, as Geuble recalled: 'It is impossible to describe our first meeting and the senseless joy that we indulged in after the long separation, having forgotten all the grief and the terrible situation in which we were.'[30]

On 4 April Pauline and Ivan were married in Chita's chapel. Commandant Leparskii acted as nuptial godfather and Natalia Fonvizina as nuptial god-mother. Ivan's leg chains were removed for the ceremony. Afterwards, the prisoners went back to the prison, while the women met in Pauline's small apartment. Volkonskaia described her in her memoirs as young, beautiful, able to seek out the funny side in others, and with a deep love for Annenkov. The next day the commandant allowed the newlyweds to meet for two hours. This was an exception – normally husbands were brought to their wives only in case of serious illness.

Now there were eight women in Chita. They played an important role in prison life as a source of strength, providing comfort and support to everyone. Iakushkin especially remembered Aleksandra Muravieva and her warmth of heart, which spread to everyone around her. She was often ill, but as soon as she heard that someone was sick or upset, she forgot her own ailment and rushed to the suffering.[31] The fact that the women participated in the lives of the prisoners and at the same time had their own rights gave the incarcerated Decembrists some power that prisoners did not normally have. The wives could complain to the commandant when things were bad.

Basargin recalled that they would round on Leparskii and tell him that if he did not wish to be regarded as a common jailer, who sold himself for money, he should alleviate their lot. Apparently, he took this to heart. Furthermore, the wives had contacts and could also complain to the government, which did not want any negative publicity. The women also managed the entire correspondence with the prisoners' relatives.[32] Most fell to the lot of Volkonskaia and Trubetskaia, since they knew many of the relatives personally. They would write as many as thirty letters at a time. All were left unsealed for Leparskii, who forwarded them to the Third Department, which served as the regime's secret police.

In addition to assisting the prisoners in various ways, the women engaged in household chores to which most noble women were strangers, such as cleaning, preparing meals, patching old clothes and gardening. They grew vegetables and tended fruit trees. Annenkova recalled getting so much produce from her garden that she filled up a whole room in her little house with vegetables. Volkonskaia, an excellent gardener, was also good at mending and sewing. Trubetskaia was more skilled at cooking, but Annenkova was the most accomplished cook. Not even the killing of fowl was a problem for her. She disapproved of the prison food, which consisted mainly of cabbage soup and porridge, so every day she brought her husband a dinner that she had made herself, even though she did not have a stove. Instead, she used the roasters, which were placed under a canopy by the prison.

Life in Chita was quiet and monotonous for the women. They could go for walks, but were forbidden to leave the village without permission. They saw their husbands twice weekly in a special room, accompanied by a duty officer. Often, when they heard the convicts' clanking chains, they ran to the window and 'with bitter joy' watched the men go to work.[33] The women spent a lot of time by the high stockade of sharpened logs, where they could talk to their husbands. At the beginning they had to do this secretly, in fear of discovery, but eventually they received permission to go there. These visits are mentioned in a poem by Odoevskii, dedicated to Volkonskaia and written in her album on her 24th birthday, 25 December 1829:

> There was a land dedicated to tears and sorrow,
> The Eastern land, where the rosy dawn,
> Ray of joy, in heaven born,
> Did not delight the suffering eyes;
> Where it was stifling and eternally clear,
> And the bright shelter bothered the prisoners,

And the whole view, vast and beautiful,
Painfully evoked freedom.

Suddenly angels from azure descended
With joy to the sufferers of that country,
But first they dressed their heavenly spirit
In transparent, earthly shrouds,
And the messengers of good Providence
Appeared as daughters of the earth,
And to the prisoners, with a smile of consolation,
They brought love and peace of mind.

And every day they sat down by the fence,
And through it the heavenly lips
Drop by drop sharpened the honey of consolation.
Since then, days and summers have flowed in the dungeon;
In the recluses of sorrow, everyone fell asleep,
And they were afraid only of one thing,
That the angels would fly up to heaven,
And throw off their veils.[34]

At first the women rented accommodation, but later they built their own houses in a row that became called Damskaia ulitsa, Ladies Street.[35] Annenkova's house was at the very end of the village. Behind it was a dense forest, across the street lay a terrifying precipice, and below was a beautiful meadow. The view from the windows was outstanding, and she frequently sat for hours on end, admiring it. In her new house, Pauline finally had a stove. The other women often came to see how she cooked dinner and asked her to teach them to make soup or bake a cake. Sometimes, they would arrive at Pauline's house unexpectedly with their provisions and ask her to cook something. However, according to Pauline, when it came to the point when it was necessary to chop raw beef or clean the chicken, the other women could not overcome their aversion, despite their best efforts:

Then our ladies tearfully admitted that they envy my ability to do everything, and bitterly complained about themselves for not being able to do anything, but that was not their fault, of course. They were not prepared by upbringing for the kind of life that fell to their lot, and from an early age I was accustomed to everything by need.[36]

During the long evenings the women gathered to sew, read and discuss various topics. Their friendship helped them to endure adversity. They shared everything, both sorrows and joys, and supported one another. 'The women have formed here some kind of family,' Volkonskaia observed. 'They accept each other with open arms – how misfortune brings people together!'[37] However, if there was a lot of deprivation, hard work and sorrow in Chita, there was also a lot of joy. One evening in September, when Pauline sat on her porch singing French romances, laughter suddenly broke the silence and all the women appeared, armed with huge sticks. 'The guests cheerfully announced to me that they were hungry,' she recalled, 'that they had no provisions and that I should feed them. They knew that I always had something in store.' She brought out a jellied pig and fried game, and salad was brought from the garden, Elizaveta Naryshkina bringing a lantern so that they could find it in the dark. Then dinner was ready, but there was nothing to drink. The resourceful Pauline soon solved this problem by finding some raspberry syrup. 'All this amused us and made us laugh like little girls,' she recalled. For a long time they sat around the table talking, then, 'having dined and laughed to the full, the ladies went home.'[38]

Sometimes in the winter, the extreme cold prevented them from meeting as often as they would have liked. 'Because of the frightfully low temperature I seldom see my friends,' Maria complained to her sister-in-law at the end of December 1827. For more than a month the thermometer hovered between -30 and -36°Ré. However, a week later Maria noted that the weather had been less cold, no worse than -25 to -30°Ré: 'Judge what we are reduced to since we find such a temperature mild.'[39]

Many of the women were fascinated by the Buriats whom they often saw passing through Chita, driving sheep. The Buriats, who lived in an encampment just outside the village, began after some time to visit the Russian women, bringing various goods and staying for tea.[40] Nikolai Bestuzhev compiled a Buriat–Russian dictionary, and Volkonskaia managed to learn the basic elements of the language. She felt that, 'since they are all around us and were here long before any Russian set foot in this country, we might as well learn to address them in their own tongue.' A Buriat prince called on her regularly and she came to regard him as a friend.[41]

Maria had a romanticized view of the Indigenous people. Pauline was also influenced by the Romantic exoticism of her time. Her descriptions of Buriats are patronizing and benevolent, in line with the image of 'the noble savage', the idealized figure of 'nature's gentleman', popularized in Romantic writings of the eighteenth and nineteenth centuries. This is especially true of their leader, Taisha, whom she happened to meet at a post station. Pauline was struck by his beauty and courtesy, but found him difficult to place – not European, yet not entirely Asian. 'Tall, slender, very beautiful, he bowed politely and extremely deftly to me, although not at all European. His face, although completely Asian, expressed a lot of meekness, he was dressed very elegantly and extremely richly ... His head was shaved [with] the braid, as the Chinese wear.'[42] On her way to Petrovsk Zavod, more than two years later, she met Taisha once more, 'this son of nature and steppe'. Again, she was struck by 'the extraordinary elegance of his manners'. This made her think that he 'probably knew how to love and feel ardently, like civilized people'. To her, it was this combination of being 'a man of nature' yet presenting a 'civilized' appearance and manners that made him interesting. Pauline saw him as someone who could combine the wild untamed nature with civilized behaviour and emotions.

In her memoirs, Pauline later wrote that she had several friends among the Buriats. She particularly remembered one, Natam, who was fond of his food. When he came to visit, he sat down on the floor and said, '"Let's eat" ... He ate for an hour without stopping. Finally, his face became oily, and he was flooded in sweat. He puffed in a terrible way, but nevertheless said: "Come on again," until he was so full he could not move. He got up with great difficulty and went to bed.'[43] Pauline found this ability mesmerizing. Even more fascinating, however, was the Buriats' capacity to starve, which meant that they sometimes did not eat for whole weeks.

Rozen was also interested in the Buriats, but his was a more ethnographic than an anthropological curiosity. In common with many contemporary male colonizers, Andrei was more interested in mapping and categorizing Indigenous people than in getting to know and understand them. In his memoirs, he praised their well-made felt tents, which did not let the wind through, and wrote admiringly about their ability to manage for a long time without food. Luxury for them, he wrote, was brick tea, which they drank from lacquered wooden bowls, and tobacco, which they smoked in small copper pipes: 'The Buriats broke off little bits from these lumps [of tea] with their hatchets, ground or pounded them in mortars, boiled the tea-powder in a kettle, added some flour, milk, or butter and fat, and drank this brew with much relish.' He was impressed by the Buriats' perseverance, ability to survive and unexpected skill at chess, but critical of their 'uncivilized' nomadic life. 'A small number of this nomadic race have turned to Christianity, live in houses and practise agriculture,' he wrote; 'the remainder are idolaters and are led by their priests, the Shamans, who purposely keep up their superstitions.' He also accused them of being dirty: 'The uncleanliness of the Buriats reaches the highest possible degree. They have no linen, wear furs next to their bare bodies and boots of chamois skin and . . . little fur caps.'[44]

This description may be contrasted with Andrei's portrayal of the Old Believers, a people whose ancestors were exiled to Siberia in the eighteenth century because of their sectarianism. After visiting their villages, Andrei was impressed by their wealth and wrote that it was a result of their industriousness and piety. He also made an interesting comparison with America. 'The riches and prosperity of these peasants made me feel as if I was looking at Russians at work in America, rather than in Siberia,' he noted. 'Here they are quite as well off as in America; they have a large and very fruitful territory, an industrious population, and govern themselves.'[45]

Several of the Decembrist wives became pregnant in 1828 and gave birth the following year. The old commandant's confusion about their condition amused them. 'Look, allow me to say that you have no right to be pregnant,' said Leparskii, in great confusion. However, 'when the births begin, well, then it is another matter.'[46] The women considered themselves lucky to have such a kind man as their commandant. Beneath his stern appearance, he had a warm heart. In March 1829 Annenkova had a daughter, whom she named Anna after her grandmother. That same month Muravieva gave birth to Nonushka (Sophia). The fragile Aleksandra almost died afterwards, but Volf took good care of her and she recovered. Davydova gave birth to a boy, Vaka (Vasilii), on 20 July 1829, and on 2 February 1830, after nine whole years of marriage, Trubetskaia gave birth to a girl, Sasha (Aleksandra). In July she wrote to Zinaida, telling her how happy she was. As she held the baby in her arms, she was distressed by a single thought: that she would be unable to feed the baby herself, a concern most mothers share to this day.[47]

Over time, things in Chita changed for the better. The prisoners' chains were removed in September 1828, and the Bestuzhev brothers made from them iron rings and bracelets that were worn by the Decembrist wives. Later, this became the highest fashion. The Bestuzhevs received orders not only from friends and relatives but from strangers. After the prisoners were freed from the chains, their confinement became less strict. Husbands would walk over to see their wives every day, and if a woman were ill, her husband was allowed to stay overnight. With time, the men did not live in their cells at all, but simply went to work from their wives' houses. Subsequently, the other prisoners were allowed to visit married couples, but only one household per person and day.[48]

Although they did quite well, many dreamed of escaping. Most, however, realized that such dreams were pointless. One of those planning to flee was Vasilii Ivashev, but he changed his mind when he suddenly received a request for marriage in a letter from his mother. It concerned a certain Camille Le Dantu. Her mother was a governess in the Ivashov family, and Camille had been brought up in their house with Vasilii's sisters. Owing to their different social positions, marriage would normally never have been considered, but now things were different. Nevertheless, the motive behind the marriage request is unclear. According to some accounts, Camille agreed to marry Vasilii for material reasons; others claim that she was in love with him even before the verdict. Vasilii hesitated for moral reasons, because of all the sacrifices Camille would have to make, but in the end he was persuaded by his friends to agree to the marriage.[49]

In January 1828 Volkonskaia learned that Nikolenka, her firstborn, had died in St Petersburg. Aleksandr Pushkin wrote a moving epitaph:

> In splendour and in joyful peace,
> At the throne of the Eternal Creator,
> He gazes with a smile on earthly exile,
> Blesses mother and prays for his father.[50]

Maria was hit by waves of grief and guilt, and even a year later the sense of loss was still strong: 'Three days ago was the dreadful anniversary. God's will be done. Since I had no rendezvous on that day, Sergei was not able to notice my state of mind. It was for the first time of the entire past that I was happy not to be with him, for we would only have embarrassed each other.' At this point, Maria began to worry about the future: 'I am unable to say how I feel when I think of our future. When I die, what will happen to Sergei, who has no one in this world to care for him?' She again asked her mother-in-law to help her gain permission to share a cell with her husband: 'I entrust you my fate; obtain this single favour that will assure me peace on this earth: get me a permit to be confined with Sergei and I will forget all my sorrows.'[51]

In September that year, Maria's father died. It was entirely unexpected. She recalled that 'the shock was so strong that it seemed to me that the sky fell on me.' These events affected her otherwise cheerful disposition. On New Year's Eve she did not have any expectations for the year ahead. 'Our fate will not be changed,' she wrote. 'My simple wish is that I will be able to share the prison cell with Sergei.'[52] However, more deaths would occur.

On 10 July 1830 Maria gave birth to a baby girl, Sophia, but she lived for only two days owing to a defective heart valve. She was buried in a small wooden coffin on a hill overlooking the Ingoda River. Maria was again overwhelmed by grief.

> In the entire surrounding landscape I can see only one thing... the new cross on the grave of my child. How will I ever find enough courage to live here and continue to look after Sergei, whose health has again taken a turn for the worse? Soniushka would have given me strength to continue. I am very lonely these days.[53]

## The journey to Petrovsk Zavod

In early June 1830 the Decembrists were informed that they would be transferred to a permanent prison 725 kilometres (450 mi.) from Chita. In this new prison, they would have their own cells and their wives would be allowed to move in with them, but husbands and wives could no longer meet outside the prison. This was a change for the worse. The wives wrote letters to Alexander von Benckendorff, head of the Gendarmes and the Secret Police, requesting that they be allowed to continue to see their husbands in their homes. The women presented different arguments, but they had clearly discussed the issue among themselves and submitted similar requests. Most of them appealed to contemporary gender roles. Some spoke of men's duty to protect and support weaker women; others emphasized the sacrifices they had made for love, gave health reasons or mentioned the difficulties of living with children in prison. Although the requests were denied, this is yet another example of the resourcefulness of the Decembrist wives.

The journey to the new prison was expected to take about a month. The prisoners went on foot, making about 21–32 kilometres (13–20 mi.) per day, with every third day reserved for resting.[54] They travelled in two convoys escorted by soldiers. Lieutenant Colonel Leparskii, nephew of their commandant, led the first group, which left on 7 August, and the commandant himself led the second, leaving two days later. Pauline Annenkova and her children travelled with the second group. As they set out from the Ingoda River, she could see the first group far ahead. 'Leparskii rode a white horse. Then followed the prisoners all dressed in a very original way, however, quite beautiful; some were even very comical.' Basargin, who was in the first group, recalled that they were dying with laughter looking at our costumes and our comic procession. First came Zavalishin in a round hat with an enormous brim and a black dress of his own invention, like a Quaker's caftan. Being small, he held in one hand a stick much taller than he was and in the other the book he was reading. Behind him was Iakushkin in a children's jacket and Volkonskii in a woman's jacket; some wore long-brimmed sequin frock coats, others Spanish robes.[55]

The women of each group travelled ahead of the men on wagons and peasant carts loaded with kitchen utensils and other necessities. They rode slowly, waiting, as Annenkova recalled, for an opportunity to see their husbands, 'but the commandant, noticing such a manoeuvre on our part, ordered us to go ahead and even forbade colliding at the stations, and sent a Cossack with an order to prepare horses for us to prevent deliberate stops or unintentional delays.'[56]

The Decembrists' representations of Eastern Siberia from the journey convey the imperialist outlook typical of its time. Basargin depicted both nature and people in classic imperialist terms, focusing on 'the picturesque' and 'the exotic'. The chosen campsites, he wrote, were near a river or spring in a meadow, and always in 'picturesque surroundings'. In the evening, the camp presented 'a beautiful picture for the eyes'. Around it was a chain of sentries; fires were lit in different places, where the Buriats sat, including women, 'with their Asian faces and strange costumes'. They had been hired to transport equipment, build fires and erect tents: 'Lights shone in our yurts and the whole interior . . . was visible through their open entrance.' Most of the prisoners walked about in small groups near the fires, talking with the Buriats or among themselves.[57] Several of the Decembrists were engaged in the imperial practices of mapping the local flora and collecting insects. The Borisov brothers compiled a huge collection of insects, whereas Iakushkin was the foremost botanist.

When the Decembrists looked back on this journey in their memoirs, they had very fond memories of it. The weather was fine most of the time and they had lots of sun, fresh air, exercise and good, plentiful food. The hike was beneficial for their health and not particularly strenuous. Living outdoors and socializing with friends in the open air gave them a sense of freedom. According to Iakushkin, it was a pleasure for them to spend the greater part of the day in the open air and, when night came, not to be locked up in a stuffy cell. Moreover, it reminded them of life in the army. They stayed in yurts or in houses in the villages they passed. Bestuzhev recalled that the yurt he shared with four others had folding beds, a table and chairs that they had made themselves, as well as a lunch basket.

Typically, they left their camp at three o'clock in the morning. After walking 10 kilometres (just under 2 mi.) or so, they stopped for breakfast. Then, the married men brought out vodka and cold veal or fried chicken that their wives had provided and shared with everyone. At eight or nine, they settled down to rest. In each party, a host was chosen who went ahead with assistants to prepare lunch and samovars at the resting place. When the others arrived at the camp, they unpacked, made up their beds and went to bathe. After lunch, they rested for a couple of hours, and when it cooled down they went out for a walk to admire the surroundings. Then they drank tea, bathed and conversed again until evening.

During the journey, the Decembrists were joined by Maria Iushnevskaia and Anna Rozen, who had arrived late in Siberia because they had tried to bring their children with them into exile. Anna had been further delayed by a terrible flood. For ten days she lived in a barn, in a miserable village, until the waters subsided.[58]

Anna suffered immensely from the separation from her four-year-old son, whom she had left behind with her sister. Her letters from the journey are very moving. She writes somewhat incoherently; thoughts and experiences are intertwined in a stream of words. A barely restrained sense of despair is constantly present, the despair of a young woman forced to leave her child behind. In a letter to her husband written shortly after the separation from her child and sister, she writes,

> I confess that when I saw the retreating carriage, which contained everything that was dear to me, I felt the earth tremble beneath me . . . The sky was covered with clouds, the sun did not show, but it was even a consolation for me that the sun, like God, shares my grief and does not shine on the day of my separation.[59]

The thought of her child absorbs her. She cannot resist writing about him all the time, telling Andrei about a toy horse he left behind; that she looks for his tender gaze in the moon; or that she dreams of his little hands around her neck when she falls asleep. Her only hope is that they will meet again: 'I hope and look forward to seeing him soon, not knowing when it will be and where; and this is also the grace of Heaven, without which I would hardly have been able to bear the burden of separation.' In moments of grief, when Anna feels the separation most acutely, she hears the words of the priest Piotr Myslovskii, who told her to go and fulfil her sacred duty and through selflessness redeem the suffering of a beloved friend. At those moments, she feels ashamed.

Fortunately, Anna did redeem her husband's suffering. Andrei recalls her arrival in his memoirs. He was sitting on a bunk in a yurt, resting after lunch, when he heard a cart on the bridge nearby:

> I heard, in the distance, the bells of post-horses, then the sound of carriage-wheels; I looked through a slit in the tent and catching sight of a green veil, I threw on my coat and ran out to meet the carriage. Nikolai Bestuzhev hastened after me, but did not get up to me; the sentries before the tents threw themselves in front of me to stop me, but it was in vain – I managed to slip through. The carriage stopped a few steps from the sentries: a moment later and my wife was in my arms.[60]

It was 'a touching rendez-vous', Vladimir Shteingel recalled.[61] The commandant let the couple stay together in a peasant's hut.

Maria Iushnevskaia, who was forty years old, had made a slow journey to Siberia. However, when she heard that Anna Rozen was already in Verkhneudinsk, she rented a mail carriage and rushed to the peasant hut where her husband was staying. It took time for her to come to Siberia because she had wanted to bring her daughter Sofia from her first marriage. In a petition to the Governor General of Western Siberia, P. M. Kaptsevich, she wrote that she wished to fulfil her most sacred duty and share her husband's plight:

> Out of the feeling of gratitude that I have for him, I would not only willingly take upon myself all the calamities in the world, and poverty, but would willingly give my life to only ease his lot... The presence of his [step]daughter, to whom he is so attached, will no less make him happy.[62]

Iushnevskaia was eventually given permission to go, but not with her daughter.

At the very end of the long journey to the new prison, the Decembrists heard the first news of the July Revolution in France. Their reactions to this event illustrate that for them Russia was part of Europe, and also that they continued to believe that the days of autocracy were numbered. Reading in the newspapers about the events in France, they felt both excited and optimistic. The prisoners managed to get hold of sparkling wine and everyone drank a glass to the revolution. Then they sang the Marseillaise, while the sentries were at a loss as to how they could be in such a good mood while approaching the prison. But their hearts were full of hope for a better future for Europe, which to their minds also meant a better future for Russia.[63]

## Petrovsk Zavod

The Decembrists arrived at the new prison on 23 September, about six weeks after leaving Chita.[64] As they approached the settlement, they could see from a distance a large village in a deep valley, a factory, a wooden church, a river and, behind it, the red roof of the prison. 'As we drew nearer,' Rozen recalled, 'we could see an enormous building with a number of brick chimneys, and stone foundations reaching high up into the wall. It was windowless, save one small projecting part, in which were the entrance, main-guard and guard-room.'[65] Petrovsk Zavod (now Petrovsk-Transbaikalia) was a large settlement of 2,000 inhabitants with government buildings for the manufacture of iron, a foundry, a lake and two or three hundred huts. It was much larger than Chita. The prison was near the iron and silver mines to which the prisoners sentenced to penal servitude were sent. It made a deeply negative impression on some of the travellers. Annenkova later described it as perfect hell: 'There is no rest here day or night, the monotonous, constant hammering never stops, black dust from iron is everywhere.'[66]

Surrounded by high fences, the prison consisted of about sixty solitary cells in twelve buildings, separated to prevent the forming of close associations among the prisoners. Maria Volkonskaia describes it as 'a huge prison in the shape of a horseshoe ... It seemed gloomy; not a single window faced outwards.'[67] The casemates occupied one side of the rectangle and half of the two side wings, and in the centre of the front facade was a guardroom. There was a long corridor along the entire building, with windows facing on to the prison yard. The corridor was divided by walls into twelve sections, each of which contained the doors of five or six cells, and one door that led to the yard. The yard was divided by a high palisade into eight separate courtyards, each with its own gate. The cells themselves had no windows, only small barred openings over the doors. The dim light from the corridor reached the cells only if their doors were open; when the cell doors were shut, total darkness prevailed.[68] The contrast with the long walk in the open air and sun could not have been greater.

It was so dark in the cells that it was impossible to read, let alone see the hands of a watch. During the day, the prisoners were allowed to open the doors to the corridor, and in warm weather they spent a lot of time there. However, the frosts began as early as September and lasted until June, which meant that the prisoners had to sit in the dark or in candle-light. Each cell was locked at 10 p.m., although this was later changed for fear of fire, so that only the sections were locked at night.[69]

The prisoners had not expected the new prison to be so disagreeable: 'How could we imagine that after we had spent nearly four years in the small but endurable prison of Chita, we should . . . be punished by removal to a far worse abode and even be deprived of daylight?'[70] In her first letter from Petrovsk Zavod, Volkonskaia noted ironically, 'Here I am finally in the promised land.'[71] Trubetskoi was happy nonetheless. Rozen recalled him saying: 'What are windows to us when we have four suns!', referring to the four women who lived in their section.[72]

The prisoners' community became even better organized in Petrovsk Zavod. Svistunov described it ironically as their own Lilliputian state. The artel was a 'parody of our dreams', said Svistunov, where they were 'playing at a republic'.[73] The public opinion of the artel was its highest court. Three chief administrators – a host, a buyer and a treasurer – were elected by secret ballot to manage the artel. They also elected a provisional committee, which would check the accounts from time to time, as well as a gardener and a direc-tor of reading.[74] Continual correspondence with the outside world through the women made it possible to receive financial aid, but also mental suste-nance. The library was constantly expanded with both books and journals. Even prohibited books reached them. A common trick to fool the prison authorities, according to Zavalishin, was to replace the contents page of a banned book with one from a work on archaeology, botany or similar.[75]

The academy that had started in Chita continued to give lectures, and the string quartet organized concerts. The prisoners grew flowers, fruit and vegetables in the courtyards, but the climate was nowhere near as favour-able for cultivation as in Chita, and this was reflected in the harvest. The prison had a spacious yard for the prisoners' exercise. In the winter, slopes were made allowing them to slide downhill, and an area was flooded for those who liked to skate. The women living in the prison also took part in these amusements.

Still, most of the Decembrists were less happy than before. Petrovsk Zavod was a permanent prison and probably felt more like a real one than Chita, where everything was temporary. The prisoners had a lot more space now, but it also made them more isolated. They lived more privately, too. Instead of eating together in the communal hall, they had section tables in each corridor. A guard was given a salary to bring food from the kitchen, prepare lunch and dinner, and wash the dishes. Not much food was served. A plate of cabbage soup and a tiny piece of beef constituted the typical repast, and supper was even scantier. Most prisoners had their own cell, which was the greatest luxury, but it did not suit everyone. 'Though we gained in quiet and space by having our cells to ourselves,' Rozen noted, 'yet the ideal charm which had brightened our life at Chita was wanting here; increasing years and decreasing health had perhaps something to do with it; also the fact that, as we lived apart, we were not so dependent on each other.'[76]

At Commandant Leparskii's initiative, the women had been given permission to build their own homes in Petrovsk Zavod, and all had done so except the newly arrived Anna Rozen and Iushnevskaia, who lived in rented rooms. Ekaterina Trubetskaia's house had small windows facing the prison walls and the mountains in the distance. From there, 'the prison looked like a muddy hole, and the mountains did not offer a cheering sight either.'[77] Aleksandra Muravieva built a spacious house that managed to stay warm during the harsh winter.[78] However, since the husbands were not allowed to come to their wives' houses, the wives moved in with their husbands in their cells.

To the women, the conditions in the prison seemed gruesome. It was dark, damp (being built on a swamp) and cold. Moreover, in the absence of windows, the rooms could not be ventilated. Muravieva told her father that conditions in Petrovsk Zavod were a thousand times worse than in Chita. Although the stove was heated twice a day, it did not produce enough warmth. In fact, the prison was so cold that the inmates were freezing even in warm boots, padded hoods and caps.[79] The women worried about both their own health and that of their husbands. Fonvizina, who was pregnant, thought it would be a miracle if everyone remained healthy. She prayed to God to save her future child.[80] Trubetskaia was concerned about her husband's health and that dampness, chill and lack of fresh air in the prison might affect his health further. Iushnevskaia also worried about her husband. He had lost a lot of weight in Siberia and now she was afraid he would fall ill with consumption (tuberculosis).[81] Naryshkina was concerned about her own health. Less than a week after their arrival, she had developed a severe cough.[82]

The situation for the women in the prison was complicated, especially for those with children. They were torn between the need to be with their children and loyalty to their imprisoned husbands. As a result, they divided their time between prison and home. Muravieva described how, when she was seven months pregnant, she was running from prison to home and from home to prison all day: 'My soul hurts for the child who remains at home alone. On the other hand, I suffer for Nikita and would never agree to see him only three times a week.'[83] Trubetskaia, too, was running back and forth. She did not fully trust the woman who looked after her daughter in her absence. 'I live in a very small room with one window,' she told her mother. 'It opens on to a corridor, lit by small windows. The darkness in the room is such that we cannot see without candles at noon. There are many cracks in the walls, the wind blows from everywhere and the dampness is so great that it penetrates to the bones.' But, she adds, 'the physical suffering that the prison may cause seems insignificant in comparison with the cruel need to be separated from my child and the anxiety I feel all the time that I do not see her.'[84]

Contrary to what one might expect, the period spent in prison was positive for some couples. According to Andrei Rozen, his wife later loved to recall their life in prison, 'during which we spent more time together than falls to the lot of most married people in the course of twenty years'. They became close and shared each other's lives in a way that they would not have done in normal circumstances. Anna would set out to her hired quarters every day at ten o'clock in the morning to attend to her housekeeping. At midday, she was back for dinner. The cook took the food to the guardroom, from where the sentry brought their meals into the corridor.[85]

Despite the many difficulties, the women tried to make the cells as pleasant as possible. Volkonskaia covered the walls with the silk curtains she had had sent from St Petersburg. 'I had a piano, a bookcase, two sofas, in a word, it was almost elegant,' she wrote in her memoirs.[86] But she could not make up for the absence of windows, something she found unbearable. The new quarters 'let in barely sufficient light to enable us to eat a piece of rye bread and not miss our mouth'.[87] Because the only light came in through the door, they had to place the table by the entrance and read or work there. The door was left open all day, but this was not possible when it got colder. The women appealed to Leparskii for the installation of windows. They also wrote to their relatives in St Petersburg for assistance in this matter.

Finally, the women's efforts bore fruit. In the spring of 1831 an order came to install windows in each cell, and at the same time to plaster the inner walls. The 64 cells were provided with narrow openings just below the ceiling, but even then, 'only a postage-stamp of God's light was admitted.' The windows were so high that they had to raise themselves using trestles to reach them. Still, Volkonskaia noticed that there was a big difference when she moved back to the prison at the end of October 1831. The improvements really had been successful. The air was cleaner, the temperature higher and the room dry.[88]

In the summer of 1831 Camille Le Dantu arrived in Petrovsk Zavod, and barely a week later she married Vasilii Ivashev. The newlyweds were allowed to live by themselves for a month before they moved into the prison. Volkonskaia noted in her memoirs that the wedding took place under less gloomy circumstances than that of Pauline Annenkova. Vasilii did not have to wear shackles on his legs; 'the groom entered solemnly with his best men (albeit accompanied by soldiers). I was the nuptial mother of the young couple; all our ladies took them to church. We drank tea with the young people and dined with them the next day.' Odoevskii wrote a poem dedicated to Camille, 'The Distant Road', in which the protagonist, Camille, describes Vasilii as 'my light in the darkness of the grave'.[89]

When a woman was about to give birth, she left the prison. Andrei Rozen lamented that he had to separate from his wife after a year together in the prison when childbirth was approaching. However, he later received permission to be with her a week before she gave birth. On 5 September 1831 Anna gave birth to a son, who was named Kondratii after Ryleev. As soon as she was able to leave the bed, Andrei had to return to prison. He was allowed to visit only twice a week. Alone in the cell, he started to worry about the future of their children. Later, after the birth of their second child in Siberia, he took it upon himself to educate the children, to give them a chance to make their own way in the world.[90] Volkonskaia had two more children in Petrovsk Zavod, a boy, Mikhail, born in March 1832, and a daughter, Elena, born three and a half years later.

The fact that the women were forced to rush back and forth between the prison and their houses had fatal consequences. On 22 November 1832 Aleksandra Muravieva passed away. Although only 28 years old, she was fragile and often ill, and had given birth many times. Like many contemporary women, she had suffered grievously from the death of her children. Her second child in Siberia was Olga, born in December 1830. Olga died in 1831, and after her death Aleksandra lost her energy. The church where Olga was buried stood on a hill and was visible from everywhere. Aleksandra was thus constantly reminded of her little Olenka.[91] Aleksandra soon became pregnant again, but this time the child was born prematurely and died soon after a difficult birth. One day in October, returning home from the prison,

Aleksandra caught a cold, which led to complications. She declined over the following weeks. 'I am so dizzy that I cannot sit up even for a moment,' she wrote to her mother-in-law, 'and if my handwriting is not good it is because I lie down. Prince Volkonskii had the courtesy of giving me a bottle of porter, and they force me to take a little every day.'[92]

Yet nothing could restore Aleksandra's health. When she realized she was dying, she asked everyone not to grieve for her because she was sure that wherever she went she would be better off. She worried only for her husband, 'Nikitushka', who would be completely orphaned without her, a prediction that came true. Aleksandra died in the arms of her inconsolable husband.[93] She was buried in the small cemetery by the local church in a coffin made by Nikolai Bestuzhev and was mourned and missed by everyone. Ivan Pushchin remembered that she always knew how to calm, comfort and give courage to others: 'In the difficult moments of the first years of our exceptional existence, unconstrained gaiety with a kind smile on her face never left her.'[94]

The authorities worried about the reaction to the death of young Aleksandra. It was therefore decided that the wives of the 'state criminals' no longer had to live in the prison, and their husbands were allowed to meet them at home every day.[95] Still, Aleksandra's death made their vulnerability apparent, and parents began to worry about what would become of their children should they die.

# Epilogue

After the Decembrists had completed their penal servitude, they were released and assigned to various places of exile as free settlers in Siberia. The men left the prison with mixed emotions. Although they appreciated their liberty, they faced an uncertain future. Some ended up in remote places without the possibility of socializing. Many found it difficult to manage financially and several suffered from poor health. The main problem for the Decembrists when they left the prison community was material deprivation. A few were wealthy, but the majority worked on the 17 hectares (42 ac) of land granted them by the government simply because they had no other means. Apart from occasional financial assistance from relatives, the only help poor exiles received came from their wealthier comrades. The Decembrists were not allowed to hold any private position, nor enter into any public business, industrial or commercial enterprises. This meant that they were deprived of rights that were generally enjoyed by Siberian exiles.

Among the first to leave for settlement were Aleksandra and Andrei Ientaltsev. The couple met a sad fate. After only a year in Chita, they were sent first to Berezov and then to Ialutorovsk. Andrei was the victim of denunciations and began to show signs of mental illness. Aleksandra tried to get permission for them to return to western Russia, but her request was denied. Even after her husband died in 1845, she was not allowed to return.[1]

At the end of 1832 prisoners of the fourth category, including Nikolai Lorer, Mikhail Fonvizin, Mikhail Naryshkin, Aleksandr Odoevskii and the Beliaev brothers, ended their prison term. Lorer later recalled the parting as sad and emotional. First, he bade farewell to Commander Leparskii, 'a good old man!' Then the prisoners in his group departed in several sleds, accompanied by their comrades who remained behind. Lorer felt 'an inexpressible melancholy' draining his heart.[2] The prisoners were taken to Irkutsk, where they met Governor General Lavinskii. He had been instructed to cast lots among them to determine who should live where. Lavinskii did not think much of the administrators in St Petersburg, who, in his opinion, knew nothing about Siberia. This meant that the deployment of the Decembrists was not well considered and they often ended up in isolated places. Mukhanov, to give just one example, was sent to Bratsk, a remote corner of Irkutsk province surrounded by impenetrable forest. At the same time, he suffered a personal tragedy. He was not allowed to marry the love of his life, Varvara Shakhovskaia, who had followed him into exile and lived with the family of her sister Praskovia Muravieva. Because her brother was married to his sister, they were considered to be too closely related to marry.

On 22 January 1833 Mukhanov left for the Bratsk fort. He believed that 'after prison, everything that is not fenced in by a palisade will seem bearable.' But he was wrong. In a letter to his mother dated 28 January, he wrote that he had never seen a place worse than the Bratsk fort: 'There is no horizon. The forest stands around like a living palisade. The peasants hardly sow anything, for there is no arable land; they are all hunters ... This village brought me such despondency that no prison has ever caused me.'[3] The village was 645 kilometres (400 mi.) from the nearest city, and there was nowhere to go for medical assistance in case of illness. In fact, there was practically no connection with the outside world. In November 1841, after repeated petitions by his mother, Mukhanov received permission to move to Ust-Kuda, not far from Irkutsk. Sadly, by this time both his beloved Varvara and his dear sister Elizaveta had died.

Lorer ended up in Miertvyi Kultuk, where he rented a room from an elderly couple who owned the only log cabin in the settlement. He quickly became depressed by 'this godforsaken place'. His future looked even bleaker when he realized that he would have to spend the whole summer there alone when the old couple went off into the woods to hunt sable. Things did not improve when he learned that groups of convicts went about in the summer, burning houses and robbing and killing people. 'They'll kill you when they find out you're rich, you know,' his host warned him.[4] Lorer recognized that his situation was hopeless. How would he defend himself with just a penknife? He lost his appetite and books no longer interested him. Then, one evening he heard someone coming. The same young Cossack who had escorted him to Miertvyi Kultuk was back to take him to Irkutsk to be transported to Kurgan in Western Siberia. It turned out that his niece A. O. Rosset, a favourite of the empress, had helped him.

Kurgan was a small town on the banks of the Tobol River, with a stone church and a population of about 2,000. It served as a frontier post and had been granted city privileges by Catherine the Great in 1782. At the beginning of the nineteenth century a school, a hospital and a fire station were built. Over the years, thirteen Decembrists were exiled to Kurgan, among them Rozen, Naryshkin, Lorer, Basargin, Shchepin-Rostovskii, Svistunov and Vilgelm Kiukhelbeker.

The Rozen family arrived in Kurgan on 19 September 1832. Anna had travelled ahead with little Konrad. As they were crossing Lake Baikal, a storm hit. The milk she was carrying for Konrad turned sour, so that he had to manage without it for five days and almost died. Andrei was delayed for several weeks. When they were finally reunited, husband and wife promised each other never to part again.[5] A little boy, Vasilii, was born in a village on the way.

Perhaps not entirely unexpectedly, on arriving in Kurgan, Andrei Rozen became depressed: 'The thought that here I must end my days as an exile, and my wife and children must spend their whole lives, made my heart sink within me.' But things improved. With the help of money received from Anna's father, they bought a wooden house for 2,900 roubles in her name. In his memoirs, Andrei describes it as a 'small house with a mezzanine'. It was 'warm, rather spacious, [and] had a large garden . . . with a covered alley of acacia trees and with shady birches and lindens'.[6] There was a bathhouse, a laundry, a barn and a stable on the plot. The Rozens had two more children during this period: a son, Vladimir, in 1834 and a daughter, Anna, in 1836. The sums of money their relatives were allowed to send them were limited, but enough for them to manage.[7]

Andrei took a great interest in horticulture. He planted new varieties of fruit tree and crossed local wild varieties with cultivated ones. According to his own account, local residents turned to him for advice on seeds and cultivation. He was also quite successful as a farmer. Part of his plot was sandy and infertile land beside a small lake, but he fertilized it with ashes and in two years the land was fruitful. He then asked for permission to buy more land, but the request was denied. The work on his plot was carried out with the help of a single farmhand, two in the summer, and harvesting was done by inviting people to a party. According to Rozen, Siberians were a pleasure-loving people.[8]

In March 1833 Mikhail and Elizaveta Naryshkin moved to Kurgan with their three-year-old adopted daughter, Uliana.[9] They rented a house near the Tobol River for 25 roubles a month. Thanks to financial assistance, in May 1833 Elizaveta bought the house for 5,650 roubles. As she proudly stated, it was built of pine logs of the best quality. They now had it rebuilt to her design, so that it became a lovely, spacious house with a dining room, two living rooms, a library and an office for each of the spouses. Adjacent to the house was a stable, barns, a greenhouse, a garden and a vegetable garden. The Naryshkins received a great deal of financial support from home and lived in better style than most of their fellow exiles. Decembrists and exiled Poles often met in their house, to share news from home and listen to music, but people of high rank in Kurgan avoided them.[10] Both Mikhail and Elizaveta devoted much time to charity. Lorer recalled that 'both husband and wife helped the poor, treated and gave the sick medication with their own money ... Their courtyard on Sundays was often full of people who were given food, clothing and money.'[11]

Some of the Decembrists, among them Aleksandr Bestuzhev and Aleksandr Odoevskii, were transferred to the Caucasus as common soldiers. In the autumn of 1837 both Naryshkin and Rozen were ordered to serve in the Caucasian army as common soldiers. Rozen was discharged in 1839 because of poor health and ordered to live in Estonia, on his brother's estate near Narva. He lived there until the amnesty of 1856. Naryshkin retired from the army in 1844 and was instructed to live in a village close to Tula. He died in 1863 or 1867 (the sources disagree), and his wife soon afterwards. Anna Rozen died in 1883 at the ripe age of 86, and her husband a year later, having turned 93.

In 1834 Natalia and Mikhail Fonvizin left Petrovsk Zavod. Ekaterina Trubetskaia felt abandoned. 'My heart sinks as I wait for next week in view of the departure of the Fonvizins, who are moving to their exile location,' she wrote to her sister. 'Her departure will be a true misfortune.'[12] The Fonvizins were sent to Ieniseisk, where they lived for almost two years. Natalia was very unhappy during the first years of settlement. The isolation, together with the loss of yet another child, affected her mental health badly. All her children born in Siberia died, and she brought up adopted children. In 1838 the couple moved to Tobolsk. Natalia was engaged in sewing, gardening and translation. She was a woman of strong religious conviction, who helped the poor and supported exiles, including the members of the Petrashevtsy circle, a group of progressive intellectuals opposed to autocracy and serfdom. In fact, her firstborn son, Dmitrii, left in Moscow, had joined this group. Perhaps this caused her to become involved in their fate. Natalia became famous for giving Fyodor Dostoyevsky, who was also a member of the circle, a copy of the New Testament when she and two other Decembrist wives met him in 1850 in the Tobolsk Transit Prison. This is said to have been of great importance to Dostoyevsky's religious development.

Sadly, the Fonvizins' first son died in 1850 and their second son in 1851, at only 25 and 26 years old respectively. Mikhail died in the spring of 1854. Three years later, at the age of 54, Natalia entered into a second marriage, with Ivan Pushchin, but after two years she was deprived of him too.

Camille and Vasilii Ivashev were settled in Turinsk, but they were unlucky and never allowed to live a happy family life. Camille's mother arrived early in 1839. At the end of that year Camille, who was eight months pregnant, caught a cold. Complications followed and she was delivered prematurely of a daughter, who lived for only one day. Camille died of the ensuing child-birth fever, at the age of 31, and Vasilii was left with three children aged two, four and six. He was inconsolable. Pushchin, who knew them both well, wrote to Evgenii Obolenskii that 'we are all orphaned without her. This early loss weighs on the heart with an involuntary murmur.'[13] A year later Vasilii died, and the children left Siberia with their grandmother.

Things went better for Pauline and Ivan Annenkov, who also left the prison in 1835, although they had their sorrows too. Pauline gave birth to eighteen children, of whom only six survived. The Annenkovs were sent into exile in Belskoe, a remote village without medical assistance. Travelling with a large family in the Siberian winter was difficult. Pauline was heavily pregnant and developed a fever when crossing Lake Baikal. Arriving in Irkutsk, she asked the governor for permission to remain there for the rest of her pregnancy. She thought Ivan would be allowed to live with her to care for her and their sick baby boy, but they were separated: 'Left alone in an unfamiliar city . . . I gave birth prematurely to twins who lived only a week and died in cruel torment.' Pauline found it hard to be without religious support. In a letter to Alexander von Benckendorff, she wrote that she had been deprived of her Church for ten years and asked for permission to move to Krasnoiarsk, where there was a Catholic church and healthcare – but to no avail.[14] Instead, the family was transferred to Turinsk.[15] After another appeal by Pauline, successful this time, Ivan was permitted to join the civil service. He became assessor of the Tobolsk Public Charity Board, where he served until 1856, when the couple moved back to western Russia. Despite giving birth to so many children, Pauline lived a relatively long life. She died in September 1876, 76 years old; Ivan died sixteen months later at the age of ninety.

Left in Petrovsk Zavod, Ekaterina Trubetskaia suffered from the beastly cold climate. The installation of double glazing and flooring made life a little easier, but her health had already been affected and she was ageing rapidly. Nevertheless, she was happy. A daughter (Elizaveta) was born in 1834 and a son (Nikita) in 1835. In a letter to her sister, Ekaterina described how they spent their days. They got up at seven and had breakfast at eight. Then Sergei gave lessons in mathematics, as well as reading and writing in Russian. After lunch, weather permitting, they went for a walk with the children and visited other children. At four, they had tea. They dined at eight, then they put the children to bed, after which Sergei and Ekaterina read or talked. Sometimes the wives would get together for an evening, have tea and either read or relax and converse. In May 1837 Ekaterina gave birth to a girl whom she named Zinaida, after her sister. In September 1838 she had another child, a boy who was baptized Vladimir.

In the summer of 1836 the prisoners of the second category left the prison. A farewell dinner was held at the home of Sergei and Maria Volkonskii, and there were many toasts and tearful goodbyes. Sergei himself had about eight months left of his sentence. At the end of his term, it was decided that he should remain at Petrovsk Zavod, but Maria protested that the schools there were inadequate. She dreaded being left behind in this gloomy place and appealed to St Petersburg that they be permitted to move to the village of Urik, about 20 kilometres (12½ mi.) from Irkutsk. Ferdinand Volf lived there in exile and they would be able to obtain from him the medical help they needed. Her request was granted, and in March 1837 they moved to Urik. As well as Volf, Mikhail Lunin, Nikita and Aleksandr Muraviev, and Iosif Poggio lived in the village.[16]

When the Volkonskiis came to Urik, they lived at first with Poggio until their house was ready. Maria had sold the house in Petrovsk Zavod to a local merchant and could therefore afford to build a larger one in Urik. On a bluff overlooking the Angara River, a wooden house of two storeys, with a front porch, six bedrooms, and separate quarters for the servants in the courtyard, was built.[17] The children's education was Maria's responsibility. She taught them French and English, and for other subjects she received help from friends. She also taught Russian to local Buriat children and cared for the sick, while Sergei occupied himself with farming.[18]

The exiles in Urik largely lived a quiet life and formed a close circle. Ekaterina Fedorovna, the mother of the Muraviev brothers, transferred a lot of money to them through Irkutsk merchants. The brothers used some of this money to support their friends. However, not all of them lived a quiet life. Lunin continued his criticism of the regime in letters to his sister. Eventually, in March 1841, he was arrested and sent to the redoubted prison in Akatui, even further east, where he died four years later. Pauline Annenkova remembered him as a wonderful person, determined and extremely independent, with a sharp and lively mind.[19] In 1843 Nikita Muraviev died. His daughter Sofia, now an orphan, was sent to her grandmother in Moscow. His brother Aleksandr stayed a while longer before he moved to Tobolsk with his wife, Josefine Brakman, governess to the Volkonskiis.

As in Urik, the Decembrists formed a close circle in other places where groups of them settled. Nikolai Basargin, who was transferred to Ialutorovsk, recalled that

> several of us were settled there: me, Pushchin, Obolenskii, Muraviev-Apostol and Iakushkin. Three of us were family people, and we were all extremely friendly with each other. Not a day passed that we did not see each other, and we had dinner and spent evenings together four times a week. Almost everything between us was in common; everyone's joy or sorrow was shared, in a word, it was some kind of brotherhood – a moral and spiritual union.[20]

Their little community also included the widows of their comrades, Aleksandra Ientaltseva and Drosida Kiukhelbeker.

In July 1839 the last of the Decembrists were released. Although they were now all of them free, they were also older and realized that their lives had changed permanently. Prison existence had taken its toll, and many of them suffered from various ailments. Their every move was watched, their correspondence checked. Maria and Aleksei Iushnevskii left for a village near Irkutsk. Aleksei died suddenly in 1844, but Maria was not allowed to return to European Russia until 1855. She stayed in Siberia, earning a living by giving lessons.[21] The assigned location for the Trubetskoi family was a village called Oek, about 30 kilometres (19 mi.) from Irkutsk. The family left Petrovsk with a sense of gratitude that they had never lost hope in God, that he would always protect them and grant them peace. Alas, this was not to be. On their way to their new home, little Volodia (Vladimir) became ill and died three days before his first birthday. Upon seeing Ekaterina Trubetskaia in Irkutsk, Fedor Vadkovskii, who also came to live in Oek, wrote that he 'found the Princess depressed, but what was far worse was that she was not only depressed, but indifferent'.[22]

The Trubetskoi family settled first in a small cottage, but they soon built a larger house, into which they moved in April 1840. At this time, they learned that Ekaterina's mother had been allowed to send them a governess, Mlle Kuz'mina. However, bad luck continued to haunt them. A year after the death of little Volodia, Nikita died of scarlet fever. He was barely five years old. Ekaterina tried to find solace in religion: 'I am thankful to Him for everything I was enabled to do. As to my sons, particularly my dear deceased Nikita, I can only imagine him among the angels, praying for us all.' As if this were not enough, she gave birth to a stillborn baby in 1841. In 1843 yet another son was born, named Ivan. A year later a daughter, Sophia, was born. No wonder Ekaterina felt old and complained that her limbs were stiff.[23]

In 1845 both Ekaterina Trubetskaia and Maria Volkonskaia received permission to live in Irkutsk with their children for reasons of health. The climate there was salubrious, dry and sunny. Using her inheritance from her mother, Maria purchased from a fur merchant a large two-storey house in the centre of town, into which she moved with her children. It was surrounded by firs and white birches and had hand-painted decorations around the windows and front door. There were large double-glazed windows to keep out the cold, high ceilings, and porcelain stoves built into the walls. There were also a number of outhouses, quarters for numerous servants, and stables.[24] In her bedroom was cedarwood panelling, blue-painted shutters and a French writing desk. Maria had an eighteenth-century pyramidal piano, a contemporary Lichtenthal piano and a music box made in Switzerland. The Trubetskois' house was nearby, overlooking the Angara River. It was built in classical style with a five-sided bay window decorated with leaves, a central risalit and a semicircular entrance door. Ekaterina's mother helped with the funds to buy it.

Ekaterina's and Maria's husbands were able to visit them in Irkutsk from time to time, with the permission of the governor. However, this turned out to be a mere formality and Sergei Trubetskoi seldom went back to Oek. By contrast, Sergei Volkonskii hardly ever visited. Maria and Sergei's relationship had deteriorated, and it was rumoured that Maria had a love affair with Alexander Poggio.

A major advantage of the move to Irkutsk was that it allowed the children to be educated. The daughters were admitted to the Girls' Institute, which had recently opened.[25] Maria applied for her son's admission to the Irkutsk gymnasium. Surprisingly, the governor supported the application and her son was admitted.[26] But the Trubetskois' misfortunes continued. In August thirteen-month-old Sophia contracted dysentery and died after just three days. Her death took a heavy toll on Ekaterina, even as she sought comfort in faith, telling herself that God 'took the child to Himself'. Ekaterina's beloved father also died at this time. She deteriorated physically and she confessed to her sister that she had 'the appearance and habits of an old woman, and I do feel terribly aged'.[27] She was only 42.

Maria Volkonskaia, too, had her misfortunes. In January 1845 she was informed that her mother had died, and shortly afterwards, she learned that her brother Nikolai had died in the Caucasus.

Life in Irkutsk was better than in other places in Siberia where Decembrists ended up. But the rules for exiles were rigid there, too. State criminals were not allowed to attend public events. This meant that they were prevented from going to the theatre or to concerts. However, with the appointment of Nikolai Muraviev-Amurskii as governor, things improved. He began to receive some of the exiles at his residence, and he and his French wife even initiated unprecedented visits to the Decembrists' homes.[28] From then on, the Decembrist wives were also allowed to entertain and could associate with Irkutsk society, which consisted of officers on the governor general's staff, officials in the administration, scientists, teachers, navy personnel, local priests and rich merchants. Trubetskaia and Volkonskaia organized literary and musical evenings to which they invited exiles living in and around Irkutsk. They spent most of their time engaged in charity work, however.

Ekaterina Trubetskaia died of cancer in 1854 at the age of 54. She had suffered in silence for a long time and her family was unaware of the seriousness of her condition. She was buried in the Znamenskii Monastery, next to the graves of her children Vladimir, Nikita and Sophia. Her death left Trubetskoi a broken man. In a letter to the Decembrist poet Gavriil Batenkov, he wrote,

> My wife was not just a woman who joined her destiny with my destiny to pass life on one common path. She merged her whole existence with mine; thoughts, feelings, rules, desires, hopes – everything in a word was common for us. She did not live for herself. She lived solely for me and the children.[29]

Thomas Atkinson, an English traveller who visited Irkutsk at the time, described Ekaterina as 'a clever and highly educated woman' who 'devoted all her energies to the education of her three daughters and a young son'.[30]

In August 1856 the new tsar, Alexander II, proclaimed amnesty for all the surviving Decembrists. By then, their number was vastly diminished, and no more than 21 men returned to European Russia. The amnesty did not restore their freedom completely, however, and they were permitted to return to western Russia only under certain restrictive conditions. They were forbidden to reside in Moscow or St Petersburg and were to remain under police surveillance. Volkonskii, who was seriously ill, hurried home. He was told to live in the village of Voron'ki, in the province of Chernihiv. Volkonskaia, whose health had deteriorated, took the chance to travel abroad for medical treatment, but to no avail; her condition worsened and she died on 10 August 1863, at the age of 58. Shortly afterwards, Sergei suffered a stroke and was confined to a wheelchair. He died suddenly on 28 November 1865, aged 77, while writing his memoirs.

Trubetskoi left Irkutsk soon after Volkonskii. Before departing, he went to his wife's grave to pay his last respects. By special permission, he looked forward to spending his last years with his daughter in Moscow. But his happiness would prove short-lived. In 1860 his daughter died of tuberculosis, and in a few months, he would follow her to the grave.[31]

# References

## Introduction

1  K. F. Ryleev, *Polnoe sobranie sochinenii* (Leipzig, 1861), p. 230; trans. in Patrick O'Meara, *K. F. Ryleev: A Political Biography of the Decembrist Poet* (Princeton, NJ, 1984), pp. 188–9.

2  A. S. Pushkin, *Polnoe sobranie sochinenii*, vol. 1 (Moscow, 1949), p. 258, translated by the author.

3  They were liberal in the sense that they advocated legally codified individual liberties, constitutional limits on executive power, equality before the law and increased representation of the people in government, among other things.

4  Anatole G. Mazour, *The First Russian Revolution, 1825: The Decembrist Movement. Its Origins, Development, and Significance* (Stanford, CA, 1961), p. 94.

5  V. I. Lenin, *Polnoe sobranie sochinenii*, 56 vols (Moscow, 1958–66), vol. XXI, p. 261.

6  Ludmilla A. Trigos, *The Decembrist Myth in Russian Culture* (New York, 2009), chs 6 and 7.

7  Ibid., p. 186. See also Iurii Lotman, 'Dekabrist v povsednevnoi zhizni', in *Besedy o russkoi kul'ture* (St Petersburg, 1994), pp. 331–84.

8  O. V. Karbasova, 'O Dukhovnom Krizise Sovremennogo Liberalnogo Dvizheniia v Rossii', *Znanie, Ponimanie, Umenie*, 2 (2013), pp. 87–97.

9  *Union of Salvation*, dir. Andrei Kravchuk, 2019. Review by Ilya Budraitskis, *Slavic Review*, LXXX/2 (Summer 2021), pp. 392–3.

## 1 State and Society

1  For literature on Alexander I and his reign, see Janet M. Hartley, *Alexander I* (London and New York, 1994); Richard S. Wortman, *Scenarios of Power: Myth and Ceremony in Russian Monarchy from Peter the Great to the Abdication of Nicholas II* (Princeton, NJ, 2006), pp. 103–19; Marie-Pierre Rey, *Alexander I: The Tsar Who Defeated Napoleon* (DeKalb, IL, 2012); Janet M. Hartley, Paul Keenan and Dominic Lieven, eds, *Russia and the Napoleonic Wars* (Basingstoke, 2015); Jan Kusber, Alexander Kaplunovsky and Benjamin Conrad, eds, *The Enigmatic Tsar and His Empire: Russia under Alexander I, 1801–1825* (Berlin, 2019); and Patrick O'Meara, *The Russian Nobility in the Age of Alexander I* (London and New York, 2019).

2  A. M. Muraviev, *Mon journal* (Moi zhurnal), in *Vospominaniia i rasskazy deiatelei tainykh obshchestv 1820-kh godov*, vol. I, ed. S. I. Chernov and Iu. G. Oksman (Moscow, 1931), pp. 89–158.

3  On serfdom in Russia and projects for reform, see Peter Kolchin, *Unfree Labor: American Slavery and Russian Serfdom* (Cambridge, MA, 1987); David Moon, *The Abolition of Serfdom in Russia, 1762–1907* (Harlow, 2001); and Susan P. McCaffray, 'Confronting Serfdom in the Age of Revolution: Projects for Serf Reform in the Time of Alexander I', *Russian Review*, LXIV/1 (2005), pp. 1–21.

4  N. K. Shil'der, *Imperator Aleksandr pervyi: Ego zhizn' i tsarstvovanie*, 4 vols (St Petersburg, 1897–8), vol. II, p. 110.

5  Marc Raeff, *Michael Speransky: Statesman of Imperial Russia, 1772–1839* (The Hague, 1957); William Benton Whisenhunt, *Mikhail M. Speranskii and the Codification of Russian Law* (Boulder, CO, 2001).

6  Ferdinand J. M. Feldbrugge, *A History of Russian Law: From the Council Code (Ulozhenie) of Tsar Aleksei Mikhailovich of 1649 to the Bolshevik Revolution of 1917* (Leiden, 2022).

7  Hartley, *Alexander I*, p. 69.

8  The Spanish Constitution of 1812 was first published in a French translation but was translated into Russian and published in *Syn otechestva* in 1813.

9  Liubov Melnikova, 'Orthodox Russia against "Godless" France: The Russian Church and the "Holy War" of 1812', in *Russia and the Napoleonic Wars*, ed. Hartley et al., pp. 181–90.

10  N. I. Lorer, 'Zapiski moego vremeni', in *Memuary dekabristov*, ed. A. S. Nemzer (Moscow, 1988), ch. 1; Vadim Parsamov, *Dekabristy i russkoe obshchestvo 1814–1825 gg* (Moscow, 2016), p. 26.

11  Nikita Muraviev told the investigating commission that the proclamation of the Allied Powers in 1813, which offered the peoples of Germany representative government, first drew his attention to free-thinking. It was subsequently approved in the speech of the emperor to the Seim; see *Vosstanie dekabristov: Materialy i dokumenty*, 22 vols (Moscow, 1925–2012), vol. I, pp. 294–5.

12  The Sejm had no power to initiate legislation.

13  Lorer, 'Zapiski', ch. 2.

14  'sur toutes les contrées que la Providence a confiées à mes soins'. P. Maikov, *Russkaia starina*, I (January–March 1903), pp. 422–5. The French original is in M. Bogdanovich, *Istoriia tsarstvovaniia Imperatora Aleksandra I i Rossii v ego vremia*, 6 vols (St Petersburg, 1869–71), vol. V, pp. 78–9.

15  Letter to Nicholas I, 11 January 1826, addressed to Levashev, 'about the disturbances and abuses they noticed during the reign of the late emperor', published as an appendix to the investigative case of V. Shteingel, in Vladimir Shteingel, *Sochineniia i pis'ma*, vol. I (Irkutsk, 1985), p. 220.

16  The interview was reported and commented on by the Belgian press. Léonce Pingaud, 'L'Empereur Alexandre Ier, roi de Pologne – la "Kongressovka" (1801–1825)', *Revue d'histoire diplomatique*, XXXII/4 (1918), p. 536; V. N. Karazin in V. I. Semevskii, *Politicheskiia i obshchestvennyia idei dekabristov* (St Petersburg, 1909), p. 152.

17  'O konstitutsii', *Syn otechestva*, 45 (1818), pp. 202–11. See Julia Berest, *The Emergence of Russian Liberalism: Alexander Kunitsyn in Context, 1783–1840* (New York, 2011), pp. 68–73.

18 Hartley, *Alexander I*, pp. 167–8; Shil'der, *Imperator Aleksandr*, vol. IV, p. 95; Semevskii, *Politicheskiia*, pp. 267, 270.

19 Richard Pipes, 'The Russian Military Colonies, 1810–1831', *Journal of Modern History*, XXII/3 (September 1950), pp. 205–19; Hartley, *Alexander I*, pp. 179–85; Semevskii, *Politicheskiia*, p. 176.

20 The assassination in February 1820 of the Duke of Berry, heir to the throne of France, intensified the monarchs' anxiety.

21 Frank W. Thackeray, *Antecedents of Revolution: Alexander I and the Polish Kingdom, 1815–1825* (New York, 1980), pp. 76–7.

22 Many of the lower ranks and some of the officers of the Semionovsky regiment were sent to the Third Corps of the Russian southern armies, where they took part in the Decembrist revolt.

23 Elise Kimerling Wirtschafter, 'Russian Perspectives on European Order: "Review of the Year 1819"', in *Russia and the Napoleonic Wars*, ed. Hartley et al., pp. 61–4.

24 Francis Ley, *Alexandre Ier et sa Sainte Alliance, 1811–1825* (Paris, 1975), pp. 261–2.

25 See Daniel Brewer, *The Flame of Freedom: The Greek War of Independence, 1821–1833* (London, 2001).

26 Vladimir Shteingel, letter to Nicholas I, 29 January 1826, in *Vosstanie dekabristov*, vol. XIV, pp. 191–3.

27 Piotr Kakhovskii in Vladimir Fyodorov, *The First Breath of Freedom* (Moscow, 1988), p. 44.

28 McCaffray, 'Confronting Serfdom', p. 10.

29 A. Skabichevskii, *Ocherki istorii russkoi tsenzury, 1700–1836 gg* (St Petersburg, 1892), pp. 89, 114; Anatole G. Mazour, *The First Russian Revolution, 1825: The Decembrist Movement. Its Origins, Development, and Significance* (Stanford, CA, 1961), pp. 32–7; Berest, *Emergence*, p. 2.

30 Shteingel, letter to Nicholas I, 11 January 1826, in *Vosstanie dekabristov*, vol. XIV, p. 188.

31 N. V. Basargin, *Vospominaniia, rasskazy, stat'i* (Irkutsk, 1988), p. 56.

32 I. D. Iakushkin, *Zapiski, stat'i, pis'ma dekabrista I. D. Iakushkina*, ed. S. Shtraikh (Moscow, 1951), p. 7.

33 Alexander Martin, 'The 1812 War and the Civilizing Process in Russia', in *Russia and the Napoleonic Wars*, ed. Hartley et al., pp. 228–42; Parsamov, *Dekabristy i russkoe obshchestvo*, p. 38; Leonid Liashenko, *Dekabristy: Novyi vzgliad* (Moscow, 2011), pp. 31–8.

34 Wortman, *Scenarios of Power*, p. 128.

35 S. G. Volkonskii, *Zapiski* (Irkutsk, 1991), pp. 358–9.

36 Marc Raeff, 'The Russian Nobility in the Eighteenth and Nineteenth Centuries: Trends and Comparisons', in *The Nobility in Russia and Eastern Europe*, ed. Ivo Banac and Paul Bushkovitch (New Haven, CT, 1983), pp. 99–121; Patrick O'Meara, *The Russian Nobility in the Age of Alexander I* (London and New York, 2019).

37 Susan Smith-Peter, *Imagining Russian Regions: Subnational Identity and Civil Society in Nineteenth-Century Russia* (Leiden, 2018); O'Meara, *Russian Nobility*, chs 5 and 6.

38 Mazour, *First Russian Revolution*, pp. 46–53; Glynn Barratt, *M. S. Lunin: Catholic Decembrist* (The Hague, 1976), p. 6; Lauren G. Leighton,

'Freemasonry in Russia: The Grand Lodge of Astraea (1815–1822)', *Slavonic and East European Review*, LX/2 (1982), pp. 244–61.

39  Joseph Bradley, *Voluntary Associations in Tsarist Russia: Science, Patriotism, and Civil Society* (Cambridge, MA, 2009); V. M. Bokova, *Epokha tainikh obshchestv* (Moscow, 2003); Oksana Kiianskaia, *Ocherki iz istorii obschestvennogo dvizheniya v Rossii v pravlenie Aleksandra I* (St Petersburg, 2008), pp. 8–10; Iurii Lotman, 'Dekabrist v povsednevnoi zhizni', in *Besedy o russkoi kul'ture* (St Petersburg, 1994), pp. 331–84; Parsamov, *Dekabristy i russkoe obshchestvo*; Joe Peschio, *The Poetics of Impudence and Intimacy in the Age of Pushkin* (Madison, WI, 2012); V. Vatsuro, *Arzamas: Sbornik v dvukh knigakh* (Moscow, 1994); Mariia Maiofis, *Vozzvanie k Evrope: Literaturnoe obshchestvo 'Arzamas' i rossiiskii modernizatsionnyi proekt, 1815–1818 gg* (Moscow, 2008); Oleg Proskurin, *Literaturnye skandaly pushkinskoi epokhi* (Moscow, 2000); M. V. Nechkina, 'Sviashchennaia artel: Kruzhok Aleksandra Muraveva i Ivana Burtsova 1814–1817 gg', in *Dekabristy i ikh vremia*, ed. M. P. Alekseeva and B. S. Meilach (Moscow, 1951), pp. 155–88; Tat'iana V. Andreeva, *Tainye obshchestva v Rossii v pervoi polovine XIX v.* (St Petersburg, 2009).

40  Patrick O'Meara, *The Decembrist Pavel Pestel: Russia's First Republican* (Basingstoke, 2003), p. 56; Polina Rikoun, 'The Maker of Martyrs: Narrative Form and Political Resistance in Ryleev's "Voinarovskii"', *Russian Review*, LXXI/3 (July 2012), p. 449; Lotman, 'Dekabrist', p. 66; Liashenko, *Dekabristy*.

41  I. Pushchin, *Zapiski o pushkine. Pis'ma* (Moscow, 1979), pp. 62–4. Lorer conveyed similar feelings; see Lorer, 'Zapiski'.

42  Nikolai Turgenev, *Rossiia i russkie*, vol. II (Moscow, 1907), pp. 54–9, quoted in O'Meara, *Russian Nobility*, p. 257.

43  See for example Yakiv Andriyevych, from his testimony to the investigating committee in *Vosstanie dekabristov*, vol. V, pp. 382–8; Natan Eidel'man, *Conspiracy against the Tsar: A Portrait of the Decembrists* (Moscow, 1985), p. 35; the testimony of Piotr Borisov in *Vosstanie dekabristov*, vol. V, p. 22; Turgenev, diary notes, 1816–20, 'Dnevniki i pis'ma Nikolaia Ivanovicha Turgeneva', in *Arkhiv brat'ev Turgenevykh*, vol. III, ed. E. I. Tarasov (St Petersburg, 1911), pp. 161–91; F. B. Volf in *Vosstanie dekabristov*, vol. XII, pp. 121–2.

44  Basargin, *Vospominaniia*, p. 51.

45  Volkonskii, *Zapiski*, pp. 358–63; Evgenii P. Obolenskii, 'Vospominaniia o Ryleeve', in *Pisateli-dekabristy v vospominaniiakh sovremennikov*, vol. I, ed. R. V. Iezuitova et al. (Moscow, 1980), p. 97.

46  Iakushkin, *Zapiski*, pp. 172–6, 41–2.

47  E. P. Obolenskii, 'Vospominaniia o Ryleeve', in *Memuary dekabristov: Severnoe obshchestvo*, ed. V. A. Fyodorov (Moscow, 1981), p. 80.

48  N. A. Bestuzhev, *Vospominaniia Bestuzhevykh*, ed. M. K. Azadovskii (Moscow-Leningrad, 1951), p. 10; Patrick O'Meara, *K. F. Ryleev: A Political Biography of the Decembrist Poet* (Princeton, NJ, 1984), pp. 52–4.

49  Mikhail S. Belousov, 'Political Allusions in the Decembrist Revolt', *Vestnik of St Petersburg University: History*, LXIII/2 (2018), p. 357. For public opinion, see also Andreeva, *Tainye obshchestva*.

50  O'Meara, *Ryleev*, pp. 219–20; Patrick O'Meara, '27 September 1825: The Funeral of Duellist K. P. Chernov', in *Days from the Reigns of Eighteenth-Century Russian Rulers*, ed. A. Cross, Study Group on Eighteenth-Century Russia Newsletter (Cambridge, 2007), part II, pp. 221–33; V. I. Semevskii et al.,

eds, *Obshchestvennye dvizheniia v Rossii v pervuiu polovinu XIX veka*
(St Petersburg, 1905), p. 294. The Decembrists also made an impact through
their everyday behaviour, trying to live according to their ideals; see Iurii M.
Lotman, 'The Decembrist in Everyday Life', in *The Semiotics of Russian
Culture*, ed. Ann Shukman (Ann Arbor, MI, 1984), pp. 71–123.

51  Lewis Bagby, *Alexander Bestuzhev-Marlinsky and Russian Byronism*
(University Park, PA, 1995), pp. 140–45; O'Meara, *Ryleev*, pp. 200–211;
M. A. Briksman, 'Agitatsionnye pesni dekabristov', in *Dekabristy i ikh vremia*,
ed. Alekseev and Meilach, pp. 7–22.

52  Shteingel, letter to Nicholas I, 11 January 1826, in *Sochineniia i pis'ma*, vol. I,
p. 223.

53  Muraviev, *Mon journal*, pp. 133–6; A. A Bestuzhev in *Vosstanie dekabristov*,
vol. I, p. 430.

54  Shteingel, letter to Nicholas I, 11 January 1826, in *Sochineniia i pis'ma*, vol. I,
p. 224.

## 2 The Decembrists

1  I. D. Iakushkin, *Zapiski, stat'i, pis'ma dekabrista I. D. Iakushkina*,
ed. S. Shtraikh (Moscow, 1951), p. 475; Glynn Barratt, *M. S. Lunin: Catholic
Decembrist* (The Hague, 1976), p. 44.

2  S. P. Trubetskoi, 'Zapiski', in *Materialy o zhizni i revoliutsionnoi deiatel'nosti*,
vol. I (Irkutsk, 1983), p. 218.

3  Anatole G. Mazour, *The First Russian Revolution, 1825: The Decembrist
Movement. Its Origins, Development, and Significance* (Stanford, CA, 1961),
pp. 66–72.

4  Nikolai Turgenev, a member of the Union of Welfare, had become acquainted
with members of the Tugendbund when he was in Prussia working for the
Allied Political Commission, led by the great reformer Heinrich Stein.

5  'Constitution of the Union of Welfare', in *Izbrannye sotsial'no-politicheskie i
filosofskie proizvedeniia dekabristov* (Moscow, 1951), pp. 237–76; trans. in Marc
Raeff, *The Decembrist Movement* (Englewood Cliffs, NJ, 1966), pp. 69–99,
First Book, para. 1.

6  *Vosstanie dekabristov: Materialy i dokumenty*, 22 vols (Moscow, 1925–2012),
vol. III, p. 117; Barratt, *Lunin*, p. 46; V. I. Semevskii et al., eds, *Obshchestvennye
dvizheniia v Rossii v pervuiu polovinu XIX veka*, vol. I (St Petersburg, 1905),
pp. 233–78.

7  Evgenii P. Obolenskii, 'Vospominaniia o Ryleeve', in *Pisateli-dekabristy v
vospominaniiakh sovremennikov*, vol. I, ed. R. V. Iezuitova et al. (Moscow,
1980), p. 97.

8  N. V. Basargin, *Vospominaniia, rasskazy, stat'i* (Irkutsk, 1988), p. 464 n. 8.

9  A. M. Muraviev, *Mon journal* (Moi zhurnal), in *Vospominaniia i rasskazy
deiatelei tainykh obshchestv 1820-kh godov*, vol. I, ed. S. I. Chernov and
Iu. G. Oksman (Moscow, 1931), pp. 132–5.

10  'Constitution of the Union of Welfare', Fourth Book, paras 26, 30, 43;
First Book, para. 10.

11  Trubetskoi, 'Zapiski', p. 224.

12  'Constitution of the Union of Welfare', First Book, para. 11.

13  *Vosstanie dekabristov*, vol. I, pp. 8–9.

14 'Constitution of the Union of Welfare', Second Book, para. 2.

15 Ibid., Fourth Book, paras 31 and 44.

16 Linda K. Kerber, *Women of the Republic: Intellect and Ideology in Revolutionary America* (Chapel Hill, NC, 1980); James F. McMillan, *France and Women, 1789–1914: Gender, Society and Politics* (London and New York, 2000).

17 For Decembrists in Ukraine, see G. D. Kazmyrchuk and Iu. V. Latysh, eds, *Dekabrysty v Ukrayini: Doslidzhennya ta materialy* (Kyiv, 2012); G. D. Kazmyrchuk and Iu. V. Latysh, *Dekabrysty v Ukrayini: Istorychni studii* (Kyiv, 2014).

18 Patrick O'Meara, *The Decembrist Pavel Pestel: Russia's First Republican* (Basingstoke, 2003), p. 61; Vladimir Fyodorov, *The First Breath of Freedom* (Moscow, 1988), p. 70; *Vosstanie dekabristov*, vol. IV, pp. 101–2.

19 O'Meara, *Pestel*, pp. 61–6; *Vosstanie dekabristov*, vol. IV, p. 91.

20 Barratt, *Lunin*, p. 47; *Vosstanie dekabristov*, vol. IV, p. 102.

21 An early example of this is found in pre-Civil War England; see Blair Worden, 'Republicanism, Regicide and Republic: The English Experience', in *Republicanism: A Shared European Heritage*, vol. I, ed. Martin van Gelderen and Quentin Skinner (Cambridge, 2002), pp. 307–27.

22 *Vosstanie dekabristov*, vol. IV, pp. 156–7; vol. X, p. 279.

23 Fyodorov, *First Breath*, p. 125; *Vosstanie dekabristov*, vol. IV, pp. 102–4.

24 This was only one of a number of reports on which Alexander I failed to act. See Patrick O'Meara, *The Russian Nobility in the Age of Alexander I* (London and New York, 2019), p. 238.

25 O'Meara, *Pestel*, p. 68; Iakushkin, *Zapiski*, p. 37; Mazour, *First Russian Revolution*, pp. 79–80.

26 N. I. Lorer, 'Zapiski moego vremeni', in *Memuary dekabristov*, ed. A. S. Nemzer (Moscow, 1988), pp. 315–545; S. G. Volkonskii, *Zapiski* (Irkutsk, 1991); Basargin, *Vospominaniia*.

27 Mazour, *First Russian Revolution*, pp. 80–86; Patrick O'Meara, *K. F. Ryleev: A Political Biography of the Decembrist Poet* (Princeton, NJ, 1984), pp. 146–54; O'Meara, *Pestel*, pp. 68–70, 76, 95, 115–21; Barratt, *Lunin*, pp. 48, 50; Iakushkin, *Zapiski*, pp. 43–6; Muraviev, *Mon journal*, pp. 134–5; Basargin, *Vospominaniia*, p. 61.

28 Obolenskii, 'Vospominaniia o Ryleeve', pp. 99–102.

29 Ibid.

30 For criticism of a unified view of the Decembrists, see Bruce Lincoln, 'A Re-Examination of Some Historical Stereotypes: An Analysis of the Career Patterns and Backgrounds of the Decembrists', *Jahrbücher für Geschichte Osteuropas*, new series, XXIV/3 (1976), pp. 357–68; Julie Grandhaye, *Les Décembristes: Une Génération républicaine en Russie autocratique* (Paris, 2011), pp. 7–33; and P. V. Il'in, ed., *Dekabristy: Aktual'nye napravleniia issledovanii* (St Petersburg, 2014).

31 O'Meara, *Russian Nobility*, chs 3 and 4; Grandhaye, *Les Décembristes*, pp. 47–54; Vadim Parsamov, *Dekabristy i russkoe obshchestvo 1814–1825 gg* (Moscow, 2016), p. 10. See also Vadim Parsamov, *Dekabristy i Frantsiia* (Moscow, 2010).

32 N. Eidel'man, *Pushkin: Iz biografii tvorchestva 1826–1837* (Moscow, 1987), p. 37; M. A Tsiavlovskii and N. A Tarkhova, eds, *Letopis' zhizni i tvorchestva Aleksandra Pushkina*, vol. I (Moscow, 1999), p. 348; V. E. Vatsuro et al.,

*A. S. Pushkin v vospominaniiakh sovremennikov*, vol. II (Moscow, 1974), p. 317; Sergei M. Volkonskii, *O dekabristakh: Po semeinym vospominaniiam* (Moscow, 1994), pp. 35–6.

33  John L. H. Keep, *Soldiers of the Tsar: Army and Society in Russia, 1462–1874* (Oxford, 1985), pp. 232, 243–4.

34  Nikolai Basargin, Nikolai Kriukov, Peter Mukhanov and Aleksandr Kornilovich, to name a few.

35  A. S. Gangeblov, *Vospominaniia dekabrista* (Moscow, 1888), pp. 7–10; O'Meara, *Pestel*, pp. 13–14.

36  *Vosstanie dekabristov*, vol. I, p. 226.

37  Ibid., pp. 8–9, 430. Lunin was another Decembrist with good knowledge of the English language, as was Nikolai Bestuzhev. Aleksandr Beliaev had learned English at school.

38  R. D. Anderson, *European Universities from the Enlightenment to 1914* (Oxford, 2004), pp. 241–3.

39  O'Meara, *Pestel*, p. 12.

40  N. I. Lorer, *Zapiski dekabrista N. I. Lorera* (Irkutsk, 1984), pp. 63–72, 90.

41  Vladimir Shteingel, letter to Nicholas I, 11 January 1826, in *Vosstanie dekabristov*, vol. XIV, pp. 147–93.

42  D. Lieven, *The Aristocracy in Europe, 1815–1914* (Basingstoke, 1992), pp. 16–19, 179–80.

43  M. A. Fonvizin, *Sochineniia i pis'ma*, vol. II (Irkutsk, 1982), pp. 180–85.

44  Letter from Aleksandr Bulgakov to his brother Konstantin Bulgakov, 8 January 1826, in *Russkii biograficheskii slovar'*, 25 vols (Moscow, 1896–1918), vol. XVII, p. 295.

45  John Keep, 'From the Pistol to the Pen: The Military Memoir as a Source on the Social History of Pre-Reform Russia', *Cahiers du monde russe et soviétique*, XXI/3–4 (1980), pp. 295–320; Keep, *Soldiers of the Tsar*, p. 244; Mikhail Velizhev, 'The Moscow English Club and the Public Sphere', in *The Europeanized Elite in Russia, 1762–1825*, ed. Andreas Schönle, Andrei Zorin and Alexei Evstratov (DeKalb, IL, 2016), pp. 234–5. See also Linda Colley, *The Gun, the Ship and the Pen: Warfare, Constitutions, and the Making of the Modern World* (New York, 2021).

46  Iakushkin, *Zapiski*, p. 8; *Vosstanie dekabristov*, vol. III, p. 44. See also A. N. Muraviev, ibid., p. 8.

47  Fonvizin, *Sochineniia*, vol. II, pp. 180–85.

48  Ryleev also refers to the campaign in France as an inspiration (*Vosstanie dekabristov*, vol. I, p. 156). See also Dmitrii Zavalishin's memoirs: D. I. Zavalishin, *Zapiski dekabrista* (St Petersburg, 1906).

49  *Vosstanie dekabristov*, vol. III, p. 44.

50  Fonvizin, *Sochineniia*, vol. II, pp. 180–85.

51  Quoted in Mazour, *First Russian Revolution*, p. 278.

52  V. F. Raevskii, *Materialy o zhizni i revoliutsionnoi deiatel'nosti*, vol. I (Irkutsk, 1980), pp. 93–101.

53  Piotr Kakhovskii, in *Iz pisem i pokazanii dekabristov: Kritika sovremennogo sostoianiia Rossii i plany budushchego ustroistva*, ed. A. K. Borozdin (St Petersburg, 1906), p. 25.

54  A. D. Borovkov (chief secretary of the investigating commission), 'Digest of the Testimony Concerning the Internal Conditions of the State Given by

the Members of the Subversive Society', in *Dekabristy: Otryvki iz istochnikov*, ed. Iu. G. Oksman (Moscow, 1926), pp. 2–9; trans. in Raeff, *Decembrist Movement*, pp. 32–43.

55  Alexander Bestuzhev, quoted in Fyodorov, *First Breath*, p. 38.

56  Shteingel, letter to Nicholas I, 11 January 1826, in *Vosstanie dekabristov*, vol. XIV, p. 191.

57  V. A. Fedorov and I. V. Porokh, eds, *Memuary dekabristov: Iuzhnoe obshchestvo* (Moscow, 1982), pp. 178–84.

58  Iakov Andreevich in *Vosstanie dekabristov*, vol. V, pp. 382–8; Fyodorov, *First Breath*, p. 49.

59  Richard Pipes, 'The Russian Military Colonies, 1810–1831', *Journal of Modern History*, XXII/3 (September 1950), pp. 205–19; 'Digest of the Testimony', in Raeff, *Decembrist Movement*, p. 40.

60  Iakushkin, *Zapiski*, p. 15.

61  Pestel, quoted in Fyodorov, *First Breath*, pp. 24–5; Trubetskoi, 'Zapiski'.

62  A. Bestuzhev, *Iz pisem i pokazanii dekabristov* (St Petersburg, 1906), p. 38.

63  Ibid.

64  Shteingel, letter to Nicholas I, 29 January 1826, in *Vosstanie dekabristov,* vol. XIV, pp. 191–3. Bestuzhev, *Iz pisem*, p. 37.

65  Quoted in Fyodorov, *First Breath*, pp. 58–62.

66  Glynn Barratt, *Voices in Exile: The Decembrist Memoirs* (Montreal, 1974), p. 5; Richard S. Wortman, *Scenarios of Power: Myth and Ceremony in Russian Monarchy from Peter the Great to the Abdication of Nicholas II* (Princeton, NJ, 2006), pp. 113–14; O'Meara, *Russian Nobility*, pp. 28–9, 296 n. 67.

67  Lorer, 'Zapiski moego vremeni', ch. 2.

68  Fonvizin, *Sochineniia*, vol. II, pp. 180–85.

69  Pestel in *Vosstanie dekabristov*, vol. IV, p. 105. See also P. G. Kakhovskii, ibid., vol. I, p. 343; E. P. Obolenskii, ibid., p. 226; M. A. Bestuzhev, ibid., p. 430; A. N. Muraviev, ibid., vol. III, p. 8. They could get information about these events in Russian newspapers (M. A. Bestuzhev, ibid., vol. IV, p. 113).

70  M. A. Fonvizin, 'Obozrenie proyavleniya politicheskoi zhizni v Rossii', in *Obshchestvennye dvizheniya v Rossii v pervoi polovine XIX veka*, vol. I, ed. P. E. Shchegoleva (St Petersburg, 1905), p. 185.

71  Derek Offord, Vladislav Rjéoutski and Gesine Argent, eds, *The French Language in Russia: A Social, Political, Cultural and Literary History* (Amsterdam, 2018).

72  Nikita Muraviev, testimony, 5 January 1826, in *Vosstanie dekabristov*, vol. I, pp. 94, 294.

73  Lunin, letter to his sister from Siberia (no. 16), September 1838, in *Dekabrist M. S. Lunin: Sochineniia i pis'ma* (Petrograd, 1923), pp. 29–60.

74  Turgenev, diary notes, 19 June 1819, 'Dnevniki i pis'ma Nikolaia Ivanovicha Turgeneva', in *Arkhiv brat'ev Turgenevykh*, vol. III, ed. E. I. Tarasov (St Petersburg, 1911), pp. 161–91.

75  Piotr Kakhovskii, quoted in Fyodorov, *First Breath*, p. 44.

76  Trubetskoi, 'Zapiski', p. 232; *Vosstanie dekabristov*, vol. I, p. 9.

## 3  Revolution in St Petersburg

1  Robert Lee, *The Last Days of Alexander and the First Days of Nicholas* (London, 1954), pp. 41–3, 45–7; N. K. Shil'der, *Imperator Aleksandr pervyi: Ego zhizn' i tsarstvovanie*, vol. IV (St Petersburg, 1898), pp. 349–429.

2  S. P. Trubetskoi, 'Zapiski', in *Materialy o zhizni i revoliutsionnoi deiatel'nosti*, vol. I (Irkutsk, 1983), p. 232.

3  Zakon (law) no. 30592, 27 November 1825, in *Polnoe sobranie zakonov Rossiiskoi imperii*, vol. XL (St Petersburg, 1830), p. 616.

4  M. A. Korff, *The Accession of Nicholas* (London, 1857), pp. 31–2, 42–9, 52; Tat'iana V. Andreeva, *Tainye obshchestva v Rossii v pervoi polovine XIX v.* (St Petersburg, 2009), pp. 533–98.

5  Trubetskoi, 'Zapiski', p. 233.

6  Iakov Gordin, *Sobytie i liudi 14 dekabria* (Moscow, 1985), pp. 37–42; Iakov Gordin, *Miatezh reformatorov* (Leningrad, 1989), p. 26; T. V. Andreeva, *Imperator Nikolai Pavlovich i graf M. A. Miloradovich* (St Petersburg, 1998), p. 234; S. V. Mironenko, *Stranitsy tainoi istorii samoderzhaviia: Politicheskaia istoriia Rossii pervoi poloviny XIX stoletiia* (Moscow, 1990), pp. 89–90; W. Bruce Lincoln, *Nicholas I: Emperor and Autocrat of All the Russias* (Bloomington, IN, 1978).

7  *The Times*, 7 January 1826, p. 2; Korff, *Accession*, pp. 117–18, 125–6.

8  Cynthia H. Whittaker, 'Chosen by "All the Russian People": The Idea of an Elected Monarch in Eighteenth-Century Russia', *Acta Slavica Iaponica*, XVIII (2001), pp. 1–18; Cynthia H. Whittaker, *Russian Monarchy: Eighteenth-Century Rulers and Writers in Political Dialogue* (DeKalb, IL, 2003).

9  A. A. Bestuzhev in *Vosstanie dekabristov: Materialy i dokumenty*, 22 vols (Moscow, 1925–2012), vol. I, pp. 187, 452.

10  Vladimir Fyodorov, *The First Breath of Freedom* (Moscow, 1988), pp. 29–30; Patrick O'Meara, *K. F. Ryleev: A Political Biography of the Decembrist Poet* (Princeton, NJ, 1984), pp. 126, 131.

11  N. A. Bestuzhev, *Vospominaniia Bestuzhevykh*, ed. M. K. Azadovskii (Moscow-Leningrad, 1951), p. 31; *Vosstanie dekabristov*, vol. I, pp. 160–61.

12  E. P. Obolenskii, 'Vospominaniia o Ryleeve', in *Pisateli-dekabristy v vospominaniiakh sovremennikov*, vol. I, ed. R. V. Iezuitova et al. (Moscow, 1980), pp. 103–4.

13  Letter from Pushchin, 12 December 1825, quoted in Patrick O'Meara, *The Russian Nobility in the Age of Alexander I* (London and New York, 2019), p. 267.

14  N. A. Bestuzhev, *Vospominaniia Bestuzhevykh*, p. 31.

15  Trubetskoi, 'Zapiski', pp. 327–8.

16  N. A. Bestuzhev, *Vospominaniia Bestuzhevykh*, p. 32; A. E. Rozen, *Russian Conspirators in Siberia: A Personal Narrative* (London, 2005), p. 27.

17  Obolenskii, 'Vospominaniia o Ryleeve', pp. 104–5.

18  A. M. Muraviev, *Mon journal* (Moi zhurnal), in *Vospominaniia i rasskazy deiatelei tainykh obshchestv 1820-kh godov*, vol. I, ed. S. I. Chernov and Iu. G. Oksman (Moscow, 2008), pp. 89–158.

19  N. A. Bestuzhev, *Vospominaniia Bestuzhevykh*, p. 34.

20  Quoted in Iurii M. Lotman, 'The Poetics of Everyday Behavior in Eighteenth-Century Russian Culture', in *The Semiotics of Russian Cultural History*,

ed. Alice Stone Nakhimovsky and Alexander D. Nakhimovsky (Ithaca, NY, 1985), pp. 67–94 (p. 87).

21 Ibid.; Lewis Bagby, *Alexander Bestuzhev-Marlinsky and Russian Byronism* (University Park, PA, 1995), pp. 150–51.

22 A. E. Rozen, *Zapiski dekabrista* (Irkutsk, 1984), pp. 123–31. According to other accounts, in the case of failure they would retreat to Kronstadt, which would serve as their island of Leon (where the Cortes was established during the First Spanish Revolution).

23 Testimony of Ryleev in *Vosstanie dekabristov*, vol. I, pp. 183–5.

24 Mikhail S. Belousov, 'Political Allusions in the Decembrist Revolt', *Vestnik of St Petersburg University: History*, LXIII/2 (2018), pp. 345–60; M. M. Safonov, *Mezhdutsarstvie: Istoricheskii opyt russkogo naroda i sovremennost'. Materialy k dokladam 19–22 iiuna 1995 g* (St Petersburg, 1995), p. 168.

25 *Vosstanie dekabristov*, vol. I, pp. 183–5.

26 Oksana Kiianskaia, *Ocherki iz istorii obshchestvennogo dvizheniya v Rossii v pravlenie Aleksandra I* (St Petersburg, 2008), pp. 156–61.

27 Richard S. Wortman, *Scenarios of Power: Myth and Ceremony in Russian Monarchy from Peter the Great to the Abdication of Nicholas II* (Princeton, NJ, 2006), p. 129.

28 N. A. Bestuzhev, *Vospominaniia Bestuzhevykh*, pp. 33–4.

29 M. M. Safonov and V. S. Parsamov, both in *Dekabristy: Aktual'nye problem i novye podkhody*, ed. Oksana Kiianskaia (Moscow, 2008).

30 M. A. Bestuzhev, *Vospominaniia Bestuzhevykh*, ed. Azadovskii, pp. 65–6.

31 Rozen, *Zapiski*, pp. 123–31.

32 Gordin, *Miatezh reformatorov*, pp. 11–13.

33 The date is given in the Old Style, that is, according to the Julian calendar used in Russia at the time.

34 N. A. Bestuzhev, *Vospominaniia Bestuzhevykh*, pp. 36–7; O'Meara, *Ryleev*, pp. 236–8.

35 M. A. Bestuzhev, *Vospominaniia Bestuzhevykh*, pp. 64–72.

36 Obolenskii, 'Vospominaniia o Ryleeve', pp. 103–4.

37 Belousov, 'Political Allusions', p. 13.

38 Miloradovich also received a bayonet wound inflicted by Obolenskii, but this was not fatal.

39 Report by War Minister Tatishchev on the events on Senate Square on 14 December 1825, in Gordin, *Miatezh reformatorov*, pp. 8–11.

40 Rozen, *Russian Conspirators*, pp. 27–9.

41 Ibid., p. 30; M. A. Bestuzhev, *Vospominaniia Bestuzhevykh*, p. 74.

42 O'Meara, *Ryleev*, p. 238.

43 Tatishchev, report, pp. 10–11.

44 Rozen, *Russian Conspirators*, pp. 30–31; M. A. Bestuzhev, *Vospominaniia Bestuzhevykh*, pp. 85–7.

45 Quoted in N. A. Bestuzhev, *Vospominaniia Bestuzhevykh*, p. 37.

46 Rozen, *Russian Conspirators*, p. 31.

47 Nicholas I, quoted in Fyodorov, *First Breath*, p. 192; original in *Mezhdutsarstvie 1825 goda i vosstanie dekabristov*, ed. B. E. Syroechkovskii (Moscow, 1926), pp. 21–8.

48 M. A. Bestuzhev, *Vospominaniia Bestuzhevykh*, p. 77.

49 Rozen, *Russian Conspirators*, p. 36.

50  A. P. Beliaev, *Vospominaniia dekabrista o perezhitom i perechuvstvovannom* (St Petersburg, 1882), ch. 10.

51  Glynn Barratt, *Voices in Exile: The Decembrist Memoirs* (Montreal, 1974), p. 179.

52  M. A. Bestuzhev, *Vospominaniia Bestuzhevykh*, p. 73. See also Rozen, *Russian Conspirators*, p. 33.

53  Beliaev, *Vospominaniia*, ch. 10.

54  Rozen, *Russian Conspirators*, pp. 31–4, 36, 37.

55  Nicholas I, quoted in Fyodorov, *First Breath*, p. 193; Tatishchev, report, pp. 10–11.

56  M. A. Bestuzhev, *Vospominaniia Bestuzhevykh*, p. 78.

57  Rozen, *Russian Conspirators*, pp. 34–5; Vladimir Shteingel, *Sochineniia i pis'ma*, vol. 1 (Irkutsk, 1985), pp. 158–9.

58  M. A. Bestuzhev, *Vospominaniia Bestuzhevykh*, pp. 78–9.

59  Ibid., pp. 79–80.

60  Rozen, *Russian Conspirators*, p. 35; Beliaev, *Vospominaniia*, ch. 10.

61  Quoted in N. I. Lorer, 'Zapiski moego vremeni', in *Memuary dekabristov*, ed. A. S. Nemzer (Moscow, 1988), ch. 6.

62  About eighty people died. G. S. Gabaev, 'Gvardiia v dekabr'skie dni 1825 g', in *14 dekabria 1825 goda*, ed. A. E. Presniakov (Moscow-Leningrad, 1926), pp. 195–7.

63  M. A. Bestuzhev, *Vospominaniia Bestuzhevykh*, p. 82.

64  Letter from Anne Disbrowe to Robert Kennedy, 14/26 December 1825, in Charlotte Anne Albinia Disbrowe, *Original Letters from Russia, 1825–1828* (London, 1878), p. 66.

65  Ibid., 16/28 December 1825.

66  Ibid., 21 December 1825/2 January 1826.

67  Letters from Aleksandr Bulgakov to his brother Konstantin Bulgakov, 2 January 1826, in *Brat'ia Bulgakovy. Perepiska*, vol. II, ed. Anna Tancharova (Moscow, 2010), available at http://decabristy-online.ru.

## 4 Revolution in Ukraine

1  For a recent biography of the brothers Muraviev-Apostol, see Oksana Kiianskaia, *Liudi dvadtsatykh godov: Dekabrist Sergei Muraviev-Apostol* (Moscow, 2023).

2  Glynn Barratt, *M. S. Lunin: Catholic Decembrist* (The Hague, 1976), pp. 53, 49; *Vosstanie dekabristov: Materialy i dokumenty*, 22 vols (Moscow, 1925–2012), vol. IV, pp. 107, 283; vol. IX, p. 381; Patrick O'Meara, *The Decembrist Pavel Pestel: Russia's First Republican* (Basingstoke, 2003), p. 134.

3  S. G. Volkonskii, *Zapiski* (Irkutsk, 1991), p. 370.

4  *Vosstanie dekabristov*, vol. IX, pp. 44, 90. Vladimir Fyodorov, *The First Breath of Freedom* (Moscow, 1988), pp. 30–31; O'Meara, *Pestel*, pp. 147–8, 152–3; L. A. Medvedskaia, *Sergei Ivanovich Murav'ev-Apostol* (Moscow, 1970), p. 110; I. V. Vasil'ev, 'Iz istorii organizatsionnoi deiatel'nosti tul'chinskoi upravy', *Osvoboditel'noe dvizhenie v Rossii*, 1 (1971), p. 50.

5  John L. H. Keep, *Soldiers of the Tsar: Army and Society in Russia, 1462–1874* (Oxford, 1985), pp. 266–7.

6 Kiianskaia, *Liudi dvadtsatykh godov*, p. 288.

7 Patrick O'Meara, 'General P. D. Kiselev and the Second Army HQ at Tul'chin, 1819–29', *Slavonic and East European Review*, LXXXVIII/1–2 (January/April 2010), pp. 261–90.

8 S. V. Mironenko, *Stranitsy tainoi istorii samoderzhaviia: Politicheskaia istoriia Rossii pervoi poloviny XIX stoletiia* (Moscow, 1990), ch. 2; O'Meara, *Pestel*, pp. 161–3; Volkonskii, *Zapiski*, pp. 375–93; N. I. Lorer, 'Zapiski moego vremeni', in *Memuary dekabristov,* ed. A. S. Nemzer (Moscow, 1988), ch. 4.

9 Lorer, 'Zapiski', ch. 5.

10 B. E. Syroechkovskii, ed., *Mezhdutsarstvie 1825 goda i vosstanie dekabristov* (Moscow, 1926), pp. 168, 206.

11 Maria Volkonskaia, *Zapiski* (Munich, 2006), p. 3.

12 'La société est découverte. Si un seul membre sera pris, je commence l'affaire.' Lorer, 'Zapiski', ch. 5.

13 O'Meara, 'General P. D. Kiselev', pp. 284, 271.

14 Lorer, 'Zapiski', ch. 5.

15 I. I. Horbachevskii (Gorbachevskii), *Zapiski, pis'ma* (Moscow, 1963), pp. 36–101; M. I. Muraviev-Apostol, *Vospominaniia i pis'ma* (Petrograd, 1922), pp. 50–85; Anatole G. Mazour, *The First Russian Revolution, 1825: The Decembrist Movement. Its Origins, Development, and Significance* (Stanford, CA, 1961), pp. 182–95.

16 'Statement of I. Rakuza', in *Krasnyi Arkhiv*, XIII (1925), pp. 34–5.

17 The Orthodox Catechism was inspired by Narcisse-Achille de Salvandy's novel *Don Alonso, ou L'Espagne: Histoire Contemporaine* (1824) about Napoleon's occupation. See Isabel de Madariaga, 'Spain and the Decembrists', *European Studies Review*, III/2 (1973), pp. 141–56. It was also influenced by the Spanish catechism *A Civil Catechism; or, A Brief Summary of the Duties of the Spaniard* (1808), which was printed in a Russian translation in 1812 in *Syn otechestva*, 2. Muraviev-Apostol and Bestuzhev-Riumin also wrote a proclamation inspired by the Spanish *pronunciamento*. Here, it is stated that all the miseries of the Russian people had come from autocratic government.

18 See Maurizio Isabella, 'Citizens or Faithful? Religion and the Liberal Revolutions of the 1820s in Southern Europe', *Modern Intellectual History*, XII/3 (2015), pp. 555–78. For Spanish influences on Russian liberals, see Richard Stites, 'Decembrists with a Spanish Accent', *Kritika: Explorations in Russian and Eurasian History*, XII/1 (Winter 2011), pp. 5–23.

19 M. V. Dovnar-Zapol'skii, *Idealy Dekabristov* (Moscow, 1907), pp. 303–6.

20 I. V. Karatsuba, 'Pravoslavnyi katekhizis S. I. Murav'eva-Apostola: kommentarii', in *Dekabristy: Aktual'nye problemy i novye podkhody*, ed. Oksana Kiianskaia (Moscow, 2008), pp. 460–76.

21 A. K. Borozdin, ed., *Iz pisem i pokazanii dekabristov: Kritika sovremennogo sostoianiia Rossii i plany budushchego ustroistva* (St Petersburg, 1906), pp. 85–7; Oksana Kiianskaia, *Iuzhnyi bunt: Vosstanie Chernigovskogo pekhotnogo polka* (Moscow, 1997), pp. 103–4.

22 Richard Stites, *The Four Horsemen: Riding to Liberty in Post-Napoleonic Europe* (Oxford, 2014), p. 16.

23 Horbachevskii, *Zapiski*, pp. 79–88; F. F. Vadkovskii, in S. I. Chernov and Iu. G. Oksman, eds, *Vospominaniia i rasskazy deiatelei tainykh obshchestv*

*1820-kh godov*, vol. I (Moscow, 1931), pp. 215–28; Muraviev-Apostol, *Vospominaniia*, pp. 53–5.

24 Volkonskii, *Zapiski*, pp. 390–92.

## 5 Liberty, Rule of Law and Representative Government

1 Letter dated 7 May 1824, from A. A. Bestuzhev to P. A. Viazemskii, in N. V. Snytko, 'Literaturnye korrespondenty P. A. Viazemskogo', *Vstrechi s proshlym*, vol. III (Moscow, 1960), pp. 333–4.

2 For recent overviews of liberalism in pre-revolutionary Russia, see Vanessa Rampton, *Liberal Ideas in Tsarist Russia: From Catherine the Great to the Russian Revolution* (Cambridge, 2020); Susanna Rabow-Edling, *Liberalism in Pre-Revolutionary Russia: State, Nation, Empire* (London, 2019).

3 Nathaniel Wolloch, 'Romanticism, Nationalism and Liberalism', in *Moderate and Radical Liberalism: The Enlightenment Sources of Liberal Thought* (Leiden, 2022), pp. 593–675.

4 For the significance of noble sentiment and friendship to the Decembrists, see Emily Wang, *Pushkin, the Decembrists, and Civic Sentimentalism* (Madison, WI, 2023); Stanislav Tarasov, 'Noble Feelings of Dissent: Russian Emotional Culture and the Decembrist Revolt of 1825', PhD thesis, Georgetown University, 2021.

5 Julie Grandhaye emphasizes the significance of republican thought in their thinking. See her *Les Décembristes: Une Génération républicaine en Russie autocratique* (Paris, 2011) and *Russie: La République interdite. Le Moment décembriste et ses enjeux* (Paris, 2012).

6 In contrast to *Russian Justice*, which was approved by the members of the Southern Society, *A Project for a Constitution* was never approved by all members of the Northern Society, but it was widely known and reflected the view of many members.

7 Also sometimes called *Russian Law*. The first drafts of the document were written in 1820, but Pestel started work on it as early as 1817. Two versions of the text have been found, the first dating from 1822–3, the second from 1824–5. None were completed. Five of the ten projected chapters exist only in outline, including the sections on state governance. In 1819–20 Pestel wrote a political memorandum on state government, in which he developed ideas on a constitutional monarchy and the structure of central administration. Patrick O'Meara, *The Decembrist Pavel Pestel: Russia's First Republican* (Basingstoke, 2003), pp. 72–6.

8 Marc Raeff, *The Decembrist Movement* (Englewood Cliffs, NJ, 1966), pp. 167–8.

9 Nikita Muraviev, *A Project for a Constitution*, ch. iii, in *Izbrannye proizvedeniia dekabristov*, vol. I (Moscow, 1951), pp. 295–329. Extract trans. in Raeff, *Decembrist Movement*, pp. 103–18, and *A Documentary History of Russian Thought: From the Enlightenment to Marxism*, ed. W. J. Leatherbarrow and D. C. Offord (Ann Arbor, MI, 1987), pp. 42–50.

10 Pavel Pestel, *Russian Justice*, ch. v, para. 10, in *Vosstanie dekabristov: Materialy i dokumenty*, 22 vols (Moscow, 1925–2012), vol. VIII, pp. 112–209. Extract trans. in Raeff, *Decembrist Movement*, pp. 124–56, and *Documentary History*, ed. Leatherbarrow and Offord, pp. 51–8.

11 Muraviev, *Project*, ch. iii, para. 19–24; Pestel, *Russian Justice*, ch. v, paras 7, 10.

12  Prince Sergei Petrovich Trubetskoi, 'A Manifesto', in *Vosstanie Dekabristov*, vol. I, pp. 107–8; trans. in Anatole G. Mazour, *The First Russian Revolution, 1825: The Decembrist Movement. Its Origins, Development, and Significance* (Stanford, CA, 1961), pp. 283–4.

13  Ibid.

14  'The Political Constitution of the Spanish Monarchy', *Cobbett's Political Register*, XVI (July–December 1814), ch. ii, art. 12; *Russian Justice*, ch. v, para. 19.

15  Maurizio Isabella, 'Citizens or Faithful? Religion and the Liberal Revolutions of the 1820s in Southern Europe', *Modern Intellectual History*, XII/3 (2015), pp. 555–78 (p. 563). For an account of religious toleration in the Russian Empire, see Paul Werth, *The Tsar's Foreign Faiths: Toleration and the Fate of Religious Freedom in Imperial Russia* (New York, 2014).

16  P. I. Pestel, *Russkaia Pravda* (St Petersburg, 1906), pp. 109–13, 116–18, 235–6; John P. LeDonne, 'Regionalism and Constitutional Reform, 1819–1826', *Cahiers du Monde Russe*, XLIV/1 (January–March 2003), pp. 27–8.

17  O'Meara, *Pestel*, p. 87; LeDonne, 'Regionalism', p. 29; Mazour, *First Russian Revolution*, p. 108.

18  Susan P. McCaffray, 'Confronting Serfdom in the Age of Revolution: Projects for Serf Reform in the Time of Alexander I', *Russian Review*, LXIV/1 (2005), pp. 1–21; Andreas Schönle, 'Political Economy, Civic Virtue, and the Subjective World of the Elite, 1780–1825', *Russian Review*, LXXVII/1 (2018), pp. 109–30; Roderick E. McGrew, 'Dilemmas of Development: Baron Heinrich Friedrich Storch on the Growth of Imperial Russia', *Jarhbücher für Geschichte Osteuropas*, XXIV/1 (1976), pp. 31–71.

19  Other economic liberals were K. F. German, K. I. Arsenev and M. A. Balugianskii.

20  Other examples were Fonvizin and Pestel.

21  N. I. Turgenev, 'Dnevniki i pis'ma Nikolaia Ivanovicha Turgeneva', in *Arkhiv brat'ev Turgenevykh*, vol. III, ed. E. I. Tarasov (St Petersburg, 1911), pp. 161–91.

22  Quoted in Vladimir Fyodorov, *The First Breath of Freedom* (Moscow, 1988), pp. 46–7. Original in V. F. Raevskii, *Materialy o zhizni i revoliutsionnoi deiatel'nosti*, vol. I (Irkutsk, 1980), pp. 93–101.

23  S. P. Trubetskoi, 'Zapiski', in *Materialy o zhizni i revoliutsionnoi deiatel'nosti*, vol. I (Irkutsk, 1983), p. 220.

24  'A Manifesto', in Mazour, *First Russian Revolution*, p. 283.

25  Muraviev, *Project*, ch. iii, para. 13.

26  Pestel, *Russian Justice*, ch. iii, para. 6.

27  In later versions of the constitution, Muraviev included conditions for allocating land to the peasants.

28  *Vosstanie dekabristov*, vol. VII, pp. 47, 199, 187.

29  Muraviev, *Project*, ch. iii.

30  'A Manifesto', p. 283.

31  Pestel, *Russian Justice*, ch. iii, paras 7, 8.

32  M. Laserson, *The American Impact on Russia, Diplomatic and Ideological, 1784–1917* (New York, 1950), p. 118; A. Walicki, *A History of Russian Thought from the Enlightenment to Marxism* (Stanford, CA, 1979), p. 59.

33  'Constitution of the Union of Welfare', in *Izbrannye sotsial'no-politicheskie i filosofskie proizvedeniia dekabristov* (Moscow, 1951), pp. 237–76; trans. in Raeff, *Decembrist Movement*, pp. 69–99, First Book, para. 11.

34 A. K. Borozdin, ed., *Iz pisem i pokazanii dekabristov: Kritika sovremennogo sostoianiia Rossii i plany budushchego ustroistva* (St Petersburg, 1906), pp. 37–8.

35 Laserson, *American Impact*, pp. 117–18.

36 A. E. Rozen, *Russian Conspirators in Siberia: A Personal Narrative* (London, 2005), p. 48.

37 Pestel, *Russian Justice*, introduction, para. 12.

38 Muraviev, *Project*, ch. ix.

39 Rogers Brubaker, *Citizenship and Nationhood in France and Germany* (Cambridge, MA, 1992), pp. 12, 6.

40 E. J. Sieyès, *What Is the Third Estate?* (London, 1963), p. 58.

41 Pestel, *Russian Justice*, ch. iii.

42 Ibid.

43 Muraviev, *Project*, ch. iii.

44 Pestel, *Russian Justice*, ch. iii.

45 Muraviev, *Project*, ch. iii, x.

46 Pestel, *Russian Justice*, introduction.

47 Ibid., ch. iii, para. 4.

48 Ibid., para. 3.

49 Muraviev, *Project*, ch. iii, ix; Pestel, *Russian Justice*, ch. iii, paras 4, 6.

50 E. Hobsbawm, *Nations and Nationalism* (Cambridge, 1992), p. 87; A. Kemiläinen, *Nationalism: Problems Concerning the Word, the Concept and Classification* (Jyväskylä, 1964), pp. 55–6, 30, 16.

51 Jean-Jacques Rousseau, *The Political Writings of Jean-Jacques Rousseau*, vol. 1, ed. C. E. Vaughan (Cambridge, 1915), book 1, ch. 8.

52 Muraviev, *Project*, ch. i.

53 Ibid., ch. ix.

54 Ibid., ch. vi.

55 'Political Constitution of the Spanish Monarchy', ch. ii, art. 13; Pestel, *Russian Justice*, introduction.

56 Muraviev, *Project*, ch. x.

57 Ibid., ch. ix, para. 92; 'Political Constitution of the Spanish Monarchy', ch. iv, art. 171.

58 'Political Constitution of the Spanish Monarchy', ch. iii, art. 131; Muraviev, *Project*, ch. ix; Pestel, *Russian Justice*, ch. v.

59 'Political Constitution of the Spanish Monarchy', ch. iv, art. 172; Muraviev, *Project*, ch. 10.

60 Muraviev, *Project*, introduction, ch. i.

61 Pestel, *Russian Justice*, introduction.

62 Letter from Piotr Kakhovskii to General Levashev, 24 February 1826, in Mazour, *First Russian Revolution*, pp. 274–7.

63 Franco Venturi, 'Destutt de Tracy and the Liberal Revolutions', in *Studies in Free Russia* (Chicago, IL, 1982), pp. 59–93 (p. 59); M. F. Orlov, 'Zapiski o tainom obshchestve', in *Memuary dekabristov*, vol. 1, ed. M. V. Dovnar-Zapol'skii (Kyiv, 1906), p. 10.

64 It was first published in English in 1811 by Thomas Jefferson.

65 A.L.C. Destutt de Tracy, *A Commentary and Review of Montesquieu's Spirit of Laws* (Philadelphia, PA, 1811, repr. New York, 1969), pp. 12–14, 18–19.

66 Pestel, *Russian Justice*, ch. iv, para. 14; Nikita Muraviev in *Vosstanie dekabristov*, vol. 1, p. 293.

67  Muraviev, *Project*, ch. ii, para. 3.

68  Pestel, *Russian Justice*, ch. iv, paras 14, 15.

69  *Vosstanie dekabristov*, vol. x, pp. 91–2; O'Meara, *Pestel*, p. 156.

70  Muraviev, *Project*, ch. ix, para. 81; Pestel, *Russian Justice*, ch. iv, paras 14, 16.

71  Muraviev, *Project*, ch. ii, para. 5.

72  P. I. Pestel, *Russkaia Pravda/La Legge Russa di Pavel Pestel* (Moscow, 1993), p. 183.

73  Pestel, *Russian Justice*, ch. ii, para. 2.

74  Muraviev, *Project*, ch. ii, iii.

75  A. D. Smith, *Nations and Nationalism in a Global Era* (Oxford, 1995), p. 186.

76  Pestel, *Russkaia Pravda* (1993), p. 183.

77  Pestel, *Russian Justice*, ch. ii, para. 2.

78  Ibid., para. 10.

79  *Vosstanie dekabristov*, vol. VII, pp. 146–8.

80  Pestel, *Russkaia Pravda* (1993), p. 183; Muraviev, *Project*, ch. ii, para. 8.

81  Abbé Grégoire, 'Rapport sur la nécessité et les moyens d'anéantir les patois et d'universaliser l'usage de la langue francaise', quoted in Brubaker, *Citizenship*, p. 7.

82  See Bertrand Barère de Vieuzac, 'Report to the Committee of Public Safety, January 1794', in Hobsbawm, *Nations*, p. 21.

83  Destutt de Tracy, *Review of Montesquieu*, pp. 82–3.

84  Pestel, *Russian Justice*, ch. i.

85  Thomas Jefferson had similar ideas about democratic township politics.

86  Pestel, *Russkaia Pravda* (1906), pp. 107–19, 235–8. See also LeDonne, 'Regionalism', pp. 5–34.

87  N. N. Bolkhovitinov, 'Dekabristy i Amerika', *Voprosy istorii*, XIII/4 (April 1974), pp. 91–2.

88  Muraviev, *Project*, introduction, ch. iv; Peter S. Onuf, *Statehood and Union: A History of the Northwest Ordinance* (Bloomington, IN, 1987).

89  Friedrich List, *Oxford English Dictionary VII*, pp. 175–6, quoted in Hobsbawm, *Nations*, pp. 30–31.

90  Pestel, *Russian Justice*, ch. i.

91  See Destutt de Tracy, *Review of Montesquieu*, pp. 82, 181, 232; Sieyès, *What Is the Third Estate?*; E. J. Sieyès, *Dire – sur la question du veto royal – a l'Assemblée Nationale* (Paris, 1789). See also O'Meara, *Pestel*, pp. 77–8, 83; K. M. Baker, *Inventing the French Revolution: Essays on French Political Culture in the Eighteenth Century* (Cambridge, 1990); Brubaker, *Citizenship*.

92  Hobsbawm, *Nations*, pp. 34–5. See also Smith, *Nations*, p. 186.

93  Destutt de Tracy, *Review of Montesquieu*, pp. 91–2.

94  Hobsbawm, *Nations*, p. 41; Nicholas Onuf and Peter Onuf, *Nations, Markets, and War: Modern History and the American Civil War* (Charlottesville, VA, and London, 2006), p. 332. See J. Appleby, 'What Is Still American in the Political Philosophy of Thomas Jefferson', *William and Mary Quarterly*, XXXIX/2 (1982), pp. 287–309.

95  Pestel, *Russian Justice*, ch. ii, para. 9.

96  Ibid., ch. i, paras 1, 2.

97  Brubaker, *Citizenship*, pp. 1, 7.

## 6 Republican Thought

1 Julie Grandhaye, *Les Décembristes: Une Génération républicaine en Russie autocratique* (Paris, 2011) and *Russie: La République interdite. Le Moment decembriste et ses enjeux* (Paris, 2012); N. D. Potapova, 'Dekabristy i respublikanskaya traditsiya', *Peterburgskii istoricheskii zhurnal*, 2 (2019), pp. 194–211; O. Kharkhordin, *Republicanism in Russia: Community before and after Communism* (Cambridge, MA, 2018).

2 S. S. Volk, *Istoricheskie vzgliady dekabristov* (Moscow, 1958), pp. 155–207.

3 I. D. Iakushkin, *Zapiski, stat'i i pis'ma dekabrista I. D. Iakushkina*, ed. S. Shtraikh (Moscow, 1951), p. 20; Piotr Kakhovskii in *Vosstanie dekabristov: Materialy i dokumenty*, 22 vols (Moscow, 1925–2012), vol. I, pp. 335–89.

4 Elise Wirtschafter, *The Play of Ideas in Russian Enlightenment Theater* (DeKalb, IL, 1997), pp. 166–71; Richard Stites, *Serfdom, Society and the Arts in Imperial Russia* (New Haven, CT, 2005), pp. 181–9.

5 Martin van Gelderen and Quentin Skinner, eds, *Republicanism: A Shared European Heritage*, 2 vols (Cambridge, 2002), vol. I, pp. 1–6; T. Paine, *A Letter to the Earl of Shelburne* (London, 1791), pp. 33, 35.

6 These poems circulated widely in manuscript form among the Decembrists, and many of them referred to Pushkin as a source of inspiration after the rising. T. C. Prousis, *Russian Society and the Greek Revolution* (DeKalb, IL, 1994), pp. 136–8.

7 Walter Vickery, 'Decembrist Poetry', in *The Modern Encyclopedia of Russian and Soviet Literatures*, vol. V, ed. Harry B. Weber (Gulf Breeze, FL, 1981), pp. 99–106.

8 A. A. Pokrovskii, Predislovie [Preface], in *Vosstanie dekabristov*, vol. I, pp. i–xix; T. G. Snytko, 'Iz neopublikovannykh sledstvennykh del o dekabristakh', in *Dekabristy-literatory*, vol. LIX, ed. A. M. Egolin et al., *Literaturnoe nasledstvo* (Moscow, 1954), p. 212.

9 F. N. Glinka, 'To a Nightingale in a Cage' [1819], in *Stikhotvoreniia* (Leningrad, 1951), pp. 105–6. Translations are by the author unless stated otherwise.

10 F. N. Glinka, 'Lament of the Captive Hebrews', in *Stikhotvoreniia*, p. 89; trans. in W. E. Brown, *A History of Russian Literature of the Romantic Period*, vol. I (Ann Arbor, MI, 1986), p. 290.

11 F. N. Glinka, *Velzen*, in *Izbrannye proizvedeniia* (Leningrad, 1957), p. 58; trans. in Brown, *Russian Literature*, vol. I, p. 286.

12 Quoted in Glynn Barratt, *Voices in Exile: The Decembrist Memoirs* (Montreal, 1974), p. 165. See also B. Bailyn, *Ideological Origins of the American Revolution* (Cambridge, MA, 1967).

13 P. A. Viazemskii, *Stikhotvoreniia* (Leningrad, 1958), p. 137; trans. in Brown, *Russian Literature*, vol. II, p. 63.

14 Glinka, *Velzen*, p. 60.

15 Radishchev's treatise with the same title was inspired by the American Revolution and the English Civil War.

16 A. S. Pushkin, *Polnoe sobranie sochinenii*, vol. I (Moscow, 1949), pp. 258–60. Henceforth *P.s.s.*; trans. in *The Complete Works of Alexander Pushkin*, 15 vols (Downham Market, 2001–3), vol. I, pp. 268–71.

17 Pushkin, *P.s.s.*, vol. I, pp. 338–9.

18  M. Viroli, *For Love of Country: An Essay on Patriotism and Nationalism* (Oxford, 1995); M. G. Dietz, 'Patriotism', in *Political Innovation and Conceptual Change*, ed. Terence Ball et al. (Cambridge, 1989), pp. 177–93.

19  Viroli, *Love of Country*, pp. 19, 63.

20  Nikolai Basargin, *Vospominaniia, rasskazy, stat'i* (Irkutsk, 1988), p. 54.

21  Quoted in Vladimir Fyodorov, *The First Breath of Freedom* (Moscow, 1988), p. 48; *Vosstanie dekabristov*, vol. v, pp. 382–8.

22  V. F. Raevskii, *Materialy o zhizni i revoliutsionnoi deiatel'nosti*, vol. 1 (Irkutsk, 1980), pp. 93–101.

23  Quoted in Barratt, *Voices in Exile*, pp. 126, 149.

24  N. I. Turgenev, 'Dnevniki i pis'ma Nikolaia Ivanovicha Turgeneva', in *Arkhiv brat'ev Turgenevykh*, vol. III, ed. E. I. Tarasov (Petrograd, 1921), p. 81.

25  Ibid., pp. 225–6. The liberal constitution of 1812 was adopted for the second time.

26  O. V. Orlik, *Dekabristy i evropeiskoe osvoboditel'noe dvizhenie* (Moscow, 1975), pp. 54–7.

27  'Constitution of the Union of Welfare', in *Izbrannye sotsial´no-politicheskie i filosofskie proizvedeniia dekabristov* (Moscow, 1951), pp. 237–76; trans. in Marc Raeff, *The Decembrist Movement* (Englewood Cliffs, NJ, 1966), pp. 69–99, Fourth Book, para. 30.

28  Ibid., First Book, para. 10.

29  Letter from A. P. Iushnevskii to S. P. Iushnevskii, 23 January 1820, in *Arkhiv dekabrista Iushnevskogo/Bunt dekabristov*, ed. V. M. Bazilievich (Leningrad, 1926), pp. 323–6.

30  N. A. Bestuzhev, 'Vospominanie o Ryleeve', in *Vospominaniia Bestuzhevykh*, ed. M. K. Azadovskii (Moscow-Leningrad, 1951), p. 25. For a study of the significance of politically engaged feeling to the Decembrists and their friends, see Emily Wang, 'Ryleev, Pushkin, and the Poeticization of Russian History', *Russian Review*, LXXVIII/1 (January 2019), pp. 62–81.

31  K. F. Ryleev, *Polnoe sobranie sochinenii* (Moscow-Leningrad, 1934), p. 239.

32  K. F. Ryleev, *Dumy*, ed. L. G. Frizman (Moscow, 1975), p. 92; trans. in Patrick O'Meara, *K. F. Ryleev: A Political Biography of the Decembrist Poet* (Princeton, NJ, 1984), p. 182.

33  Ryleev, *Dumy*, p. 25; trans. in O'Meara, *Ryleev*, p. 180.

34  Quoted in L. G. Leighton, *Russian Romanticism: Two Essays* (The Hague, 1975), p. 70.

35  K. F. Ryleev, *Sochineniia* (Moscow, 1988), p. 90.

36  Ryleev, *Dumy*, p. 87; trans. in O'Meara, *Ryleev*, p. 175.

37  Several fragments of Nalivaiko made it past the censor and were published in the *Polar Star* for 1825.

38  Ryleev, *Sochineniia*, p. 250; trans. in O'Meara, *Ryleev*, p. 192.

39  Viroli, *Love of Country*, pp. 30–38.

40  From Glinka's *Velzen*; trans. in S. Karlinsky, *Russian Drama from Its Beginnings to the Age of Pushkin* (Berkeley, CA, 1985), p. 219.

41  V. K. Kiukhel'beker, *Izbrannye proizvedeniia v dvukh tomakh*, 2 vols (Moscow, 1967), vol. II, pp. 175–274, 677–729. See Brown, *Russian Literature*, vol. II, pp. 24–9 for a discussion of this drama.

42  P. A. Katenin, *Izbrannye proizvedeniia* (Moscow-Leningrad, 1965), pp. 361–422.
    See also Brown, *Russian Literature*, vol. I, pp. 43, 53–7; vol. II, pp. 24–9;
    Karlinsky, *Russian Drama*, pp. 220–22.

43  Pushkin, *P.s.s.*, vol. I, p. 267; trans. in Pushkin, *Complete Works*, vol. I, p. 272.

44  Ryleev, *Sochineniia*, pp. 265–6; trans. in O'Meara, *Ryleev*, p. 194.

45  A. I. Odoevskii, *Stikhotvoreniia* (Moscow, 1982), p. 66; trans. in Brown,
    *Russian Literature*, vol. II, p. 113.

46  A. S. Pushkin, *Polnoe sobranie sochinenii*, vol. I (Moscow, 1949), p. 258,
    translated by the author.

47  Orlik, *Dekabristy*, p. 74.

48  M. A. Dodolev, 'Russia and the Spanish Revolution of 1820–1823', *Russian
    Studies in History*, VIII/3 (Winter 1969–70); M. A. Dodolev, 'Rossiia i
    voina ispanskogo naroda za nezavisimost', *Voprosy Istorii*, 11 (1972),
    pp. 33–44; Isabel de Madariaga, 'Spain and the Decembrists', *European
    Studies Review*, III/2 (1973), pp. 141–56; Richard Stites, 'Decembrists with
    a Spanish Accent', *Kritika: Explorations in Russian and Eurasian History*,
    XII/1 (Winter 2011), pp. 5–23; Derek Offord, 'The Response of the Russian
    Decembrists to Spanish Politics in the Age of Ferdinand VII', *Historia
    Constitucional*, 13 (2012), n.p.; Susanna Rabow-Edling, 'The Decembrist
    Movement and the Spanish Constitution of 1812', *Historia Constitucional*,
    13 (2012), pp. 143–61.

49  Quoted in Anatole G. Mazour, *The First Russian Revolution, 1825: The
    Decembrist Movement. Its Origins, Development, and Significance* (Stanford,
    CA, 1961), p. 48.

50  M. V. Nechkina, *Dvizhenie dekabristov*, vol. I (Moscow, 1955), p. 305.

51  Mazour, *First Russian Revolution*, p. 56.

52  V. F. Raevskii, *Stikhotvoreniia* (Leningrad, 1952), pp. 134–5; trans. in Brown,
    *Russian Literature*, vol. II, pp. 104–5.

53  Kiukhel'beker, *Izbrannye*, vol. I, p. 144; trans. in Brown, *Russian Literature*,
    vol. II, p. 16.

54  Ryleev, *Polnoe sobranie sochinenii*, p. 417. See also I. M. Toibin,
    'O prozaicheskikh nabroskakh Ryleeva filosofsko-istoricheskogo
    soderzhaniia', *Uchenye zapiski Kurskogo gosudarstvennogo pedagogicheskogo
    instituta*, 3 (1954), pp. 32–57.

55  For a discussion of Ryleev's conception of history, see Polina Rikoun, 'The
    Maker of Martyrs: Narrative Form and Political Resistance in Ryleev's
    "Voinarovskii"', *Russian Review*, LXXI/3 (July 2012), pp. 436–59. See also
    Wang, 'Ryleev, Pushkin'.

56  Pushkin, *P.s.s.*, vol. II, p. 29; trans. in Brown, *Russian Literature*, vol. II,
    p. 116.

57  The poem 'One spark will start a flame' was written in the late 1820s or early
    1830s.

58  Odoevskii, *Stikhotvoreniia*, p. 73; trans. in Brown, *Russian Literature*, vol. II,
    p. 116.

59  Quoted in Brown, *Russian Literature*, p. 148.

60  Ryleev, *Sochineniia*, p. 214; trans. in O'Meara, *Ryleev*, pp. 188–9.

61  K. F. Ryleev, *Stikhotvoreniia* (Moscow, 1956), pp. 165, 330.

62  Ibid., p. 330; trans. in O'Meara, *Ryleev*, p. 178.

63  Kiukhel'beker, *Izbrannye*, vol. II, pp. 175–274, 677–729.

64 Brown, *Russian Literature*, vol. I, pp. 289, 307.

65 Glinka, *Stikhotvoreniia*, pp. 76–9.

66 Glinka, *Velzen*, p. 58; trans. in Brown, *Russian Literature*, vol. I, p. 286.

67 Ryleev, quoted in O'Meara, *Ryleev*, p. 180.

68 See G. W. Bowersock, 'The Roman Emperor as Russian Tsar: Tacitus and Pushkin', *Proceedings of the American Philosophical Society*, CXLIII/1 (March 1999), pp. 130–47.

69 Pushkin, *P.s.s.*, vol. I, p. 338.

70 O'Meara, *Ryleev*, p. 191.

71 Kiukhel'beker, *Izbrannye*, vol. I, pp. 158–61; trans. in Brown, *Russian Literature*, vol. II, p. 17.

72 Ryleev, *Sochineniia*, p. 266; trans. in O'Meara, *Ryleev*, pp. 194–5. The Spanish patriot Rafael del Riego was killed in 1823.

73 Letter from Piotr Kakhovskii to General Levashev, 24 February 1826, in Mazour, *First Russian Revolution*, pp. 274–7.

74 'Messieurs, je vous félicite: Riego est fait prisonnier.' 'Quelle heureuse nouvelle, Sire.' Basargin, *Vospominaniia*, p. 71.

75 *Vosstanie dekabristov*, vol. I, p. 373; vol. XVIII, p. 299.

76 Pushkin, *P.s.s.*, vol. I, pp. 338–9; trans. in Pushkin, *Complete Works*, vol. II, pp. 47–8.

77 Lorenz Erren argues that Russian political culture was faithful to a set of values that were more Roman than European, but he does not present much evidence for this. Lorenz Erren, 'Russia a Republic? Some Remarks on the National Consciousness of the Decembrists', in *The Enigmatic Tsar and His Empire: Russia under Alexander I, 1801–1825*, ed. Jan Kusber, Alexander Kaplunovsky and Benjamin Conrad (Berlin, 2019), p. 267.

78 Volk, *Istoricheskie vzgliady dekabristov*; H. Lemberg, *Die nationale Gedankenwelt der Dekabristen* (Cologne and Graz, 1963); A. Walicki, *A History of Russian Thought from the Enlightenment to Marxism* (Stanford, CA, 1979), pp. 53, 67, 59; Prousis, *Russian Society*, pp. 137–8.

79 H. T. Colbourn, *Lamp of Experience: Whig History and the Intellectual Origins of the American Revolution* (Chapel Hill, NC, 1965).

80 P. Maier, *From Resistance to Revolution: Colonial Radicals and the Development of American Opposition to Britain, 1765–1776* (New York, 1972); Bailyn, *Ideological Origins*.

81 J. P. Greene, 'Empire and Identity from the Glorious Revolution to the American Revolution', in *The Oxford History of the British Empire*, vol. II: *The Eighteenth Century*, ed. P. J. Marshall (Oxford, 1998), pp. 208–30 (p. 228); H. Kohn, *The Idea of Nationalism* (New York, 1945), pp. 206–7, 167. See also Gabriel de Mably, *Observations sur l'histoire de France* (Geneva, 1765).

82 A. Walicki, *Russia, Poland and Universal Regeneration: Studies on Russian and Polish Thought of the Romantic Epoch* (Notre Dame, IN, 1991), p. 12.

83 V. F. Raevskii, *Polnoe sobranie stikhotvorenii* (Moscow-Leningrad, 1967), pp. 151–5; trans. in Brown, *Russian Literature*, vol. II, p. 107.

84 Walicki, *History of Russian Thought*, pp. 67, 59.

85 Glinka, *Stikhotvoreniia*, p. 77.

86 Natalie O. Kononenko, 'The Influence of the Orthodox Church on Ukrainian Dumy', *Slavic Review*, L/3 (1991), pp. 566–75; Ed Weeda, 'The Boundaries of Advice Literature: The Theme of Vadim Novgorodskii

in Literary Texts and the Discussion on Autocracy, Liberty and Equality, 1786–1831', *Slavonic and East European Review*, LXXXVII/2 (April 2009), pp. 227–58 (pp. 252–5).

87  K. F. Ryleev, *Polnoe sobranie stikhotvorenii* (Leningrad, 1971), p. 330; trans. in O'Meara, *Ryleev*, p. 178.

88  A. I. Odoevskii, *Polnoe sobranie stikhotvorenii* (Leningrad, 1958), pp. 127–8. See Brown, *Russian Literature*, vol. II, p. 112.

89  D. Saunders, *Russia in the Age of Reaction and Reform, 1801–1881* (New York, 1992), p. 98.

90  G. A. Hosking, *Russia: People and Empire* (Cambridge, MA, 1997), p. 177; Janet M. Hartley, *Alexander I* (London and New York, 1994), p. 209; Walicki, *History of Russian Thought*, p. 67.

91  *Vosstanie dekabristov*, vol. VII, p. 129.

## 7 Incarceration

1  A. S. Pushkin, 'To the Emperor Nicholas I', in *Pushkin Threefold: Narrative, Lyric, Polemic, and Ribald Verse*, trans. Walter Arndt (New York, 1972), p. 27.

2  A. D. Margolis, *Tiur'ma i ssylka v imperatorskoi Rossii: Issledovaniia i arkhivnye nakhodki* (Moscow, 1995), pp. 61–2; Patrick O'Meara, '*Vreden sever*: The Decembrists' Memories of the Peter-Paul Fortress', in *St Petersburg, 1703–1825*, ed. Anthony Cross (Basingstoke, 2003), p. 165; M. V. Nechkina, *Den' 14 dekabria 1825 goda* (Moscow, 1985), p. 212.

3  Anna von Rozen, née Malinovskaia, was the daughter of the director of the Tsarskoe Selo Lyceum, V. F. Malinovsky. She was very well educated and knew both English and French.

4  A. E. Rozen, *Russian Conspirators in Siberia: A Personal Narrative* (London, 2005), p. 41.

5  According to Rozen, it was his brother M. A. Bestuzhev who had this exchange with Nicholas (ibid., p. 43).

6  Quoted in Jean Henri Schnitzler, *Histoire Intime de la Russie sous les Empereurs Alexandre et Nicolas* (Paris, 1847). The translation is my own ('Je pourrais vous pardonner, et si j'avais assurance de posséder en vous désormais un fidèle serviteur, je le ferais … Voilà précisément ce dont nous nous plaignons, que l'Empereur puisse tout, et qu'il n'y ait point de loi pour lui. Au nom de Dieu, laissez à la justice son libre cours et que le sort de vos sujets ne dépende plus à l'avenir de vos caprices ou de vos impressions du moment.').

7  N. I. Lorer, 'Zapiski moego vremeni', in *Memuary dekabristov*, ed. A. S. Nemzer (Moscow, 1988), p. 313.

8  N. V. Basargin, *Vospominaniia, rasskazy, stat'i* (Irkutsk, 1988), p. 83; Pauline Annenkova, *Zapiski* (Petrograd, 1915); B. E. Syroechkovskii, ed., *Mezhdutsarstvie 1825 goda i vosstanie dekabristov* (Moscow, 1926), pp. 32–3.

9  Syroechkovskii, *Mezhdutsarstvie*, p. 34.

10  Ibid., pp. 32–3.

11  Lorer, 'Zapiski', ch. 6.

12  A. S. Gangeblov, *Vospominaniia dekabrista* (Moscow, 1888), p. 72.

13  Glynn Barratt, *Voices in Exile: The Decembrist Memoirs* (Montreal, 1974), p. 139.

14  O'Meara, '*Vreden sever*', pp. 169–70; Patrick O'Meara, *The Decembrist Pavel Pestel: Russia's First Republican* (Basingstoke, 2003), p. 169; *Vosstanie*

*dekabristov: Materialy i dokumenty*, 22 vols (Moscow, 1925–2012), vol. VIII, p. 375; Syroechkovskii, *Mezhdutsarstvie*, pp. 19, 33.

15 A. M. Muraviev, *Mon journal* (Moi zhurnal), in *Vospominaniia i rasskazy deiatelei tainykh obshchestv 1820-kh godov*, vol. 1, ed. S. I. Chernov and Iu. G. Oksman (Moscow, 1931), pp. 135–40; *Vosstanie dekabristov*, vol. XVI, pp. 138, 160.

16 A ravelin is an outwork of fortifications, with two faces forming a salient angle, constructed beyond the moat and in front of the curtain.

17 O'Meara, '*Vreden sever*', pp. 171–2; A. D. Margolis, *Peterburg dekabristov* (St Petersburg, 2000); Lorer, 'Zapiski', ch. 9; Rozen, *Russian Conspirators*, pp. 58–9.

18 Lorer, 'Zapiski', ch. 9.

19 Quoted in Barratt, *Voices in Exile*, p. 102; P. E. Shchegolev, *Dekabristy: Sbornik statei* (Leningrad, 1926), pp. 266–9.

20 Lorer, 'Zapiski', ch. 7.

21 Basargin, *Vospominaniia*, p. 85.

22 A. V. Podzhio [Poggio], *Zapiski, pis'ma* (Irkutsk, 1989).

23 Rozen, *Russian Conspirators*, pp. 46–7.

24 Ibid., p. 53; Gangeblov, *Vospominaniia dekabrista*, p. 88; R. V. Iezuitova et al., eds, *Pisateli-dekabristy v vospominaniiakh sovremennikov*, vol. 1 (Moscow, 1980), pp. 92–111.

25 N. A. Bestuzhev, *Vospominaniia Bestuzhevykh*, ed. M. K. Azadovskii (Moscow-Leningrad, 1951), p. 38.

26 Lorer, 'Zapiski', ch. 9.

27 Evgenii P. Obolenskii, 'Vospominaniia o Ryleeve', in *Pisateli-dekabristy*, ed. Iezuitova et al., pp. 97–110.

28 Ibid.; Gangeblov, *Vospominaniia dekabrista*, p. 84.

29 Lorer, 'Zapiski'; Muraviev, *Mon journal*.

30 Muraviev, *Mon journal*.

31 Ibid.

32 Ol'ga V. Edel'man, *Sledstvie po delu dekabristov* (Moscow, 2010).

33 According to Edel'man, confrontation was used to solve contradictions in testimony, mainly on the subject of regicide. However, in more than half of the cases confrontation failed (ibid.).

34 O'Meara, '*Vreden sever*', p. 168; Rozen, *Russian Conspirators*, p. 42.

35 Rozen, *Russian Conspirators*, pp. 53–5; Gangeblov, *Vospominaniia dekabrista*, p. 110; Basargin, *Vospominaniia*, pp. 92–100; Bestuzhev, *Vospominaniia Bestuzhevykh*, p. 38.

36 Marc Raeff, *The Decembrist Movement* (Englewood Cliffs, NJ, 1966), p. 31; Muraviev, *Mon journal*.

37 Letter from S. P. Trubetskoi to E. I. Trubetskaia, 15 December 1825, in S. P. Trubetskoi, *Materialy o zhizni i revoliutsionnoi deiatel'nosti*, vol. 1 (Irkutsk, 1983), pp. 103–217.

38 Trubetskaia to Trubetskoi, 16 December 1825, ibid., p. 334 n. 1.

39 Ibid., 25 December 1825, p. 335–6 n. 3.

40 Trubetskoi, *Materialy o zhizni*, p. 336 n. 1.

41 Trubetskaia to Trubetskoi, 27 December 1825, ibid.

42 Ibid., 31 December 1825, p. 337 n. 2.

43 Trubetskoi to Trubetskaia, 5 January 1826, ibid., pp. 109–10.

44 Ibid., 31 December 1825 and 6 January 1826, pp. 108, 110–11.

45 Trubetskaia to Trubetskoi, 1 and 2 January 1826, ibid., p. 337 n. 1; Trubetskoi to Trubetskaia, 5 January 1826, ibid., pp. 109–10.

46 Trubetskaia to Trubetskoi, 1 and 2 January 1826, ibid., p. 337 n. 1.

47 Trubetskoi to Trubetskaia, 6 January 1826, ibid., p. 110.

48 Ibid., 22 April 1826, p. 156.

49 Ibid., 5 April 1826, p. 148.

50 Ibid., 28 April 1826, p. 160.

51 Patrick O'Meara, *K. F. Ryleev: A Political Biography of the Decembrist Poet* (Princeton, NJ, 1984), pp. 245–6.

52 Bestuzhev, *Vospominaniia Bestuzhevykh*, pp. 38–9.

53 Letter from N. M. Ryleeva to K. F. Ryleev, 21 December 1825, in K. F. Ryleev, *Polnoe sobranie sochinenii*, vol. II (Moscow, 1907), pp. 121–46.

54 Ibid., 26 December 1825.

55 Letter from Ryleev to Ryleeva, 25 December 1825, ibid.

56 Ibid., 17 March 1826.

57 Ibid., 15 February 1826; 13 March 1826.

58 Ibid., 24 May 1826.

59 Letter from Ryleeva to Ryleev, 25 January 1826, ibid.

60 Letter from Ryleev to Ryleeva, n.d., ibid.

61 Nikita was not in St Petersburg during the revolt.

62 Letter from Nikita Muraviev to Aleksandra Muravieva, 29 December 1825, in Nikita Muraviev, *Pis'ma dekabrista 1813–1826 gg* (Moscow, 2001), pp. 212–13.

63 Letter from Aleksandra Muravieva to Nikita Muraviev, 2 January 1826, www.hrono.ru, accessed 6 August 2024; E. A. Pavliuchenko, *V dobrovol'nom izgnanii: O zhenakh i sestrakh dekabristov* (Moscow, 1986), pp. 15–16.

64 Ibid (letter from Muravieva to Muraviev).

65 Letter from Muraviev to Muravieva, 3 January 1826, in Muraviev, *Pis'ma dekabrista*, p. 214.

66 Ibid., 5 January 1826, p. 215.

67 Ibid., mid-February 1826, p. 229.

68 Ibid., 19 January [1826?], pp. 221–2. After this first visit, Muravieva was allowed to visit her husband regularly. Subsequently, his mother and children also came to see him in the Fortress.

69 Ibid., 10 January 1826, p. 219.

70 Ibid., 9 January 1826, p. 217.

71 Ibid., 18 January 1826, p. 221.

72 Ibid., 3 January 1826, p. 214.

73 Ibid., May 1826, p. 236.

74 Note from Muraviev to Ekaterina and Aleksandra Muravieva, ibid., May 1826, p. 235–6: 'Aleksandra's brother Zakhar Chernyshev was a Decembrist. At the time of the uprising he was on leave in Oriol province, but he was arrested and sentenced to one year of hard labour and exile.'

75 Ibid.

76 Rozen, *Russian Conspirators*, p. 57.

77 Ibid., pp. 50, 56–7, 59.

78 Barratt, *Voices in Exile*, p. 105.

79 Lorer, 'Zapiski', ch. 7.

80 Rozen, *Russian Conspirators*, pp. 53–5.

81 M. A. Fonvizin, *Sochineniia i pis'ma*, vol. II (Irkutsk, 1982), pp. 194–8.

## 8 Sentencing

1   Anatole G. Mazour, *The First Russian Revolution, 1825: The Decembrist Movement. Its Origins, Development, and Significance* (Stanford, CA, 1961), pp. 212–13; Natan Eidelman, in *Conspiracy against the Tsar: A Portrait of the Decembrists* (Moscow, 1985), p. 75, states that there were 123 'state criminals'. According to Tat'iana V. Andreeva, 570 arrests were made, of whom 299 people were acquitted: *Tainye obshchestva v Rossii pervoi treti XIX veka: Gosudarstvennaia politika i obshchestvennoe mnenie* (St Petersburg, 2009), pp. 888, 518–29.

2   Patrick O'Meara, *The Decembrist Pavel Pestel: Russia's First Republican* (Basingstoke, 2003), pp. 177–8.

3   Alexander Herzen, *My Past and Thoughts* (Los Angeles, CA, 1982), p. 43.

4   Roman Koropeckyj, *Adam Mickiewicz: The Life of a Romantic* (Ithaca, NY, 2008), p. 72; Richard S. Wortman, *Scenarios of Power: Myth and Ceremony in Russian Monarchy from Peter the Great to the Abdication of Nicholas II* (Princeton, NJ, 2006), pp. 131–2; O'Meara, *Pestel*, pp. 177–8.

5   *Vosstanie dekabristov: Materialy i dokumenty*, 22 vols (Moscow, 1925–2012), vol. VI. A group of noble officers from the Southern Society were also convicted by military courts and sent to Siberia with common criminals. A. D. Margolis, *Tiur'ma i ssylka v imperatorskoi Rossii: Issledovaniia i arkhivnye nakhodki* (Moscow, 1995), p. 59; S. V. Mironenko, *Dekabristy. Biograficheskii spravochnik* (Moscow, 1988), pp. 34, 114, 168–9, 171–2.

6   *Vosstanie dekabristov*, vol. XVII, p. 280.

7   Nevertheless, a small group of civilians did see the hanging. Ludmilla Trigos, 'The Spectacle of the Scaffold: Performance and Subversion in the Execution of the Decembrist', in *Times of Trouble: Violence in Russian Literature and Culture*, ed. M. Levitt and T. Novikov (Madison, WI, 2007), pp. 42–56 (p. 44).

8   N. V. Basargin, *Vospominaniia, rasskazy, stat'i* (Irkutsk, 1988), p. 101.

9   N. I. Lorer, 'Zapiski moego vremeni', in *Memuary dekabristov*, ed. A. S. Nemzer (Moscow, 1988), ch. 8; A. E. Rozen, *Russian Conspirators in Siberia: A Personal Narrative* (London, 2005), pp. 59–60.

10  Ibid. Lorer and his friends were placed in Alekseevskii ravelin.

11  A. V. Podzhio [Poggio], *Zapiski, pis'ma* (Irkutsk, 1989).

12  Lorer, 'Zapiski', ch. 7.

13  A. M. Muraviev, *Mon journal* (Moi zhurnal), in *Vospominaniia i rasskazy deiatelei tainykh obshchestv 1820-kh godov*, vol. I, ed. S. I. Chernov and Iu. G. Oksman (Moscow, 1931), pp. 131–60.

14  M. S. Lunin, *Sochineniia i pis'ma* (St Petersburg, 1923), pp. 60, 47, 53; Glynn Barratt, *M. S. Lunin: Catholic Decembrist* (The Hague, 1976).

15  Sergei Muraviev-Apostol, 'Prison Diary', *Russkii arkhiv*, V/1 (1887), pp. 49–52.

16  2 Timothy 4:6–7.

17  Quoted in N. A. Bestuzhev, *Vospominaniia Bestuzhevykh*, ed. M. K. Azadovskii (Moscow-Leningrad, 1951), p. 39.

18  Letter from K. F. Ryleev to N. M. Ryleeva, 13 July 1826, in K. F. Ryleev, *Polnoe sobranie sochinenii*, vol. II (Moscow, 1907), pp. 121–46.

19  Ibid.

20  Lorer, 'Zapiski', ch. 8.

21 Record of N. A. Blagoveshchenskii, *Istoricheskii vestnik*, 1 (1904), pp. 80–86.

22 E. P. Obolenskii, 'Vospominaniia o Ryleeve', in *Pisateli-dekabristy v vospominaniiakh sovremennikov*, vol. 1, ed. R. V. Iezuitova et al. (Moscow, 1980), pp. 108–10.

23 Lorer, 'Zapiski', ch. 8; V. I. Shteingel, *Zapiski*, vol. 1 (Irkutsk, 1985), p. 172; Basargin, *Vospominaniia*, p. 103.

24 Rozen, *Russian Conspirators*, p. 63; Glynn Barratt, *Voices in Exile: The Decembrist Memoirs* (Montreal, 1974), p. 201; Lorer, 'Zapiski'; N. I. Grech, *Zapiski* (Moscow, 1990), pp. 331, 334–5; N. V. Basargin, *Zapiski* (Krasnoiarsk, 1985), p. 79.

25 See the diary of Dowager Empress Maria Fedorovna, in *Mezhdutsarstvie 1825 goda i vosstanie dekabristov*, ed. B. E. Syroechkovskii (Moscow, 1926), pp. 100–102; M. N. Myslovskii, 'Iz zapisnoi knizhki protoieriya', in *Shchukinskii sbornik* (Moscow, 1905), pp. 29–40.

26 Record of N. A. Blagoveshchenskii; Lorer, 'Zapiski', ch. 8; Basargin, *Vospominaniia*, p. 106; Shteingel, *Zapiski*, p. 172.

27 Witnesses disagree as to the identity of those who fell, but according to the official report of the Governor General of St Petersburg, Golenishchev-Kutuzov, it was Ryleev, Kakhovskii and Muraviev-Apostol. *Pisateli-dekabristy*, ed. R. V. Iezuitova et al., pp. 252–3 n. 1–2.

28 N. Ramazanov, 'Kazn' dekabristov. Rasskazy sovremennikov', *Russkii arkhiv*, 2 (1881), pp. 341–6; S. E. Erlikh, *Istoriia mifa. 'Dekabristskaia legenda' Gertsena* (St Petersburg, 2006), p. 214; Trigos, 'The Spectacle of the Scaffold', p. 55.

29 Maria Volkonskaia, *Zapiski* (Moscow, 1977).

30 Record of N. A. Blagoveshchenskii. An *oprichnik* was a member of Ivan the Terrible's personal guard, who terrorized the civilian population and suppressed the rising boyar aristocracy in the sixteenth century. An aiguillette is a braided cord, usually made from gold or silver, worn on a uniform as a symbol of honour.

31 Bestuzhev, *Vospominaniia Bestuzhevykh*.

32 Basargin, *Vospominaniia*, p. 112 n. 86.

33 N. K. Shil'der, *Imperator Nikolai pervyi: Ego zhizn' i tsarstvovanie*, vol. 1 (St Petersburg, 1903), pp. 256–8, 704–6.

34 Ibid., pp. 456–8.

35 Letter from Aleksandr Bulgakov to his brother Konstantin Bulgakov, 19 July 1826, in *Brat'ia Bulgakovy. Perepiska*, vol. II, ed. Anna Tancharova (Moscow, 2010), available at http://decabristy-online.ru.

36 Herzen, *My Past and Thoughts*, p. 44.

37 Wortman, *Scenarios of Power*.

38 Interest in this doctrine has resurfaced in Putin's Russia. See Fiona Hill and Clifford G. Gaddy, *Mr Putin: Operative in the Kremlin* (Washington, DC, 2015), pp. 64–8. See also Paul Robinson, *Russian Conservatism* (Ithaca, NY, 2019), ch. 3.

39 Wortman, *Scenarios of Power*, pp. 120, 128–33. Some of the Decembrists' families struggled to save their sons by sending numerous petitions to the tsar. Nicholas also wanted to be seen as a caring father to his people. One example of this is his offer to support Natalia Ryleeva by giving her a pension of 3,000 roubles a year until she remarried in 1833. Patrick O'Meara, *K. F. Ryleev: A Political Biography of the Decembrist Poet* (Princeton, NJ, 1984), p. 309.

40  Nicholas V. Riasanovsky, *A Parting of Ways: Government and the Educated Public in Russia, 1801–1855* (Oxford, 1976).

41  Patrick O'Meara, '*Vreden sever*': The Decembrists' Memories of the Peter-Paul Fortress', in *St Petersburg, 1703–1825*, ed. Anthony Cross (Basingstoke, 2003), p. 185.

42  Basargin, *Vospominaniia*, p. 110.

43  Letter from Nikita Muraviev to Ekaterina and Aleksandra Muravieva, October 1826, in Nikita Muraviev, *Pis'ma dekabrista 1813–1826 gg* (Moscow, 2001), pp. 244–5.

44  Rozen, *Russian Conspirators*, p. 85.

45  Basargin, *Vospominaniia*, p. 109; A. P. Beliaev, 'Vospominaniia dekabrista', in A. D. Margolis, *Peterburg dekabristov* (St Petersburg, 2000), p. 349. French translations of Scott and Cooper were popular.

46  Lorer, 'Zapiski', ch. 9.

## 9  To Siberia

1  V. A. Fedorov, ed., 'Krestnyi put' dekabristov v Sibir': Dokumenty ob otpravke osuzhdennykh na katorgu i v ssylku i ob usloviiakh ikh soderzhaniia 1826–1837gg', *Istoricheskii arkhiv*, 6 (2000), pp. 46–56. Most convicts passed through Yaroslavl, Perm, Yekaterinburg, Tobolsk, Tara, Kainsk, Kolyvan, Tomsk, Krasnoyarsk and Irkutsk.

2  A. E. Rozen, *Russian Conspirators in Siberia: A Personal Narrative* (London, 2005), p. 79.

3  Obolenskii, quoted in Glynn Barratt, *Voices in Exile: The Decembrist Memoirs* (Montreal, 1974), pp. 201–2.

4  It consisted of three concentric fortress chains and had been built to protect St Petersburg.

5  The Bestuzhev brothers were transferred on 7 August 1826 and stayed for a year in Shlisselburg.

6  Vladimir Shteingel, *Sochineniia i pis'ma*, vol. 1 (Irkutsk, 1985), p. 137. Gavriil Batenkov, Nikolai Panov, Aleksandr Sutgof, Dmitrii Shchepin-Rostovskii, Vladimir Bechasnov and Ivan Povalo-Shveikovskii were also sent there.

7  Aleksandr Barsukov, *Rodoslovie Sheremetevyh* (St Petersburg, 1899), p. 21.

8  Quoted in Barratt, *Voices in Exile*, p. 205.

9  Ibid., pp. 218–19.

10  P. E. Annenkova, *Vospominaniia* (Moscow, 2003), ch. 7.

11  A. M. Muraviev, *Mon journal* (Moi zhurnal), in *Vospominaniia i rasskazy deiatelei tainykh obshchestv 1820-kh godov*, vol. 1, ed. S. I. Chernov and Iu. G. Oksman (Moscow, 1931), pp. 131–60.

12  Rozen, *Russian Conspirators*, pp. 84, 206–7.

13  Quoted in Daniel Beer, *The House of the Dead: Siberian Exile under the Tsars* (London, 2016), p. 71.

14  M. A. Bestuzhev, quoted in Mark Bassin, 'Inventing Siberia: Visions of the Russian East in the Early Nineteenth Century', *American Historical Review*, XCVI/3 (June 1991), pp. 763–94 (p. 778).

15  See Bassin, 'Inventing Siberia'.

16  Rozen, *Russian Conspirators*, pp. 89–90.

17  N. V. Basargin, *Vospominaniia, rasskazy, stat'i* (Irkutsk, 1988), pp. 117–18.

18  The husbands of both these women took common-law wives in their settlements in 1838–9, and had new families, but returned to Russia after the amnesty.

19  Anatole G. Mazour, *Women in Exile: Wives of the Decembrists* (Tallahassee, FL, 1975), p. 65.

20  Letter from N. M. Ryleeva to K. F. Ryleev, 8 May 1826, in K. F. Ryleev, *Polnoe sobranie sochinenii*, vol. II (Moscow, 1907), pp. 121–46.

21  Christine Sutherland, *The Princess of Siberia: The Story of Maria Volkonsky and the Decembrist Exiles* (London, 1985), p. 124.

22  Quoted in Mazour, *Women in Exile*, p. 63.

23  Barbara Evans Clements, *A History of Women in Russia: From Earliest Times to the Present* (Bloomington, IN, 2012), p. 67; Barbara Alpern Engel, *Women in Russia, 1700–2000* (Cambridge, 2004), pp. 31–4.

24  Letter from Aleksandra Muravieva to Nikita Muraviev, 2 January 1826, in E. A. Pavliuchenko, *V dobrovol'nom izgnanii: O zhenakh i sestrakh dekabristov* (Moscow, 1986), pp. 15–16; E. A. Pavliuchenko, *Zhenshchiny v russkom osvoboditel'nom dvizhenii: Ot Marii Volkonskoi do Very Figner* (Moscow, 1988).

25  Letters from E. I. Trubetskaia to S. P. Trubetskoi, 1 and 2 January 1826, in S. P. Trubetskoi, *Materialy o zhizni i revoliutsionnoi deiatel'nosti*, vol. I (Irkutsk, 1983), p. 337 n. 1.

26  Letter from Trubetskoi to Trubetskaia, 11 May 1826, ibid., pp. 167–8. Daniel Beer writes that Trubetskoi used emotional blackmail to compel his wife to follow him into exile; that he appealed to her love for him, but even more to her religious sense of duty as a wife (*House of the Dead*, pp. 65–7). However, the feelings Trubetskoi expressed in his letter from the Fortress appear truthful and, moreover, Trubetskaia made her own decision very early to share his fate.

27  Ibid., 12 July 1826, p. 205.

28  Petition by M. K. Iushnevskaia to the Governor General of Western Siberia, P. M. Kaptsevich, 30 July 1826.

29  O. Popova, 'Istoriia zhizni M. N. Volkonskoi', in *Zven'ia*, vols III–IV (Moscow, 1934), pp. 21–128 ( p. 43).

30  Nikolai Basargin recalled that he read Ryleev's poem *Voinarovskii* to his wife when it had recently been published, and that she told him she would also come to console him and share his fate should he be arrested. Unfortunately, Maria Basargina died in August 1825 while giving birth to their daughter Sophia.

31  Letter from Maria Volkonskaia to Sergei Volkonskii, 28 June 1826, in *Pamiati dekabristov: Sbornik materialov*, vol. II (Leningrad, 1926), p. 95. Iurii Lotman notes that following the exiled husband to Siberia existed as a norm in the customs of common people in Russia. See Iurii Lotman, 'Dekabrist v povsednevnoi zhizni', in *Besedy o russkoi kul'ture* (St Petersburg, 1994), pp. 353–4.

32  Sutherland, *Princess of Siberia*, p. 108. See also Popova, 'Istoriia zhizni', pp. 28–60; M. D. Filin, *Maria Volkonskaia* (Moscow, 2006), pp. 143–53.

33  A. E. Rozen, *Zapiski dekabrista* (Irkutsk, 1984), pp. 123–31.

34  N. V. Basargin, *Vospominaniia, rasskazy, stat'i* (Irkutsk, 1988), p. 75.

35  Maria Volkonskaia, *Zapiski* (Moscow, 1977), pp. 32–40, 50–55, 58–71.

36  Annenkova, *Vospominaniia*, ch. 9.

37 Letters from Nikita Muraviev to Aleksandra Muravieva, mid-February and May 1826, in Nikita Muraviev, *Pis'ma dekabrista 1813–1826 gg* (Moscow, 2001), pp. 229, 236–7.

38 Basargin, *Vospominaniia*, p. 79.

39 Maria Volkonskaia, *Zapiski* (Munich, 2006), p. 10.

40 Thomas W. Atkinson, *Travels in the Regions of the Upper and Lower Amoor, and the Russian Acquisitions on the Confines of India and China* (London, 1860), pp. 374–5, 378.

41 Barratt, *Voices in Exile*, pp. 224–5, 227.

42 Beer, *House of the Dead*, pp. 81–2; Andrew A. Gentes, *Exile to Siberia, 1590–1822* (Basingstoke, 2008), pp. 101, 108, 125; E. Anisimov, *Dyba i knut: Politicheskii sysk i russkoe obshchestvo v XVIII veke* (Moscow, 1999), pp. 654–5.

43 Letter from Trubetskoi to Trubetskaia, Irkutsk, 5 October 1826, in S. P. Trubetskoi, *Materialy o zhizni i revoliutsionnoi deiatel'nosti*, vol. II (Irkutsk, 1987), pp. 70–71.

44 Mazour, *Women in Exile*, p. 23; Rozen, *Russian Conspirators*, p. 99.

45 Mukhanov was sent to Sveaborg and then to Vyborg fortress. Not until 5 October 1827 was he sent to Siberia. In 1833 he appealed for permission to marry Varvara but was denied.

46 Obolenskii, quoted in Barratt, *Voices in Exile*, p. 228.

47 Letter from Trubetskoi to Trubetskaia, Nizhne-Zarentuevskaia station, 30 *versts* from the Nerchinsk factories, 26 October 1826, in Trubetskoi, *Materialy o zhizni*, vol. II, pp. 73–4.

48 Letter from Trubetskoi to Trubetskaia, Blagodatsk Mine, 29 October 1826, ibid., pp. 74–6.

49 Mazour, *Women in Exile*, p. 26.

50 6,500 *versts*. 1 *verst* = 1.07 kilometres (⅔ mi.).

51 Muraviev, *Mon journal*, pp. 145–9; V. A. Fyodorov, ed., *Memuary dekabristov: Severnoe obshchestvo* (Moscow, 1981), pp. 136–40.

52 A. S. Pushkin, *Eugene Onegin*, trans. Douglas Hofstadter (New York, 1999), ch. 1, p. 33. Scholars disagree on whether these lines are really about Maria. The same goes for other poems said to be dedicated to or inspired by her. See M. N. Virolainen et al., eds, *Legendy i mify o Pushkine* (St Petersburg, 1995); V. V. Nabokov, *Kommentarii k 'Evgeniiu Oneginu' Aleksandra Pushkina*, ed. A. N. Nikoliukin (Moscow, 1999), pp. 127–48.

53 Volkonskaia, *Zapiski* (1977), pp. 32–40, 50–55, 58–71.

54 Mazour, *Women in Exile*, pp. 3–7, 65; S. V. Maksimov, *Sibir i katorga* (St Petersburg, 1900), part 3, pp. 205–6; M. M. Khin, 'Zheny dekabristov', *Istoricheskii vestnik*, XII (1884), pp. 659–60.

55 Letter from Maria Volkonskaia to her sister, quoted in Sutherland, *Princess of Siberia*, p. 154.

56 Letter from Volkonskaia to her mother-in-law (Aleksandra), 28 May 1827, in *Russkie propilei*, vol. I (Moscow, 1915), p. 20.

57 Mazour, *Women in Exile*, p. 27.

58 'To I. I. Pushchin', in Alexander Pushkin, *Selected Lyric Poetry*, trans. James E. Falen (Evanston, IL, 2009), p. 110.

59 Letter from Aleksandra Muravieva to E. P. Chernysheva, 4 February 1827, www.hrono.ru, accessed 6 August 2024.

60  Letter from Muraviev to Muravieva, January 1827, in Muraviev, *Pis'ma dekabrista*, p. 245.
61  Brick tea was a form of compressed tea pressed into blocks, produced in China and used as a form of currency in China, Tibet, Mongolia, Central Asia and Siberia.
62  Sutherland, *Princess of Siberia*, p. 156.
63  Letter from Maria Volkonskaia, 12 February 1827, in *Russkie propilei*, vol. I, pp. 5–6; Volkonskaia, *Zapiski* (2006), p. 12.
64  Volkonskaia, *Zapiski* (2006), p. 12; letter from Trubetskoi to Trubetskaia, Blagodatsk Mine, 29 October 1826, in Trubetskoi, *Materialy o zhizni*, vol. II, p. 76.
65  Volkonskaia, *Zapiski* (2006), p. 12. See also E. P. Obolenskii, 'Vospominaniia', in *Obshchestvennye dvizheniia Rossii v pervuiu polovinu XIX veka*, ed. P. E. Shchegoleva, vol. I (St Petersburg, 1905).
66  Letter from Maria Volkonskaia to Aleksandra Volkonskaia, 12 February 1827, in *Russkie propilei*, vol. I, pp. 5–6.
67  Ibid., 28 May 1827, pp. 19–21.
68  Ibid., 2 September 1827, pp. 37–8.
69  Volkonskaia, *Zapiski* (2006), p. 13; letter from Trubetskoi to Trubetskaia, Blagodatsk Mine, 5 November 1826, in Trubetskoi, *Materialy o zhizni*, vol. II, p. 78.
70  Fedorov, *Memuary dekabristov*, p. 107.
71  Obolenskii, 'Vospominaniia'.
72  Volkonskaia, *Zapiski* (2006), p. 16.
73  Mazour, *Women in Exile*, p. 25; Rozen, *Russian Conspirators*, p. 96.

## 10  Prison Life

1  A. E. Rozen, *Russian Conspirators in Siberia: A Personal Narrative* (London, 2005), pp. 91, 95–6.
2  ¾ *arshin* = 53.34 centimetres.
3  Rozen, *Russian Conspirators*, p. 97. See also P. E. Annenkova, *Vospominaniia* (Moscow, 2003).
4  M. A. Bestuzhev, *Vospominaniia Bestuzhevykh*, ed. M. K. Azadovskii (Moscow-Leningrad, 1951), pp. 143, 155. Andrew Gentes argues that Mikhail Bestuzhev was exaggerating because the Decembrists lived either separately with their wives or with two or three others in private quarters: Andrew A. Gentes, *Exile to Siberia, 1590–1822* (Basingstoke, 2008), p. 97. This seems to be an unfair accusation. There were at most eight women in Chita, and the rules for meetings were not relaxed until a year after Bestuzhev's arrival. There is no evidence that the other prisoners lived in private quarters.
5  Iakushkin, quoted in Glynn Barratt, *Voices in Exile: The Decembrist Memoirs* (Montreal, 1974), pp. 222–3.
6  Letters from Maria Volkonskaia to her mother-in-law (Aleksandra), 9 September and 2 October 1827, in *Letopisi: Dekabristy* (Moscow, 1938), book III, pp. 89–90.
7  Letter from Maria Volkonskaia to Aleksandra Volkonskaia, 12 February 1827, in *Russkie propilei*, vol. I (Moscow, 1915), pp. 5–6; Maria Volkonskaia, *Zapiski* (Irkutsk, 1973), p. 17.

8   Letter from Aleksandra Muravieva to Ekaterina Muravieva, 17 May 1827, www.hrono.ru, accessed 6 August 2024.

9   I. D. Iakushkin, *Zapiski, stat'i, pis'ma dekabrista I. D. Iakushkina*, ed. S. Shtraikh (Moscow, 1951), pp. 167–71.

10  Rozen, *Russian Conspirators*, pp. 97–8. The Muravievs' son Mikhail died on 26 February 1827, but they did not receive the news until much later.

11  Letters from Aleksandra Muravieva to Ekaterina Muravieva, 17 May 1827, 11 January 1831, www.hrono.ru, accessed 6 August 2024.

12  Annenkova, *Vospominaniia*.

13  Maria Volkonskaia, *Zapiski* (Irkutsk, 1977), pp. 50–55, 58–71.

14  Letter from Maria Volkonskaia to her mother-in-law, Chita, 26 September 1827, quoted in Anatole G. Mazour, *Women in Exile: Wives of the Decembrists* (Tallahassee, FL, 1975), p. 107.

15  Letters from Maria Volkonskaia to her sister in-law (Sofia), 20 and 27 December 1827, in *Russkie propilei*, vol. I, pp. 51–2, 54–5.

16  Letters to Maria Volkonskaia from her mother-in-law, 2 October and 19 November 1827; letter from Volkonskaia to her sister-in-law, 27 December 1827, ibid., pp. 54–5.

17  Mazour, *Women in Exile*, pp. 31–2.

18  Letter from Maria Volkonskaia to Aleksandra Volkonskaia, 12 January 1829, in *Russkie propilei*, vol. I, p. 59.

19  Ibid., 14 November 1827, pp. 46–7.

20  Letter from Maria Volkonskaia to Sofia Volkonskaia, 27 December 1827, ibid., pp. 54–5.

21  Bestuzhev, *Vospominaniia Bestuzhevykh*, p. 146.

22  N. V. Basargin, *Zapiski* (Krasnoiarsk, 1985), p. 185; Barratt, *Voices in Exile*, p. 254.

23  A .V. Sobolev, 'Vel'mozhnaia katorga i ee artel'noe khoziastva', *Voprosy istorii*, 2 (2000), pp. 127–35.

24  John L. H. Keep, *Soldiers of the Tsar: Army and Society in Russia, 1462–1874* (Oxford, 1985), p. 238.

25  Rozen, *Russian Conspirators*, pp. 95, 98–9, 102–3, 123; Basargin, *Zapiski*, pp. 127–8, 167–70; Maria Volkonskaia, *Zapiski* (Munich, 2006), p. 19.

26  Military strategy and tactics, mathematics, chemistry, anatomy, physics, history, astronomy, literature and mechanics.

27  Rozen, *Russian Conspirators*, pp. 103–5; A. P. Beliaev, *Vospominaniia dekabrista o perezhitom i perechuvstvovannom* (St Petersburg, 1882); Basargin, *Zapiski*, pp. 130–31; Bestuzhev, *Vospominaniia Bestuzhevykh*, pp. 158–9, 161.

28  Volkonskaia, *Zapiski* (2006), p. 18; P. N. Svistunov, *Sochineniia, pis'ma 1825–1840*, vol. I (Irkutsk, 2002).

29  Rozen, *Russian Conspirators*, p. 106. Aleksandra Davidova lived to the age of 93.

30  Annenkova, *Vospominaniia*, ch. 14.

31  Iakushkin, *Zapiski*, pp. 167–71; Annenkova, *Vospominaniia*, ch. 15; Volkonskaia, *Zapiski* (2006), p. 18.

32  Basargin, *Zapiski*, p. 129.

33  Annenkova, *Vospominaniia*; letter from Maria Volkonskaia to Sofia Volkonskaia, 27 December 1827, in *Russkie propilei*, vol. I, pp. 54–5.

34  A. I. Odoevskii, 'To Princess M. N. Volkonskaia', Chita, 25 December 1829, trans. by the author. See www.culture.ru, accessed 2 March 2023.

35  Rozen, *Russian Conspirators*, p. 110.

36  Annenkova, *Vospominaniia*.
37  Letter from Maria Volkonskaia to her mother, Chita, 26 September 1827, quoted in Christine Sutherland, *The Princess of Siberia: The Story of Maria Volkonsky and the Decembrist Exiles* (London, 1985), p. 191.
38  Annenkova, *Vospominaniia*.
39  Letters from Maria Volkonskaia to Sofia Volkonskaia, 20 and 27 December 1827, in *Russkie propilei*, vol. I, pp. 51–2, 54–5. Volkonskaia probably used the Réaumur scale, which means that it was even colder (-30°Réaumur = -37.5°C).
40  Annenkova, *Vospominaniia*.
41  Sutherland, *Princess of Siberia*, pp. 218–22.
42  Annenkova, *Vospominaniia*.
43  Ibid.
44  Rozen, *Russian Conspirators*, pp. 111–12.
45  Ibid., p. 118; Barratt, *Voices in Exile*, pp. 317–18. This depiction appears to be based on Thomas Jefferson's vision of America. Similar comparisons were made by other Decembrists.
46  Annenkova, *Vospominaniia*, pp. 182–5.
47  Mazour, *Women in Exile*, p. 31.
48  Bestuzhev, *Vospominaniia Bestuzhevykh*, pp. 158–9; Basargin, *Zapiski*, p. 182.
49  Iakushkin, *Zapiski*, pp. 172–6; O. K. Bulanova-Trubnikova, *Roman dekabrista: Dekabrist V. P. Ivashev i ego sem'ia* (Moscow, 1933). Sergei Erlikh has argued that Madame Ivasheva bought Camille to be her son's wife, primarily based on the testimony of Dmitrii Zavalishin: S. E. Erlikh, 'The Decembrists in Historical Memory (2000–2014)', PhD thesis, St Petersburg Institute of History of the Russian Academy of Sciences, 2015.
50  A. S. Pushkin, 'Epitafiia mladentsu/Epitaph to an Infant' (1828), in A. S. Pushkin, *Sobranie sochinenii v 10 tomakh*, vol. II, p. 244; trans. in Ilia Vinitskii, *Ghostly Paradoxes* (Toronto, 2009), p. 75.
51  Letter from Maria Volkonskaia to Aleksandra Volkonskaia, 19 January 1829, in *Russkie propilei*, vol. I, p. 61.
52  Quoted in Mazour, *Women in Exile*, p. 69; *Russkaia starina*, vol. VI (1878), p. 340.
53  Quoted in Sutherland, *Princess of Siberia*, p. 218. According to her grandson, she wrote, 'In the entire surrounding landscape only one native thing can be detected – the grass on the grave of my child.' Sergei M. Volkonskii, *O dekabristakh. Po semeinym vospominaniiam, Neizdannye materialy* (St Petersburg, 1922), p. 65.
54  20–30 *versts*.
55  Basargin, *Zapiski*, p. 146.
56  Annenkova, *Vospominaniia*.
57  Basargin, *Zapiski*, p. 147.
58  Bestuzhev, *Vospominaniia*, pp. 325–35; Rozen, *Russian Conspirators*, pp. 110–14; Barratt, *Voices in Exile*, pp. 276–81; B. L. Modzalevskii and Iu. G. Oksman, eds, *Dekabristy neizdannye materialy i stat'i* (Moscow, 1925), pp. 131–2.
59  G. Nevelev, *Dekabristskii kontekst. Dokumenty i opisaniia* (St Petersburg, 2012), pp. 420–35.
60  Rozen, *Russian Conspirators*, p. 114.
61  Quoted in Modzalevskii and Oksman, *Dekabristy neizdannye materialy*, p. 141.

62  Petition from Maria Iushnevskaia, dated 30 July 1826. D. I. Bahalij, *Dekabrysty na Ukraïni*, vol. II (Kyiv, 1930).

63  Basargin, *Zapiski*, p. 150.

64  Letter from E. P. Naryshkina to V. M. Naryshkina, 27 September 1830, in *Dekabristy na katorge i v ssylke: Sbornik novykh naterialov i statei*, ed. S. Shtraikh (Moscow, 1925), pp. 9–56.

65  Rozen, *Russian Conspirators*, p. 118.

66  Annenkova, *Vospominaniia*.

67  Volkonskaia, *Zapiski* (2006), p. 22.

68  George Kennan, *Siberia and the Exile System*, vol. IX (London, 1891), pp. 278–318; Mazour, *Women in Exile*, pp. 70–71.

69  Basargin, *Zapiski*, p. 152; Iakushkin, *Zapiski*, pp. 126–7.

70  Rozen, *Russian Conspirators*, p. 119.

71  'Me voilà enfin dans la terre promise.' Quoted in Mazour, *Women in Exile*, p. 70.

72  Rozen, *Russian Conspirators*, p. 119.

73  Quoted in Daniel Beer, *The House of the Dead: Siberian Exile under the Tsars* (London, 2016), p. 119.

74  Iakushkin, *Zapiski*, pp. 129–30.

75  Rozen, *Russian Conspirators*, pp. 124–5; D. I. Zavalishin, *Zapiski dekabrista* (St Petersburg, 1906), pp. 268–9.

76  Iakushkin, *Zapiski*, p. 130; Basargin, *Zapiski*, pp. 167–8; Rozen, *Russian Conspirators*, p. 123.

77  Basargin, *Zapiski*, p. 153; Mazour, *Women in Exile*, pp. 37, 42.

78  Letter from Aleksandra Muravieva to Ekaterina Muravieva, 11 January 1831, www.hrono.ru, accessed 9 August 2024.

79  Letter from Aleksandra Muravieva to G. I. Chernyshev, 1 October 1830, in *Dekabristy na katorge*, ed. Shtraikh, pp. 45–6.

80  Letter from N. D. Fonvizina to N. N. Sheremeteva, 28 September 1830, ibid., pp. 43–4.

81  *Russkaia starina*, vol. III (1896), p. 610; letter from M. K. Iushnevskaia to S. P. Iushnevskii, 27 September 1830, in *Dekabristy na katorge*, ed. Shtraikh, pp. 38–40.

82  Letter from E. P. Naryshkina to V. M. Naryshkina, 27 September 1830, ibid., pp. 36–7.

83  Letter from A. G. Muravieva to G. I. Chernyshev, 1 October 1830, ibid., pp. 45–6.

84  Letter from E. I. Trubetskaia to A. G. Laval, 28 September 1830, ibid., pp. 41–2.

85  Rozen, *Russian Conspirators*, p. 122.

86  Maria Volkonskaia, *Zapiski* (2006), p. 23.

87  Bestuzhev, *Vospominaniia Bestuzhevykh*, p. 248.

88  Letter from Maria Volkonskaia to her mother-in-law, 30 October 1831, in *Russkie propilei*, vol. I, pp. 80–81; Bestuzhev, *Vospominaniia Bestuzhevykh*, p. 248.

89  Basargin, *Zapiski*, p. 174; Iakushkin, *Zapiski*, pp. 172–6.

90  Rozen, *Russian Conspirators*, pp. 122–3.

91  Aleksandra's own mother died in 1828 and her father in 1831.

92  Letter from Aleksandra Muravieva to Ekaterina Muravieva, 4 November 1832, www.hrono.ru, accessed 9 August 2024. Apparently, porter was considered a salubrious drink. Maria Volkonskaia asked her mother-in-law to send some 'Porter Anglais' to Sergei, since he needed 'fortifiants' for his health.

93 Iakushkin, *Zapiski*, pp. 167–71.

94 I. I. Pushchin, *Zapiski o Pushkine i pis'ma iz Sibiri* (Moscow-Leningrad, 1927), p. 172.

95 Iakushkin, *Zapiski*, pp. 167–71.

# Epilogue

1 Anatole G. Mazour, *Women in Exile: Wives of the Decembrists* (Tallahassee, FL, 1975), pp. 93–4; G. Kubalov, 'Dekabristy i amnistiya', *Sibirskie ogni*, V (1924), pp. 143–59. See also V. P. Boiko, *Dekabristy v Sibiri: Predprinimatel'stvo, obraz zhizni, sotsiokul'turnyi oblik* (Tomsk, 2013).

2 Quoted in Glynn Barratt, *Voices in Exile: The Decembrist Memoirs* (Montreal, 1974), pp. 304–5.

3 Letter from P. A. Mukhanov to N. A. Mukhanova, 28 January 1833, in P. A. Mukhanov, *Sochineniia, pis'ma* (Irkutsk, 1991), pp. 296–8.

4 Barratt, *Voices in Exile*, pp. 309–10.

5 A. E. Rozen, *Russian Conspirators in Siberia: A Personal Narrative* (London, 2005), pp. 128–32.

6 Ibid., pp. 137, 142.

7 The allowed sum was 300 silver roubles a year; 600 for a married man.

8 Rozen, *Russian Conspirators*, pp. 140, 146–7; Glynn Barratt, 'A Note on N. A. Bestuzhev and Academy of Chita', *Canadian Slavonic Papers*, 12 (Spring 1970), pp. 47–59; Rozen, *Russian Conspirators*, p. 140.

9 The Naryshkins, who were childless, had adopted the girl when she was six months old.

10 Barratt, *Voices in Exile*, pp. 312–13.

11 N. I. Lorer, 'Zapiski moego vremeni', in *Memuary dekabristov,* ed. A. S. Nemzer (Moscow, 1988), p. 442.

12 Mazour, *Women in Exile*, p. 40.

13 O. K. Bulanova-Trubnikova, *Roman dekabrista: Dekabrist V. P. Ivashev i ego sem'ia* (Moscow, 1933); I. D. Iakushkin, *Zapiski, stat'i, pis'ma dekabrista I. D. Iakushkina*, ed. S. Shtraikh (Moscow, 1951), pp. 172–4; letter from Ivan Pushchin to I. P. Obolenskii, in I. I. Pushchin, *Zapiski o Pushkine i pis'ma iz Sibiri* (Moscow-Leningrad, 1927), p. 128. Their first son died in 1832.

14 Letter from Pauline Annenkova to Count A. Benckendorff, 15 September 1837, in Mazour, *Women in Exile*, pp. 85–90.

15 Vasilii Ivashev, Nikolai Basargin, Ivan Pushchin, Evgenii Obolenskii, Alexander Briggen, V. I. Vranitskii and S. M. Semenov were also exiled to Turinsk.

16 Mazour, *Women in Exile*, pp. 41–3, 72–3. Giuseppe's brother Alessandro (Aleksandr) was sent to Urik when he was released from Shlisselburg fortress, where he had spent several years in solitary confinement.

17 *Pamiati dekabristov: Sbornik materialov*, vol. III (Leningrad, 1926), pp. 124–31; *Russkaia starina*, vol. IX (1903), pp. 706–16; vol. X (1903), pp. 221–39; *Minuvshie gody*, vols V–VI (1908), p. 523.

18 Christine Sutherland, *The Princess of Siberia: The Story of Maria Volkonsky and the Decembrist Exiles* (London, 1985), p. 257. Maria also adopted a girl from the Chukchi people; she had been found abandoned in the forest.

19 P. E. Annenkova, *Vospominaniia* (Moscow, 2003), ch. 18.

20 N. V. Basargin, *Zapiski* (Krasnoiarsk, 1985), p. 262; Pushchin, *Zapiski o Pushkine*, p. 243.

21 Iakushkin, *Zapiski*, p. 297.

22 Mazour, *Women in Exile*, pp. 44–5.

23 Letter from Ekaterina Trubetskaia to her sister Zinaida, quoted in Mazour, *Women in Exile*, pp. 45–7.

24 The prohibition against having servants had now been removed.

25 The head of the Institute was the old governess to the Trubetskoi family.

26 Upon Mikhail's graduation, General Muraviev-Amurskii, who had become governor of Eastern Siberia in 1847, included Mikhail in his administration.

27 Quoted in Mazour, *Women in Exile*, pp. 50–51.

28 Ibid., pp. 51–2.

29 Letter from S. P. Trubetskoi to G. S. Batenkov, 26 February 1855, in S. P. Trubetskoi, *Materialy o zhizni i revoliutsionnoi deiatel'nosti*, vol. II (Irkutsk, 1987), p. 233.

30 Thomas W. Atkinson, *Travels in the Regions of the Upper and Lower Amoor, and the Russian Acquisitions on the Confines of India and China* (London, 1860), p. 379.

31 B. G. Kubalov, *Dekabristy i amnistiia* (Novonikolaevsk, 1925); S. V. Kodan, 'Amnistiia dekabristam 1856 g', *Voprosy istorii*, 4 (1982), pp. 178–82; Mazour, *Women in Exile*, pp. 53–5, 76–7.

# Select Bibliography

Bagby, Lewis, *Alexander Bestuzhev-Marlinsky and Russian Byronism* (University
    Park, PA, 1995)
Barratt, Glynn, *Voices in Exile: The Decembrist Memoirs* (Montreal, 1974)
—, *The Rebel on the Bridge: A Life of the Decembrist Baron Andrey Rozen,
    1800–1884* (London, 1975)
—, *M. S. Lunin: Catholic Decembrist* (The Hague, 1976)
Beer, Daniel, *The House of the Dead: Siberian Exile under the Tsars* (London, 2016)
Bradley, Joseph, *Voluntary Associations in Tsarist Russia: Science, Patriotism, and
    Civil Society* (Cambridge, MA, 2009)
Fyodorov, Vladimir, *The First Breath of Freedom* (Moscow, 1988)
Grandhaye, Julie, *Les Décembristes: Une Génération républicaine en Russie
    autocratique* (Paris, 2011)
—, *Russie: La République interdite. Le Moment decembriste et ses enjeux*
    (Paris, 2012)
Hartley, Janet M., *Alexander I* (London and New York, 1994)
—, Paul Keenan and Dominic Lieven, eds, *Russia and the Napoleonic Wars*
    (Basingstoke, 2015)
Keep, John L. H., *Soldiers of the Tsar: Army and Society in Russia, 1462–1874*
    (Oxford, 1985)
Leatherbarrow, William J., and Derek C. Offord, eds, *A Documentary History of
    Russian Thought: From the Enlightenment to Marxism* (Ann Arbor, MI, 1987)
Lee, Robert, *The Last Days of Alexander and the First Days of Nicholas* (London,
    1954)
McCaffray, Susan P., 'Confronting Serfdom in the Age of Revolution: Projects for
    Serf Reform in the Time of Alexander I', *Russian Review*, LXIV/1 (2005),
    pp. 1–21
Mazour, Anatole G., *The First Russian Revolution, 1825: The Decembrist Movement.
    Its Origins, Development, and Significance* (Stanford, CA, 1961)
—, *Women in Exile: Wives of the Decembrists* (Tallahassee, FL, 1975)
Moon, David, *The Abolition of Serfdom in Russia, 1762–1907* (Harlow, 2001)
Offord, Derek, 'The Response of the Russian Decembrists to Spanish Politics in
    the Age of Ferdinand VII', *Historia Constitucional*, 13 (2012), n.p.
O'Meara, Patrick, *K. F. Ryleev: A Political Biography of the Decembrist Poet*
    (Princeton, NJ, 1984)
—, *The Decembrist Pavel Pestel: Russia's First Republican* (Basingstoke, 2003)

—, '*Vreden sever*: The Decembrists' Memories of the Peter-Paul Fortress', in *St Petersburg, 1703–1825*, ed. Anthony Cross (Basingstoke, 2003), pp. 165–89

—, *The Russian Nobility in the Age of Alexander I* (London and New York, 2019)

Rabow-Edling, Susanna, *Liberalism in Pre-Revolutionary Russia: State, Nation, Empire* (London, 2019)

Raeff, Marc, *The Decembrist Movement* (Englewood Cliffs, NJ, 1966)

Rozen, A. E., *Russian Conspirators in Siberia: A Personal Narrative* (London, 2005)

Stites, Richard, 'Decembrists with a Spanish Accent', *Kritika: Explorations in Russian and Eurasian History,* XII/1 (Winter 2011), pp. 5–23

—, *The Four Horsemen: Riding to Liberty in Post-Napoleonic Europe* (Oxford, 2014)

Sutherland, Christine, *The Princess of Siberia: The Story of Maria Volkonsky and the Decembrist Exiles* (London, 1985)

Trigos, Ludmilla A., *The Decembrist Myth in Russian Culture* (New York, 2009)

Wang, Emily, *Pushkin, the Decembrists, and Civic Sentimentalism* (Madison, WI, 2023)

Wortman, Richard S., *Scenarios of Power: Myth and Ceremony in Russian Monarchy from Peter the Great to the Abdication of Nicholas II* (Princeton, NJ, 2006)

# Acknowledgements

I started this book when alternative futures for Russia at least seemed possible. The anti-government protests of 2011–13 had not yet receded into distant memory. But as these words are written, Russia is involved in a full-scale invasion of neighbouring Ukraine. The country is moving even further towards authoritarianism and is turning its back on Western political values. This makes it all the more important to highlight that there exists in Russia's past also a liberal tradition.

The book took longer than planned, and I have incurred many debts in the process. Along the way, distractions and challenges both private and professional caused unexpected delays. Acting as director of studies at the Institute for Russian and Eurasian Studies (IRES), Uppsala University, and struggling to keep the show on the road during the COVID-19 pandemic took much time and energy, but I was fortunate to work with supportive and professional administrators. I owe particular thanks to Jevgenija Gehsbarga.

I would like to thank the director of IRES, Claes Levinsson, who in the final stages ensured that I had time to complete the book, and all my colleagues at the Institute for creating such a supportive and stimulating research environment. I am particularly grateful to my colleague Matthew Kott, who agreed to replace me as director of studies at short notice.

I am immensely grateful to the people who took time out of their busy schedules to read and comment on the whole or parts of the manuscript. Max Edling, Leo Granberg and Katarina Rehn provided helpful comments on style and content. Mark Bassin read and commented on Chapters Nine and Ten and shared with me his expertise on Siberia. Derek Offord's careful reading and insightful comments on the introduction as well as on Chapters Five and Six improved and clarified my argument. I would like to extend a special thanks to Patrick O'Meara. When I contacted him out of the blue, he generously brought to bear on my manuscript his unsurpassed expertise with regard to the Decembrists. Both Derek and Patrick also provided me with much-needed encouragement.

Two master's students assisted me in the initial phase of the book project. Anna Appelberg searched for the image of the Decembrists in contemporary Russian media. Anastasia Artamonova wrote a literature review and conducted a pilot study of contemporary Russian views of the Decembrists. Thank you both.

I am grateful to Dave Watkins at Reaktion Books, who made the bold suggestion that I write a book about the Decembrist revolt. Had it not been for his initiative, this book would not have seen the light of day.

Finally, I wish to extend a special thanks to Max Edling, who helps me keep things in perspective. He read an early version of the manuscript and provided me with many excellent suggestions for improvements, but, above all, made me realize that the book was far from finished.

Chapter Five is partly based on my article 'The Decembrists and the Concept of the Civic Nation', published in *Nationalities Papers*, XXXV/2 (May 2007). It is reprinted with permission (copyright © 2007 by Cambridge University Press).

# Photo Acknowledgements

The author and publishers wish to express their thanks to the sources listed below for illustrative material and/or permission to reproduce it. Some locations of artworks are also given below, in the interest of brevity:

All-Russian Museum of A. S. Pushkin (Vserossiiskii muzei A. S. Pushkina), St Petersburg: pp. 46, 184; © S. Ballard 2024: pp. 65, 88; Grispb/AdobeStock: p. 149; Heritage Image Partnership Ltd/Alamy Stock Photo: p. 127 (The Institute of Russian Literature (Pushkin House), St Petersburg); private collection: p. 167; The State A. S. Pushkin Museum, Moscow: p. 84; The State Hermitage Museum, St Petersburg: p. 72; State Historical Museum, Moscow: pp. 14, 102, 200.

# Index

Page numbers in *italics* refer to illustrations